D0042185

STRANGERS
IN A
STRANGE
LAND

STRANGERS
IN A
STRANGE
LAND

Living the Catholic Faith in a Post-Christian World

CHARLES J. CHAPUT

HENRY HOLT AND COMPANY   NEW YORK

Henry Holt and Company
Publishers since 1866
175 Fifth Avenue
New York, New York 10010

www.henryholt.com

Henry Holt ® and 🅜® are registered trademarks of
Macmillan Publishing Group, LLC.

Distributed in Canada by Raincoast Book Distribution Limited

Library of Congress Cataloging-in-Publication Data

Names: Chaput, Charles J., author.
Title: Strangers in a strange land : living the Catholic faith in a post-Christian
world / Charles J. Chaput.
Description: New York : Henry Holt and Company, [2017] | Includes
bibliographical references.
Identifiers: LCCN 2016030808| ISBN 9781627796743 (hardcover) |
ISBN 9781627796750 (electronic book)
Subjects: LCSH: Christian life—Catholic authors. | Christian life—United
States. | Christianity and politics—Catholic Church. | Christianity and
politics—United States. | Church and state—United States.
Classification: LCC BX1406.3 .C43 2017 | DDC 282/.7309051—dc23
LC record available at https://lccn.loc.gov/2016030808

Our books may be purchased in bulk for promotional, educational, or business
use. Please contact your local bookseller or the Macmillan Corporate and
Premium Sales Department at (800) 221-7945, extension 5442, or by e-mail at
MacmillanSpecialMarkets@macmillan.com.

First Edition 2017

Designed by Meryl Sussman Levavi

Printed in the United States of America

1 3 5 7 9 10 8 6 4 2

IN MEMORY OF RONALD LAWLER, O.F.M. Cap.

Mentor and friend

As for me, I believe in a good God and in a life that is on the side of good, a life in which it is not a matter of indifference whether one takes one path or another.

—PAUL CLAUDEL

CONTENTS

STRANGERS
IN A
STRANGE
LAND

CHAPTER 1

RESIDENT ALIENS

We, the ordinary people of the streets, believe
with all our might that this street, this world, where
God has placed us, is our place of holiness.

—MADELEINE DELBRÊL

C HRISTIANS HAVE MANY GOOD REASONS FOR HOPE. OPTI-
mism is another matter. Optimism assumes that, sooner or
later, things will naturally turn out for the better. Hope has no
such illusions.

That sounds like an oddly nervous way to start a book about
our life as Catholic Christians. After all, the Gospel is supposed
to be good news, a message of joy. And so it clearly is. The
Christian faith is expanding rapidly across the Southern Hemi-
sphere. In Africa, 9 million converts enter the Catholic Church
each year. By 2030, if current trends hold, China may have the
largest Christian population in the world.[1]

Even in France, once the "eldest daughter of the Church"
and now the secular heart of an aging continent, signs of a
living Church persist—small, implausible, but real. And in the
United States, while many parishes are struggling to survive in
the nation's Rust Belt and eastern cities, many others in the
South and West are thriving. The Church in America has an

impressive number of movements and new communities ener-
getically alive, and some extraordinary young leaders, both
clergy and lay.

In other words, outside Europe, Christianity is very much
alive and growing. And it's not a passive faith. Jesus left us with
a mandate to transform creation.

But doing that, of course, is easier said than done, even—
or maybe especially—in a nation like the United States.

My goal when I wrote *Living the Catholic Faith* (2001) was
simple. I wanted to help Catholics recover the basics of their
faith so they could live it more fully. In *Render Unto Caesar*
(2008, 2012) I wanted to help readers apply their religious and
moral convictions more vigorously in the public square as good
citizens. Looking back, I think much in both books remains
useful. But if that's so, why do a new book?

The reason is time. Time passes. Times change. Watersheds
happen. In June 2015, in its *Obergefell v. Hodges* decision, the
U.S. Supreme Court ruled that states must license same-sex
marriages and recognize similar marriages when lawfully performed out of state. The Court struck down the nation's traditional understanding of marriage. That much was obvious. But
in its effect, the Court actually went much further. It changed
the meaning of family by wiping away the need for the natural
relationships—husband and wife, mother and father—at the
heart of these institutions.

With *Obergefell*, marriage and family no longer precede and
limit the state as humanity's basic social units grounded in
nature. Instead, they now mean what the state says they mean.
And that suggests deeper problems, because in redefining
marriage and the family, the state implicitly claims the authority to define what is and isn't properly human.

Buried in *Obergefell* is the premise that who we are, how

we mate, and with whom we mate are purely matters of personal choice and social contract. Biology is raw material. Gender is fluid. Both are free of any larger truth that might limit our actions. And the consequences of that premise will impact every aspect of our shared political, economic, and social life.

Why so? Benedict XVI explained it simply and well: "[The] question of the family is not just about a particular social construct, but about man himself—about what he is and what it takes to be authentically human . . . When such commitment is repudiated, the key figures of human existence likewise vanish: father, mother, child—essential elements of the experience of being human are lost."[2]

Obviously *Obergefell* is only one of many issues creating today's sea change in American public life. But it confirmed in a uniquely forceful way that we live in a country very different from that of the past. The special voice that biblical belief once had in our public square is now absent. People who hold a classic understanding of sexuality, marriage, and family have gone in just twenty years from pillars of mainstream conviction to the media equivalent of racists and bigots.

So what do we do now?

Patriotism, rightly understood, is part of a genuinely Christian life. We're creatures of place. The soil under our feet matters. Home matters. Communities matter. The sound and smell and taste of the world we know, and the beauty of it all, *matter.* As G. K. Chesterton would say, there's something cheap and unworthy—and inhuman—in a heart that has no roots, that feels no love of country.

Thus, believers don't have the luxury of despair. And the idea that we can retire to the safety of some modern version of a cave in the hills isn't practical. Our task as Christians is to be healthy cells in society. We need to work as long as we can, in whatever way we can, to nourish the good in our country and to encourage the seeds of a renewal that can enliven our young people.

Americans learn from an early age that democracy is the gold standard of human governance. And its advantages are obvious. Every citizen has (in theory) an equal voice in the course of our nation's affairs. But if America is (or was) "exceptional," something unique in history, it's not because this country is a New Jerusalem, or a redeemer nation, or has a messianic mission. Those things are vanities and delusions. When John Winthrop wrote his famous homily for Puritan colonists nearly four hundred years ago, the "city upon a hill" he imagined building in the New World was something genuinely new. It was the hope of a common life that had its foundations in humility, justice, mutual support, and the love of God.

That biblical vision has always helped shape the American story. The very idea of the "person" has religious origins. Even the concept of the individual—the building block of Western political life—has its early seeds in biblical faith.[3] America has always been a mixed marriage of biblical and Enlightenment ideas.

The trouble is that liberal democratic states also have a less visible, internal dynamic. In a democracy, political legitimacy comes from the will of sovereign individuals. Their will is expressed through elected representatives. Anything that interferes with their will, anything that places inherited or unchosen obligations on the individual—except for the government itself, which embodies the will of the majority of individuals—becomes the target of suspicion.

To protect the sovereignty of individuals, democracy separates them from one another. And to achieve that, the state sooner or later seeks to break down any relationship or entity that stands in its way. That includes every kind of mediating institution, from fraternal organizations, to synagogues and churches, to the family itself. This is why Alexis de Tocqueville, the great French observer of early American life, said that "despotism, which is dangerous at all times, [is] particularly to be feared in democratic centuries."[4]

Tocqueville saw that the strength of American society, the force that kept the tyrannical logic of democracy in creative check, was the prevalence and intensity of religious belief. Religion is to democracy as a bridle is to a horse. Religion moderates democracy because it appeals to an authority higher than democracy itself.[5]

But religion only works its influence on democracy if people really believe what it teaches. Nobody believes in God just because it's socially useful. To put it in Catholic terms, Christianity is worthless as a leaven in society unless people actually believe in Jesus Christ, follow the Gospel, love the Church, and act like real disciples. If they don't, then religion is just another form of self-medication. And unfortunately, that's how many of us live out our Baptism.

Until recent decades, American culture was largely Protestant. That was part of the country's genius. But it also meant that Catholics and other minorities lived through long periods of exclusion and prejudice. The effect of being outsiders has always fueled a Catholic passion to fit in, to find a way into the mainstream, to excel by the standards of the people who disdain us. Over time, we Catholics have succeeded very well—evidently too well. And that very success has weakened any chance the Church had to seize a "Catholic moment" when Catholics might fill the moral hole in our culture created by the collapse of a Protestant consensus.

As a result, Tocqueville's fear about democracy without

religious constraints—what he called its power to kill souls and prepare citizens for servitude[6]—is arguably where we find ourselves today.

Many factors have added to the problem, things we can't easily control. To cite just one example: The political impact of new technologies has been massive. They shape the nature of our reasoning and our discourse. They've moved us away from a public square tempered by logic, debate, and reflection based on the printed word, to a visual and sensory one, emotionally charged and spontaneous. And given the nature of our culture—as we'll see later in these pages—technology's influence will continue to grow.

The credibility of a liberal democracy depends on its power to give people security and freedom—with "freedom" measured largely by the number of choices within each person's private control. The goal of modern technology is to expand those choices by subduing the natural world; to put nature at the service of society in general, and individual consumers in particular. As a result, modern democracy isn't just "open" to modern technology; it now depends on it. The two can't be separated.

Their cooperation leads in unforeseen directions. As the progress of democracy and technology go hand in hand, the political influence of polling, focus groups, behavioral experts, and market research grows. The state gradually takes on elements of a market model that requires the growth of government as a service provider. The short-term needs and wants of voters begin to displace long-term purpose and planning.

In effect, democracy becomes an expression of consumer preference shaped and led by a technology-competent managerial class. It has plenty of room for personal "values." But it has very little space for appeals to higher moral authority or shared meaning.[7] For the state, this is convenient. Private belief—unlike communities of faith—can fit very comfortably in a consumer-based, technocratically guided democracy. Private beliefs make no public demands; and if they do, those demands can easily be ignored or pushed to the margins.

Where does that lead?

Judges 2:6–15 is the story of what happens after the Exodus and after Joshua wins the Promised Land for God's people. Verse 10 says that Joshua "and all that generation also were gathered to their fathers; and there arose another generation after them, who did not know the Lord or the work which he had done for Israel."

It's a Bible passage worth pondering. Every generation leaves a legacy of achievement and failure. In my lifetime, many good men and women have made the world better by the gift of their lives to others. But the biggest failure of so many people of my (baby boomer) generation, including parents, teachers, and leaders in the Church, has been our failure to pass along our faith in a compelling way to the generation now taking our place.

The reason the Christian faith doesn't matter to so many of our young people is that—too often—it didn't really matter to us. Not enough to shape our lives. Not enough for us to suffer for it. As Catholic Christians, we may have come to a point today where we feel like foreigners in our own country—"strangers in a strange land," in the beautiful English of the King James Bible (Ex 2:22). But the deeper problem in America isn't that we believers are "foreigners." It's that our children and grandchildren *aren't*.

✄

SOME YEARS AGO, the singer Bobby McFerrin had a hit tune called "Don't Worry, Be Happy." The lyrics were less than complex. Basically he just sang the words "Don't worry, be happy" more than thirty times in the space of four minutes. But the song was fun and innocent, and it made people smile. So it was very popular.

That was in 1988. Before the First Iraq War. Before 9/11. Before Al Qaeda, Afghanistan, the Second Iraq War, the 2008 economic meltdown, the Benghazi fiasco, the Syria fiasco, the IRS scandal, the HHS mandate, *Obergefell*, refugee crises, Boko Haram, ISIS, and the 2015 and 2016 attacks in Paris, San Bernardino, Orlando, and elsewhere.

And yet, in a way he never intended, McFerrin had it right. Despite all the conflicts in the world and in our own nation, Christians *shouldn't* worry. We *should* be happy. John Paul II, in the first moments of his pontificate, urged us to "be not afraid." This from a man who lived through the Second World War and the two worst murder regimes in history. And when Pope Francis called us back to the "joy of the Gospel"—as he did in his first apostolic exhortation—he, too, reminded us that, as Christians, we have every reason to hope. We have no excuse to look as though we've just come back from a funeral.[8]

Given the turmoil in the world, this stubborn faith in the goodness of life can seem naive. Skeptics tend to think of religion as either organized sentimentality or a kind of mental illness. But Christian faith rightly lived has never been an escape from reality, an emotional crutch, or a weapon for hurting others. It's true that people can and do misuse religion to do terrible things. We see that happening in the Middle East and elsewhere today. If and when we Christians do that, though, we betray the Gospel we claim to serve.

More than fifty years after Vatican II, the world is a bloody and fractured place. Some of those fractures reach deeply into the Church herself.

But this isn't news. It's always been so. Scripture is a record of the same story told again and again, in different ways but always with the same theme, for more than three thousand years. God loves man. Man betrays God. Then God calls man back to his friendship. Sometimes that call involves some very painful suffering, and for good reason. God respects our freedom. But he will not interfere with our choices or their consequences, no matter how unpleasant. As a result, the struggle in the human heart between good and evil—a struggle that seems burned into our chromosomes—projects itself onto the world, to ennoble or deform it. The beauty and the barbarism we inflict on one another leave their mark on creation.

But still God loves us, and his love endures forever.

It's worth rereading paragraphs 84–86 in *Evangelii Gaudium* because in it, Pope Francis forcefully warns us against the kind of pessimism about the world that can turn the hearts of good people into slabs of stone. "Nobody can go off to battle," Francis writes, "unless he is fully convinced of victory beforehand. If we start without confidence, [we've] already lost half the battle . . . Christian triumph is always a cross, yet a cross which is at the same time a victorious banner borne with aggressive tenderness against the assaults of evil. The evil spirit of defeatism is brother to the temptation to separate, before its time, the wheat from the weeds; it is the fruit of an anxious and self-centered lack of trust."[9]

There are no unhappy saints, and joy and hope are constant themes in the work of Pope Francis. Like Saint Paul, he sees the source of Christian joy in the act of preaching the Gospel, in a passion for living the Good News and actively sharing the person of Jesus Christ with others. This is why he has such urgent words for tepid Christians. This is why he can seem so impatient with believers who let their hearts grow numb. If we don't share our faith, we lose it. Without a well-grounded faith, we can't experience hope, because we have no reason to trust in the future. And without hope, we turn more and more inward and lose the capacity to love.

People typically see Jorge Bergoglio as a man formed by the example of Ignatius Loyola and Francis of Assisi. And of course that's true. His spirituality is clearly Jesuit, and his desire for a pure and simple Church close to the poor is clearly Franciscan. But his hunger for God also has other sources.

In a 2013 homily to the general chapter of the Order of Saint Augustine, Francis asked the delegates to "look into your hearts and ask yourself if you have a heart that wants great things or a heart that is asleep. Has your heart maintained [Augustine's] restlessness or has it been suffocated by things?"[10] The passion and restlessness in this Pope's own heart mirror the great Augustine who saw that our hearts can never rest until they rest in God—the God whom Augustine longed for as life's "sovereign joy."

It might seem odd to link Pope Francis and Augustine. Between them runs a canyon of imagined differences in personality and style. For the mass media, Francis is the sunny reformer dragging an ancient institution into the light of the twenty-first century, while Augustine is the grim Christian polemicist from a dark and barbarous past. But appearances can be deceiving. We should ask ourselves: What really constitutes barbarism? And which moment in history is really the one with more light? There's a paradox about Francis that reporters tend to gloss over. The Pope who smiles so often, speaks so kindly, and holds joy in such high regard also has the awkward habit of talking about the devil.

By his own account, Francis has read *Lord of the World*—Robert Hugh Benson's novel about the Antichrist and the end of the world—three or four times. And when he speaks about the devil, which he does with some frequency, he doesn't mean a symbol of evil or a metaphor about man's appetite for destruction. Francis means exactly what the Church has always taught. Satan is a real personal being, a supremely intelligent spirit, a rebel against God, and an enemy of everything human.[11]

Lord of the World was published in 1907, at the start of a young and hopeful twentieth century. It was a time when the new power of science seemed sure to bear fruit in an age of reason, peace, human dignity, and progress, without the primitive baggage of God or superstition. If the modern era had a high point of confidence in humanity's independence and possibilities, *Lord of the World* captured its pride perfectly. And yet within ten years, every shred of that confidence and an entire way of life had been annihilated by the First World War. The twentieth century, despite its accomplishments, became the bloodiest, most irrationally fanatic and destructive in history. It's hard to imagine anyone *not* believing in the existence of the devil after the Holocaust, the Gulag, or Pol Pot.

So again, what constitutes barbarism? And which moment in time is really the darker—the world of the fifth-century bishop of Hippo, or the world of today's bishop of Rome?

The irony of the present moment is that the same tools we use to pick apart and understand the natural world, we now use against ourselves. We're the specimens of our own tinkering, the objects of our social and physical sciences. In the process, we've lost two things. We've lost our ability to see anything sacred or unique in what it means to be human. And we've lost our capacity to believe in anything that we can't measure with our tools. As a result, we're haunted by the worry that none of our actions really has any larger purpose.

The post-Christian developed world runs not on beliefs but on pragmatism and desire. In effect—for too many people—the

appetite for comfort and security has replaced conviction. In the
United States, our political institutions haven't changed. Nor
have the words we use to talk about rights, laws, and ideals. But
they no longer have the same content. We're a culture of self-
absorbed consumers who use noise and distractions to manage
our lack of shared meaning. What that produces in us is a
drugged heart—a heart neither restless for God nor able to love
and empathize with others.

There's a passage from Augustine's *City of God* that's worth
remembering. In describing the Romans of the Late Empire
he wrote:

> This is [their] concern: that every man be able to increase
> his wealth so as to supply his daily prodigalities, so that the
> powerful may subject the weak for their own purposes. Let
> the poor court the rich for a living [so] that under their pro-
> tection they may enjoy a sluggish tranquility; and let the
> rich abuse the poor as their dependents, to minister to their
> pride. Let the people applaud not those who protect their
> interests, but those who provide them with pleasure. Let no
> severe duty be commanded, let no impurity be forbidden . . .
> [In] his own affairs let everyone with impunity do what he
> will . . . [and let] there be a plentiful supply of public pros-
> titutes for everyone who wishes to use them, but especially
> for those who are too poor to keep one for private use.[12]

Sound familiar? True, prostitutes for the poor may seem
like an odd government entitlement. But surely it's no more
"odd" than presidents and lawmakers today who help poor
people kill their own children with abortions at low or no cost—
not only in this country but around the globe.

Augustine began writing *City of God* in AD 413. He wanted to defend the empire's Christian community against pagans who blamed Christianity for the decline of Rome and the breakdown of the world they knew. But over the years, he built the text into what Thomas Merton called "a monumental theology of history" and "an autobiography of the Catholic Church," both timeless and universal. Despite its great size, the book's key ideas are fairly simple.

Augustine argues that when Adam sinned against God, creation fell with him. Nature, including human nature, is now crippled by evil. Sin infects all human endeavors. Man by his own efforts can't be perfected. For Augustine, Rome is a new Babylon and the symbol of earthly power for every generation. But Rome is merely the material face of another, deeper reality. In the mind of Augustine, every inhabitant of our world actually belongs to one of two invisible cities that will commingle until the end of time—the City of Man, consisting of the distracted, the confused, the indifferent, and the wicked, and the City of God, made up of God's pilgrim people on earth. In Augustine's words, "The two cities have been formed by two loves; the earthly city by the love of self, even to the contempt of God; the heavenly by the love of God, even to the contempt of self. The former, in a word, glories in itself, the latter in the Lord. For the one seeks glory from men; but the greatest glory of the other is God, the witness of conscience."[13]

Sinners hide among the saints, and saints among the sinners. Only God knows the truth of each person. And only he can winnow the wheat from the chaff at the end of time. Meanwhile, the two cities interpenetrate and overlap. That leaves Christians with the task of seeking to live their faith well in a fallen world. And it brings us finally to what Augustine says to us today.

Can an African bishop dead for nearly sixteen hundred years offer anything useful to American Christians who live in a very different world?

Augustine might answer this way:

First, he would say that we don't in fact live in such a different world. Many of the details of daily life have changed—our tools, memories, and expectations; our frames of thought and our command of nature. But the human condition is the same. We're born; we grow; we die. We ask what our lives mean. We wonder whether any larger purpose guides the world, and why the people we love age and weaken and then pass on. Beauty still pierces our hearts. Hurting the poor and the weak still shames us. Augustine's two cities are still with us. And in their essentials, they're still very much the same.

Second, Augustine would remind us that as long as the City of God and the City of Man are commingled, "we [believers] also enjoy the peace of Babylon." In other words, the temporal peace and security provided by the state allow us to sojourn, imperfectly but more or less unmolested, toward heaven.[14] Therefore Christians have a duty to pray for earthly rulers. And when possible, we should help to make the structures of this world as good as they can be.

Which raises the issue of politics. Augustine's attitude toward politics was a mixture of deep skepticism and a sense of moral obligation. For Augustine, sin infects even the best human motives. No political party is pure. No political order, no matter how seemingly good, can ever constitute a just society.

But we can't simply withdraw from public affairs. Saint Benedict could retreat to the Italian countryside, but Augustine was a bishop intimately tied to his people and their society. For Augustine, the classic civic virtues named by Cicero—prudence, justice, fortitude, and temperance—can be renewed and elevated, to the benefit of all citizens, by the Christian virtues of faith, hope, and charity. Therefore, political engagement is—or at least it can be—a worthy Christian task. Public office can be an honorable Christian vocation. But any Christian involvement in politics needs to be ruled by modest expectations and a spirit of humility. Success will always be limited. No legal system will ever be fully just.[15]

Third and finally: If the key sin of the nineteenth and early twentieth centuries was an overweening pride in human progress, Augustine might say that the key sins of the twenty-first century—at least, in much of the developed world—are cynicism and despair. Not the brand of despair we see in the panic or severe depression that drives some persons to suicide. Rather, Augustine would mean the kind of despair that's really a subtle inversion of pride. He'd mean the icy, embittered vanity that defies reality and truth, despite its own failures, and that comes from the mouth of Satan in Milton's *Paradise Lost*: "The mind is its own place, and in itself can make a heaven of hell, a hell of heaven." As Satan puts it, better to rule in hell than serve in heaven.[16]

I remembered that line after the November 2015 terrorist attacks in France, when a magazine cartoonist told the world not to pray for Paris because "We don't need more religion! Our faith goes to music! Kisses! Life! Champagne and joy!"[17]

One has to wonder whether the murdered would feel the same.

That stubborn refusal to see anything beyond the horizon of this earthly life fills the air the developed world now breathes. The temptation exists even in the Church to compromise with destructive patterns of life and to reduce the beauty of Christian truths about marriage, sexuality, and other inconvenient matters to a set of attractive ideals—which then leads by little

steps to surrendering her redemptive mission. What the world
needs from believers is a witness of love and truth, not approval.
And that requires from all of us—clergy and laypersons alike—
a much greater confidence in the Word of God, the power of
grace, and the ability of people to actually model and take joy
in what the Church believes.

Again: We live in a time when the product of man's reason—
the creature we call science—now seems to turn on and attack
reason itself, to discredit free will, and to diminish anything
unique about what it means to be human. But as a culture, we
still cling to the idea that progress is somehow inevitable, that
science and technology will one day deliver us from the burdens
of being human. And our educated classes seem willing to
believe in almost anything to avoid dealing with the possibility of
God. "Anything but Jesus" could be the motto of the secular age.

Augustine would find none of this surprising, or even very
foreign. The Rome of Roman greatness, the Rome of people's
happy imagination and memory, no longer existed, and had
really never existed, when he wrote *City of God.* We need to
examine our own nation with the same hard realism. Patriotism
is a form of love, and real love sees the world as it truly is. There
is much to love, and much that's worth fighting for, in this country we call our home. As Christians, we're here in part to make
the world a better place. But our nation is *not* our home, not
really. And Augustine would tell us never to forget that.

We need to share the urgency of Pope Francis in preaching
the joy of the Gospel. And that raises the question: *What is joy?*
Joy is more than satisfaction. It's more than pleasure or con-
tentment. Even the word "happiness" doesn't really capture it.
Joy is the exhilaration we find in being overcome by great
beauty, or in the discovery of some great truth or gift, and the
passion that drives us to share this exhilaration with others,

even if we suffer in the process. In effect, we don't possess joy; joy possesses us.

One of the reasons that Pope Francis sometimes seems so frustrated with the state of the Church today may be that, in his experience, too many Christians tend to confuse doctrine and law and rituals and structures with the real experience of faith. Obviously these things are important. Augustine would say that they're very important, because without them our faith is disincarnate and little more than a collection of warm feelings. The Church is harmed by an overly sentimental or anti-intellectual spirit in her work. In an "emotivist" age, the last thing we need is a flight from clear teaching.

But Augustine would likely agree with Francis that the structural elements of Church life become empty and dead when they're not animated by love—in other words, if they don't proceed from a living relationship with Jesus Christ and the interior joy it creates. We can too easily use them as a hiding place from the real task of discipleship, which is preaching the joy of the Gospel by our lives and our actions.

Did Augustine know joy? Read his *Confessions*. In his sermons, Augustine called this earth "a smiling place." Portions of his work read like a litany to the goodness and beauty of creation.[18] His biographer Peter Brown describes him as a man immoderately in love with the world. And the reason is simple. Augustine loved the world because he was in love with the Author of the beauty and goodness he found there.

What does that mean for us today? Augustine would tell us that the real problem with the world is bigger than abortion or poverty or climate change or family breakdown, and it's much more stubborn. The real problem with the world is us.

As Augustine said in his sermons, it's no use complaining about the times, because *we are the times*. How we live shapes them. And when we finally learn to fill our hearts with something more than the noise and narcotics of the wounded societies we helped create; when we finally let our hearts rest in God as Augustine did; then—and only then—the world will begin to change, because God will use the witness of our lives to change it.

TIME PASSES. TIMES CHANGE. Watersheds happen. I sat down to write this book for everyday Catholics and others who love Jesus Christ and his Church more than they love their own opinions; people who know that something's gone wrong with their country, but don't understand why, or what to do about it.

That expression—"everyday Catholics"—needs some unpacking. In twenty-eight years as a bishop, what I've seen is this: Most of the adult Catholics I know have families and demanding jobs. They're often harried and fatigued and distracted. But they're nobody's fools. Most of us ordinary believers were born with plenty of intelligence, and today more than ever, we need to use it. If our mass-media culture works to make people shallow, gullible, angry, and dumb much of the time, it's because *we let it.*

Since you're reading this book, you're probably different. You probably like to think, and want to think, as a grown-up real person, in a mature Catholic spirit of faith. And you might suspect (wisely) that too many people aren't thinking at all. Adults deserve adult food for thought, and in these pages I'll try to honor that. To that end, I've included endnotes where useful, and they can lead to some great additional reading. But they're not exhaustive.

The structure of this book is simple. Chapter 2 revisits the America we thought we knew and in many ways did know, along with the ideals and virtues it embodied. For readers already well versed in our nation's history and the Catholic role in the story, chapter 2 might be flyover country, something to scan on the way to the rest of the book. But for the many others who, until now, have taken the Jack Nicholson approach to worthwhile but unwanted invitations—"I'd rather stick needles in my eyes"—chapter 2 is for you.[19]

Chapters 3 through 7 outline where we are now and how we got there. And chapters 8 through 12 speak to our reasons for hope, and to how we can live as Christians, with joy, in a very different world. That new world poses questions we all need to face: How do we fit into a deeply changed and changing nation? How do we grow in our faith? Where do our real loyalties lie? And how did we one day wake up in a culture we thought we knew but now seems so foreign?

We're passing through a religious revolution in America. For many generations a common Christian culture transcended our partisan struggles. It gave us a shared framework of behavior and belief. Now another vision for our nation's future has emerged. It sees no need for Christianity. And in many cases it views our faith as an obstacle to its ambitions. We've become, in Stanley Hauerwas's famous phrase, "resident aliens."[20] We're tempted to turn bitter and quit the struggle. Nobody likes to be driven from his high seat, yet this is exactly what has happened to American Christianity. Many believers are ill equipped for life on the "outside." But we need to fight this temptation. And to do so we need to approach twenty-first-century America with a spirit not of anger, but of clear judgment and of love.

Love is grateful: We need to thank God for all the good in America, not just in the past, but today.

Love is patient: We need to recognize that we're not going to "win" many of the culture-shaping struggles we face—at least, not on our own time. Only on God's time.

Love builds up: We need to do what can be done rather than anguishing over what can't.

Patriotism can be manipulated by demagogues. It can be a cheap substitute for religious faith. But at its core, it's a good thing. When Saint Paul speaks of love, he says, "Love bears all things, believes all things, hopes all things, endures all things" (1 Cor 13:7). By "love" he means the Christlike charity made possible by God's grace, and he calls us to this spirit of love in our life together as believers.

Our relationship to the nation we call America is not our relationship to Christ's body, the Church. There are things we should *not* bear, should *not* believe, should *not* endure in civic life. But we need to welcome some, and maybe a great deal, of bearing and believing and hoping and enduring, for the sake of saving what can be saved.

Because for better or worse, what happens in this country has meaning for a much wider world.

CHAPTER 2

OF BLESSED MEMORY

A MERICANS HATE THINKING ABOUT THE PAST. UNFORTUnately, we need to.

Over a lifetime we learn a lot of lessons, first from parents, later from experience and other people. One of the big lessons in life is this: A sound guide to staying married, staying friends, or simply staying sane is to remember and honor the good in things before criticizing the bad. This is a sensible way to treat people. It's also a good way to think about our country.

Memory matters because the past matters. The past is the soil out of which our lives and institutions grow. We can't understand the present or plan for the future without knowing the past through the eyes of those who made it. Their beliefs and motives matter. For the American founding, there's no way to scrub either Christianity or its skeptics out of the nation's genetic code.

Nearly all the Founders were religious believers. Most called themselves Christians. In practice, John Adams and his colleagues in revolution were men who had minds that were a "miscellany and a museum," men who could blend the old and the new, Christianity and Enlightenment ideas, without destroying either.[1] Biblical faith and language saturated the founding era. Even Thomas Jefferson, stopped by a skeptical friend on his way to church one Sunday morning, would say that "no nation has ever yet existed or been governed without religion. Nor can [it] be. The Christian religion is the best religion that has ever been given to man and I, as chief magistrate of this nation, am bound to give it the sanction of my example."[2]

Religion and sin, of course, can share the human heart quite comfortably. The evils of America's past—brutality to native peoples, slavery, racism, religious prejudice, exploitation of labor, foreign intervention—are bitter. But they're not unique to America or to religious believers. Nor do they define the nation. Nor do they void the good in the American experiment or its uniqueness in history.

Asked some years ago if he believed in "American exceptionalism," the French political scholar Pierre Manent said, "It's difficult not to, because it is the only political experiment that succeeded . . . the only successful political foundation" made through choice and design. "[I]f you are not able to treat the United States for the great political-civic achievement it is, you miss something huge in the political landscape."[3]

The good in our history is real. America's "exceptional" nature, however, doesn't imply superiority. It doesn't even suggest excellence. It implies *difference*. It involves something new in governance and liberty, rooted in the equality of persons, natural rights, and reverence for the law. And it's sustained— or was intended to be—by national traits of industriousness, religious faith, and volunteerism.

America is exceptional in another way as well: It's the only

society with no real history of its own before the age of progress.[4]
The continent, for the Founders, was not just vast and pristine.
It was a blank slate for a new kind of political order, unlike anything that had come before. When the Founders stamped the
words *novus ordo seclorum*—"a new order of the ages"—on the
national seal, they meant it. And they proved it. A special genius
of law, institutional structure, moral imagination, and an idea
of the human person animated the American founding and its
development.

From the start, religious faith has been the glue and rudder of the American experiment, its moral framework and
vocabulary—at least as people have typically experienced it.
That rudder and glue no longer seem to apply. We now really
do have a new order of the ages. And it has shaped a new kind
of human being.

THE PRINCETON SCHOLAR ROBERT P. GEORGE, a grandson of
Syrian and Italian immigrants, notes, "Part of what is unique
about this country is that our common bonds are not in blood
or ethnicity or soil, but are rather in a shared moral and political creed." A person can become a citizen of Greece or France,
but he can't really become Greek or French. By contrast, "An
immigrant who becomes a citizen of the United States can
become, not merely an American citizen, somebody who's got
the certificate, has been through the ceremony, but can become
an *American*—someone who is recognized as an American by
his fellow Americans . . . He is as American as [anyone] whose
ancestors came over on the *Mayflower*."[5]

The new nation's "shared moral and political creed" had
biblically influenced roots. As the constitutional scholar
Matthew Franck puts it, America began as "a nation made up

largely of Christian people, governed by a secular political order they [saw] as properly enmeshed in a relation of mutual support with their religious faith."

Many Founders used arguments from both Christianity and John Locke—himself ambiguously Christian—and switched back and forth between them. They believed both types of argument led to the same ends. Those who favored one type didn't see the other as a threat. Jefferson's words in the Declaration of Independence reflect this. He refers both to "Nature" and to "Nature's God." Then he claims that the truths he wants to assert are simply "self-evident," with another reference to the Creator. The question of *why* they're self-evident is left floating.

Franck offers a way to grasp how religion and the Enlightenment intertwined. He describes the founding's Christian elements as the *warp* of the nation's fabric (the threads first stretched on the weaver's loom). The secular elements were the weft, or woof (the threads woven at a right angle through the warp). The Founders didn't see a conflict. Some leaned more on Christian thought in their reasoning, others on Locke and the Enlightenment. "Sometimes their arguments traveled along the warp," Franck writes, "sometimes on the weft, but it was one fabric to them."[6]

Added to this Christian-Enlightenment mix were a commonsense moral reasoning and the common law tradition inherited from England. These qualities deepened further in the colonies, based on the colonists' unique experiences. Both gave the Founders a grounding in tradition. Both kept them from following the more extreme currents of Enlightenment thought.

Building a new life in a new world, always growing westward, made the society more meritocratic. This undermined traditional roles and positions. Colonists also shared the memory of an oppressive government unconcerned with their well-being. And the colonies' religious diversity meant that the new nation would need to find a way for different groups to live in harmony. The Enlightenment's liberal thought gave the Founders the defense of toleration they needed.

America's system of checks and balances was designed to limit the role of government. This was deliberate. The drafters of the Constitution sought to block any faction or interest from exploiting the whole. No other nation had such a thing. But where did it come from? The Founders drew their thinking from the realism of humanity's fall in Genesis 3, not from dreams of the perfectible man—dreams that later made the French Revolution a nightmare. They also borrowed from Locke's insights into the nature of politics, reflected in the fear of faction and division expressed in the *Federalist Papers*.

They drew as well from the Enlightenment's trust in man's ability to create good institutions. And they built on a biblical sense of justice in rejecting oppression. Each element reacted upon the other, leading the Founders to a form of government that enabled mutual support and liberty while restraining state power.

But America's success stems from more than the procedures the Founders put in place. Even the best process depends on the character of the people who live it. The American project needs a virtuous people. A free market economy requires trust. The people who buy and sell must be trustworthy in order for the system to work. No organizational structure can make up for dishonest people. Regulatory agencies and courts mean very little in a morally crippled culture.

American life worked so well because of the moral ideals that undergirded it and the behaviors it required. Those ideals and behaviors were rooted in faith. James Madison, in his *Memorial and Remonstrance against Religious Assessments* in

1785, said that man's duty to honor God "is precedent both in order of time and degree of obligation to the claims of civil society. Before any man can be considered as a member of civil society, he must be considered as a subject of the Governor of the universe." And as John Adams told the Massachusetts militia in 1789, "Our constitution was made only for a moral and religious people. It is wholly inadequate to the government of any other."

There's more. John Witherspoon, another of the Founders and a Presbyterian minister, preaching in 1776, said:

> Nothing is more certain than that a general profligacy and corruption of manners make a people ripe for destruction . . . [H]e is the best friend of American liberty, who is most sincere and active in promoting true and undefiled religion, and who sets himself with the greatest firmness to bear down profanity and immorality of every kind . . . I do not wish you to oppose anybody's religion, but everybody's wickedness.[7]

The "avowed enemy of God," he said, is "an enemy to his country." Even the English skeptic David Hume once said that those who tell people that God and immortality do not exist may be "good reasoners, but I cannot allow them to be good citizens and politicians"—"politicians" meaning political philosophers. For Hume, unbelievers kill a people's faith, on which a stable society depends.

America's Christian and secular threads share what historian Hugh Heclo calls a moral calculus.[8] Christians among the Founders saw religion as essential for anyone to act morally. Others may have felt that the human masses needed it, but not those Washington called in his Farewell Address the special people shaped by "refined education." But nearly all saw religion as key to what Washington called "national morality."

"For the generation of the American founding," Matthew Franck notes, "faith and reason *alike* taught the dignity of man. Christianity and the Enlightenment *both* treated the human person as a moral agent entitled to freedom and answerable to moral norms in the use of that freedom." The Christian faith, he continues,

> was the first truly global religion to appeal beyond the bounds of tribe, soil, and heritage, inviting all men and women into a redemptive relationship with the Creator. America was the first self-consciously "founded" country, similarly universal in its openness to all, and in its transcendence of the tribe—or even the sect; a nation with a credo ("We hold these truths"), to which one could come from anywhere in the world, and of which one could become a member just by paying allegiance to the ideas of universal justice in that credo. These were more than merely incidental affinities between Christian faith and American freedom; they were interwoven threads, and for many Americans today, they remain so.[9]

As Alexis de Tocqueville said, the United States "is the product . . . of two perfectly distinct elements that elsewhere have often made war with each other, but which, in America, they have succeeded in incorporating somehow into one another and combining marvelously. I mean to speak of the *spirit of religion* and the *spirit of freedom*" (emphasis in original).[10]

Tocqueville saw that self-interest is a permanent flaw in human affairs, but it could be doubly destructive in American society. The reason? The loss of the Old World hierarchies they had renounced in the New World left people isolated and alone. This made marriage and family ties vital to the health of society. Marriage curbed the selfishness so natural to humans by binding a man and woman together, and even more by binding them to their children. Religious faith offered the purpose and reinforcement to sustain family structure.

What Tocqueville sensed, and a vast amount of data has since shown, is that religious commitment strengthens marriage. More nonbelievers than churchgoers divorce or separate. Couples of the same denomination (and presumably the same religious commitment) tend to be happier. Even theological "conservatism" seems linked to greater happiness.[11]

Sound marriages and flourishing families strengthen society. This is why the Supreme Court's *Obergefell* decision was so poisonous—but also, in a sense, so faithfully democratic. Without the restraints of some higher moral law, democracy instinctively works against natural marriage, traditional families, and any other institution that creates bonds and duties among citizens. It insists on the autonomous individual as its ideal.

In the 2012 election, the Obama presidential campaign ironically proved the point. It built an interactive website called "The Life of Julia." Fictional Julia goes through life, as a writer in the *Washington Post* put it, "married to the state."[12] The government makes everything possible—school, work, support for a son, retirement. A husband is not in the picture. The Julia website was the administration's appeal to a growing demographic: unmarried women. It was also a glimpse of the future.

AMERICA'S FOUNDING HAD ITS radical voices. Thomas Paine was the harshest toward organized religion. The founding may have been a heroic age, but like any revolution, it wasn't a pretty one. Journalism and politics were as ugly then as they are now. But most Founders mixed their zeal with prudence. They were educated gentlemen: landowners, lawyers, businessmen, pastors. They were men who wanted freedom, but of a kind rooted in social stability. They wanted an "ordered liberty" that balanced individual freedom with duties to neighbors and the common good.

In building their new order, then, they fused a liberal trust in man's ability to govern himself with a biblical sense of man's appetite for sin. The Founders wanted a representative government, but one carefully limited in scope. They believed in "the people," or at least those entitled to vote. But they also believed that even the people can abuse power. So in crafting the new nation, they looked not just to the Enlightenment and biblical wisdom, but also to the classical era, especially Rome.

The political scholar Robert Kraynak names four key streams that fed the Founders' vision: republicanism, constitutionalism, natural law, and cultural tradition. These are worth sketching here.

The first stream was *republicanism*. The Founders were hostile to nobility. They disliked inherited privilege. Yet they also saw "pure" democracy as a problem, not a solution. Class distinctions were weaker in the former colonies than in Europe. But the Founders were well aware of differences in education, ownership, and pedigree, and what they could mean for public order. They lacked a history for their own novel ideas. So they looked to the ancient Roman Republic as a model for their institutions. The very words "senate" (Latin *senatus*, from *senex* for "old") and "republic" (*res publica*, state or commonwealth, literally "public matter") had roots in the Roman experience.

The Roman Republic, like the American colonies, emerged from the overthrow of a monarchy. The similarities were real, but also limited. Rome had an early system of checks and balances. Power in the republic was divided. The lower classes elected tribunes of the people, who could veto legislation. But an elite of "old families" governed the state through the Senate. They also controlled executive leadership in the consulship. And to a much greater degree than in the colonies, the Roman Republic depended on farming, slave labor, and military expansion for its survival.

For a "new order" in a new world, the example of Rome offered a Golden Age grounding. The Founders named Capitol Hill after Rome's Capitoline Hill. They used a neoclassical style for public buildings. And they created a representative, popular democracy filtered through undemocratic structures. States' rights diluted federal power. State legislatures chose senators. Supreme Court judges were appointed, not elected. Even the president was chosen indirectly by the people, through an Electoral College of state electors.

All of these efforts were designed to ensure the sovereignty of the people but also to moderate majority rule. In Kraynak's words, they sought to educate and "elevate the common people's views on politics." The new American republic was finally a democratic creature rather than an aristocratic one. And unlike Rome, it had a stronger interest in economic growth than in armed expansion. Borrowing from Enlightenment thinkers like Charles Montesquieu and others, the Founders believed that commerce served human happiness by encouraging peace and improving the conditions of everyday life.

The second stream of the Founders' vision was *constitutionalism.* For obvious reasons, the Founders drew on the English legal tradition. But the English "constitution" was unwritten. It existed in no single text. It was a collection of laws, precedents, instincts, and practices that had grown organically over time. It worked well enough in England. But it was not easily transferable to a new form of government.

The word "constitution" comes from the Latin *cum*, for "with," and *stituere*, for "set up." The Founders had the task of imagining and "setting up together" a government without precedent. The English monarchy, for all its flaws, resembled the kind of mixed-authority state Thomas Aquinas might prefer: a blend of limited kingship, aristocracy (the House of Lords), and the common people (the House of Commons). The American Founders instead invested all authority in the people.

Thus, in effect, the United States is a contract among equal citizens—but one with a semi-sacred aura.

At Sinai, God wrote the Ten Commandments onto stone tablets. The Hebrews carried them everywhere in the Ark of the Covenant. The tablets' constant presence reminded the Hebrews of their duties and identity. The Law was literally set in stone. It was irreformable and established the Jews as a people. The American Constitution, in contrast, was the work of men. The Founders saw it as foundational, but unavoidably imperfect. They made it reformable through amendment. The first ten amendments, the Bill of Rights, are an example. But they deliberately made the amendment process long and hard. They wanted to dampen the impact of people's passions on basic structures of the nation's life.

Like the Mosaic Law for the Jewish people, the Constitution established what America is. We are a nation of law. This is why arguments about what the Founders intended and what the Constitution means (or should mean) are so heated in our public life. And since the law defines who we are as a people far more firmly than ethnicity, creed, or geography, and since the law is a written text, it's also why America is a country where print literacy and its habits of thought *matter*.

The third stream of the Founders' vision was *natural law*. The Founders based their revolution on an appeal to "natural rights." The Declaration of Independence argues that human liberty and rights are not man-made. They're inherent to who we are. A phrase from the Declaration such as "All men are created equal" implies a Creator, implies that we enjoy our rights not as state entitlements but as part of our natural dignity. They spring from "the laws of nature and nature's God." They are "gifts endowed by [our] Creator." They preexist any human authority and cannot be revoked.

In natural law thinking, a greater than human moral order exists and governs the universe. Thus all human power is accountable to higher standards of good and evil. These apply to everyone. England's monarch, George III, might have loathed the American revolutionaries. But he would have understood their natural law reasoning. In the Christian world, kings were not gods. Even a king claiming "divine right" knew he would be judged by God for acts of injustice. In fact for the Founders, under the natural law, even a sovereign people were accountable to God's judgment and had the duty to act in accord with the moral order of creation.

As Kraynak notes, "the Founders believed that freedom was based on moral order, not moral relativism." They drew their natural law principles from John Locke, Cicero, and others, as well as from the strong natural law tradition in Christian thought. Thus, for Kraynak, "Without natural law—meaning an objective moral law put into nature and human nature by the Creator—the ideal of republican liberty lacks an ultimate foundation."[13]

The fourth and last stream in the Founders' vision was *cultural tradition*. The Founders believed that liberty depended on persons with the maturity to avoid both radical self-assertion and a timid reliance on the state. A strong civil society—bigger than the individual but separate from the state—with its diverse communities, traditions, memories, duties, and protections, gives oxygen to republican liberty. It binds the individual to other people, but also protects him from absorption by the state.

To put it another way: In life, as Alasdair MacIntyre once wrote, each of us enters "upon a stage which we did not design, and [where] we find ourselves part of an action that was not of our making. Each of us, being a main character in his own drama, plays subordinate parts" in the dramas of others.[14] Every person belongs to a much greater narrative than citizenship, bound into contexts such as intergenerational webs of family, faith, codes of honor, or allegiance to a civilization and its history. These connections breed humility about our place in the world and thereby foster sanity. They work against both worship of the self and worship of the state.

These four streams came together in the Founders' vision that gave birth to an entirely new kind of nation. Whether the Founders would recognize their handiwork today, in its maturity, is another matter.

⚜

WHEN WE TALK ABOUT the Christian role in the founding, we need to be clear about what we mean. Catholics were few in the colonies. Charles Carroll was the only Catholic among the fifty-six signatories to the Declaration of Independence.[15]

Americans were Protestant. Except for the University of Pennsylvania, all Ivy League schools—the cream of U.S. higher education—began as Protestant institutions. Reformed Christianity shaped colonial attitudes toward personal conscience and freedom. As Stanley Hauerwas notes, "America is the first great experiment in Protestant social formation. Protestantism in Europe always assumed and depended on the cultural habits

that had been created by Catholic Christianity. America is the
first place Protestantism did not have to define itself over against
a previous Catholic culture."[16]

In effect, America embodies the Protestant social imagination. For many Protestants—so Hauerwas argues—"faith in
God [became] indistinguishable from their loyalty to a country
that insured them that they had the right to choose which god
they would or would not believe in." America didn't need an
established church "because it was assumed that the church
was virtually established by the everyday habits of daily life."
Or, to borrow a line from G. K. Chesterton: America has always
been a nation that thinks it's a Church.

Thus it's no surprise that Protestants have typically felt at
home in America. In a sense, they own the patent. It also explains
the distrust aimed at Catholics throughout much of American
history. The Catholic Church was everything Protestants resisted:
priests, popes, pagan-seeming ceremonies, top-down authority. But as long as their numbers were small, Catholics caused
little annoyance. Some, like Charles Carroll, had wealth and
social standing. Father John Carroll—Charles's cousin—was
affluent, well educated, and well traveled. He had diplomatic
skill and was a friend of Benjamin Franklin, who recommended
him to the Holy See as America's first bishop.

In the first National Synod of Baltimore (1791), Bishop Carroll made a point of stressing Catholic patriotism and urged
public prayers for the president and government. A gifted
administrator, winning and urbane, he built good working relations with George Washington and Thomas Jefferson as well
as with his own clergy.

But the spirit of live and let live broke down under the
weight of nineteenth-century immigration. Waves of Italian, Pol-
ish, German, and especially Irish newcomers, all largely Catho-

lic, swamped the social infrastructure and reshaped the electorate of cities like New York and Boston.

The results were ghettos of poverty and crime. And they triggered a backlash. Fierce anti-Catholic calumnies appeared in the press. Mob violence and church burnings followed. Looking back from the vantage of 2016, the anti-Catholic rage of the period is hard to fathom. But it was bitterly real for the people who lived it. Allusions to prejudice and persecution figure in joint pastoral letters by the American bishops in 1829, 1837, 1840, 1866, and 1884. The Fourth Provincial Council of Baltimore (1840) noted "acts of barbarity and sacrilegious destruction," libels against the clergy, defamation, and textbooks in public schools that sought "to misrepresent our principles, to distort our tenets, to vilify our practices and to bring contempt upon our Church and its members."[17]

And yet, in the same council, the bishops spoke of "the love we bear to our civil and political institutions." While urging their people to vote, the bishops called them to think of the common good and to remember "that our republic can never be respected abroad, nor sustained at home, save by an uncompromising adherence to honor, to virtue, to patriotism and to religion."

Why were Catholics so faithful to a state biased from the start to see them as intruders?

Despite their differences, Catholics and Protestants shared the same basic faith and worldview. They had the same moral vocabulary. They shared an understanding of who man is. And Catholics came to the colonies for many of the same reasons Protestants did. Land was vast, rich, available, and cheap. Risks were high, but so was the chance for profit. There was room to breathe. There was an escape from the conflicts and suffocating class structures of Europe. People brave enough to cross an ocean could start a new life with relatively little interference from neighbors or authorities. There was a high degree of personal liberty. There were no predetermined outcomes based on privilege. America was a continent with no memory, at least for the Europeans. It had a present and future, but no past to contend with. It was raw material waiting to be worked.

American life (at its best) bred a religion-blind character of self-reliance and invention. As industry grew throughout the nineteenth century, so did economic opportunity. So did Catholic numbers—rapidly. And so did the enthusiasm for everything American, embodied by Church leaders such as Archbishop John Ireland of St. Paul, Minnesota. A Civil War hero, Ireland was a strong booster of America's democratic spirit. Which brought him, and others like him, into friction with the Holy See.

As noted previously in *Render Unto Caesar*, the nineteenth-century papacy, dealing with hostile revolutions in Europe, had a very different view of democracy.[18] Pope Gregory XVI argued that it was "insanity to believe in liberty of conscience and worship, or of the press." His successor, Pius IX, could be charming and humorous—but he was no more cordial in his views. A contemporary said that "liberal ideas filtered into his head like snow blowing in around the cracks of a closed window." And Pius's successor, Leo XIII, wrote an 1899 encyclical warning against "Americanist" errors.

America's bishops handled these worries with a mix of compliance and adroit disregard. Lord John Dalberg-Acton, the period's great English Catholic historian and politician, noted that U.S. Church leaders—happily distant from Europe—had a talent for warmly applauding Rome's words and then doing as they pleased.

Charles Morris, a chronicler of American Catholic life, wrote that "There were no more patriotic Americans than Catholics, nor any Catholics more loyal to the Pope than Americans, and the American Church developed a wonderful skill at picking its own path between those loyalties."[19] Catholics did well in America. They acknowledged their success with gratitude and loyalty to their country.

In a 1919 pastoral letter written just after the First World War, the bishops wrote that "The traditional patriotism of our Catholic people has been amply demonstrated in the day of their country's trial. And we look with pride upon the record which proves . . . the devotion of American Catholics to the cause of American freedom." They added, "The account of our men in [military] service adds a new page to the record of Catholic loyalty."

But they also included a theme that grew in urgency as the twentieth century wore on:

> The state then has a sacred claim upon our respect and loyalty. It may justly impose obligations and demand sacrifices for the sake of the common welfare which it is established to promote. It is the means to an end, not an end in itself; and because it receives its power from God, it cannot rightfully exert that power through any act or measure that would be at variance with the divine law or with the divine economy for man's salvation. As long as the state remains within its proper limits, and really furthers the common good, it has a right to our obedience . . . But it may not rightfully hinder the citizen in the discharge of his conscientious obligation, and much less in the performance of duties which he owes to God.[20]

In 1933, in the pit of the Great Depression, the bishops attacked the corporate greed of "many [who,] having a materialistic attitude toward life, and therefore [no] true moral sense of their obligations, object to any restriction of competition, even that which degrades the dignity of human labor and ignores every principle of justice."[21] They warned that "Industry [in our country] is considered to be of more importance than the moral welfare of man." Through the concentration of wealth, industry "has acquired such complete control that independent operation, even on the part of so-called owners and employers, is practically impossible."

Starting as early as 1919, the bishops also attacked growing secularist trends in the nation's life. But still their loyalty never wavered. In a December 1941 letter to President Franklin Roosevelt, dated just two weeks after Pearl Harbor, Detroit's Archbishop Edward Mooney reaffirmed the Catholic "attachment to the ideals and institutions of government we are now called upon to defend."

Mooney quoted the Third Plenary Council of Baltimore (1884) in stressing that "We believe that our country's [Revolutionary War] heroes were the instruments of the God of nations in establishing this home of freedom." He added, "We will zealously fulfill our spiritual ministry in the sacred cause of our country's service. We place at your disposal in that service our institutions and their consecrated personnel . . . that [God] may strengthen us all to win a victory that will be a blessing not for our nation alone, but for the whole world."[22]

With World War II and the Cold War, Church and national interests seemed logically to coincide. By the 1950s, American Catholics had reached a zenith in numbers and institutional strength. It was a high point of Bing Crosby–fueled sentimental appeal (thanks to films like *Going My Way* and *The Bells of*

St. Mary's); perceived moral courage (Karl Malden in *On the Waterfront*); articulate anti-Communism; and broad public respect.

In the lavish patriotism of leaders such as New York's Cardinal Francis Spellman, Church and nation "seemed to fuse . . . into a single shining ideal."[23] And with the rise of John Kennedy in 1960 as the country's first Catholic president—young, attractive, and a war hero—Catholics had finally arrived.

WRITING IN THE *Wall Street Journal* in 2015, on the 77th anniversary of Kristallnacht, John Lang recalled the nightlong Nazi violence against Jews in 1938 Berlin. Mobs roamed the streets beating up Jews and smashing and burning their businesses. As an eight-year-old Jewish boy, "I was at my grandmother's. Through the window I could see my beautiful synagogue engulfed in flames as desperate screams rose from the street below." The next morning, "Uniformed Nazis and their sympathizers were having fun" as they picked through the wreckage of their brutality. "One group looked at a large stain on the street that was said to be the blood of a Jew. Even now I can hear their laughter."

Lang was fortunate. He escaped to Britain on a *Kindertransport* train. He was taken in by the United States as a child refugee and later became a citizen. "After nearly 75 years in the U.S.," he wrote, "I am still stirred by the thought of American freedom—so precious and thrilling that I cannot imagine life without it."[24]

Stories like John Lang's are too common to number. They live in our memory. They inspire our national imagination. They shine with the best ideals of what America was intended to be: more than a clever legal structure, more than an economic machine, but rather an experiment in moral nobility.

Despite all of its failures, America has always been something unique in the world—a place where the poor could rise, where slavery could be ended, where the persecuted were welcomed, where the law mattered, where different religions could live together in peace, where liberties and rights were real because responsibilities were equally real, and where the idea of what it means to be "human" was broadly shared and anchored in things more permanent than government and more sacred than educated opinion.

These are memories rightly called blessed. They are historically unique gifts, and also infinitely fragile; which is why the bishops who built the foundations of Catholic life in the United States "conceived of a Church that would be *in* America, vehemently *for* America but never *of* America."[25]

As the great Jesuit scholar Father John Courtney Murray wrote in 1955, "God does not furnish blueprints for the future." But the future can sometimes be glimpsed in the shape of emerging problems. "[The] American constitutional commonwealth," he warned, "is not intelligible and cannot be made to work except by men who possess the public philosophy" that the Founders first brought to building it.[26]

A question facing us now is whether that commonwealth can endure. Another is whether it was ever really sustainable from the start.

CHAPTER 3

WHY IT CAN'T BE
LIKE IT WAS

O NCE UPON A TIME IN AMERICA, A PERSON COULD WALK into a grocery store, take a bottle of aspirin off the shelf, twist open the cap, and shake out a tablet or two. No plastic bands around the caps. No foil safety seals glued over the opening. It didn't matter what company made the aspirin. It didn't matter where the customer shopped. People with a headache might take a pill right in the store aisle. They'd throw the bottle into their cart and pay for it with the rest of their groceries.

Then, in the fall of 1982, seven Chicago-area people died after swallowing Tylenol capsules that had been laced with potassium cyanide. Copycat crimes soon followed. Alert to lawsuits and a loss of consumer confidence, drug makers started adding tamper-proof seals to their bottles. The FDA approved regulations requiring companies to safeguard their products from being opened without the buyer's knowing it.

In the space of a few weeks, a nation of (then) 231 million people—people who had trusted one another to respect a person's medical needs—became a country of people who wouldn't buy a bottle with a tear on the edge of a safety seal. Today, no drug company would dare propose selling medicines without those seals. The public outcry wouldn't allow it. Customers wouldn't buy the unprotected product. The social trust that preceded the Tylenol affair is gone forever.

A lot more than medicine bottles has changed from the America many of us knew as children and young adults. The differences are important, and cataloging them is a matter of prudence, not nostalgia. We tend to imagine our politics and our culture as pendulums. In politics, elections seem to swing from Democrat to Republican and back, from a focus on government action to a focus on the free market and back. Or so we like to think.

Ronald Reagan's influence was great enough to elect his Republican vice president to one term as president. But then the country elected Bill Clinton. Reacting to eight years of Clinton, it elected George W. Bush twice. Reacting to Bush, it elected Barack Obama twice. Even within the parties, swings take place. The "New Democrat" Clinton was followed by the more ideologically zealous Obama. The classically conservative Reagan was followed by the self-styled "compassionate conservatives," Bush father and son. In 2016, yet another presidential election year, both major parties engaged in civil wars over their future direction: Bernie Sanders versus another Clinton, Donald Trump versus everyone else.

The pendulum image is misleading, though. It can easily make us complacent. It suggests that if we wait long enough, things will return to normal. But "normal" is a fluid word, and societies aren't pendulums. They don't swing only so far in each direction. They're living organisms. They move through history. They grow, peak, and decline. They can become ill. They can also recover. But sometimes they die, often after a lingering sickness that eats up much of the good in their legacy. The lesson? Politics is important, but by itself it tells us very little. In fact, surface political changes can obscure deeper cultural contradictions. Conservatives may cheer new leaders who lower taxes and reduce regulation, but these changes can amount to not much more than rearranging deck chairs on the *Titanic*. They may in fact worsen a culture's health.

What's good for business is not always good for America because businesses have their own agendas. Some of America's biggest companies, for example, are the most avid in backing same-sex marriage. Corporations including Eli Lilly, Walmart, and Apple were glad to join in what amounted to a social media lynch mob against Indiana's Religious Freedom Restoration Act (RFRA) in 2015. Why? Because it allegedly harmed persons with same-sex attraction. In the words of Patrick Deneen:

> The decision to #BoycottIndiana was not made because it was the politically courageous thing to do. It was made because it was the profitable thing to do. The [business] establishment could express support for a fashionable social norm while exerting very little effort, incurring no actual cost, and making no sacrifice to secure the goal. It had the further advantage of distracting most people from the fact that corporations like Apple have no compunction doing business in places with outright oppression of gays, women and Christians. Those real forms of repression and discrimination didn't matter; Indiana's purported oppression of gays did.[1]

How did Indiana RFRA supporters (like the small-town owners of Memories Pizza) become nationally reviled thought

criminals?[2] The answer lies in cultural disruptions over the past
century that sped up rapidly after World War II.

Simply put, America *can't* be the way it once was. As we'll
see throughout these pages, changes in the country's sexual, religious, technological, demographic, and economic fabric make
that impossible. And these upheavals have further reshaped our
politics, education, and laws. Traditionally, nations depend on
the continuity of generations to transmit memories and beliefs
across time and thus sustain their identity. At least for the United
States, that pattern is now smashed. Discontinuity, more and
more, drives today's American life.

Popular wisdom tends to locate the seeds of today's social
conflicts in America's "cultural revolution" of the 1960s. Those
of us who are old enough tend to remember the sixties through
the lens of the Vietnam War. And for good reason. Other wars
had been unpopular, but Vietnam was the first big setback to
America's national confidence, to our sense of being the "good
guys" in an American century.

The war opened the first deep cracks in how Catholics
understood their patriotism. The brothers Daniel and Philip
Berrigan, both of them priests, were among the many American Catholics who saw the war as immoral and who publicly
protested it.

Vietnam was also the first war covered nonstop by global
media. And the young men who fought in it served in a *republican* army, a citizen army used for ambiguous ends that critics
claimed were imperial. The war's conscript nature democratized
the anger against it. And that anger of the young bled easily into
other deep shifts taking place in the nation's life fueled by
postwar wealth, global security commitments, the Cold War,
scientific advances, and the struggle for racial justice.

Little things, too, can have big consequences. The transistor, perfected in 1947 and hitting the popular market in the mid-1950s, transformed the field of electronics and made modern computers possible—and indirectly, all that a computer-driven society implies. A similar "little" thing was the advent of the birth control pill for public use in 1960. Looking back from the vantage point of 2016, we can see that the pill is a monument to unintended consequences. It was benign-seeming because its creators intended it to strengthen marriages by giving couples the power to space their children. But it was radical in its effect because in decoupling sexual intimacy from procreation, it sparked much deeper changes in American social attitudes and behaviors than anyone foresaw.

Feminist scholars were hardly the first to notice that sex has implications that go well beyond making babies. Sex defines and breaks relationships and personal identities. It can be a cultural glue or a powerful destabilizer. This is one of the reasons traditional societies have always surrounded sex with rigorous sacred rituals and protections.

Half a century after the sixties, many American young people are more committedly pro-life than their parents and even their grandparents. This seems ironic, but it shouldn't surprise. They've seen what abortion does. They've lived with the fact that they could have been aborted. The humanity of the unborn child is obvious on any ultrasound machine.

The bad news is that many of these same young adults are less interested in marrying than their parents were. They're far more open to same-sex relationships and behavior. They're also much more casual in pursuing active sexual lives, with or without the baggage of long-term commitment.

Of course, young adult sex as a leisure activity is hardly stunning news. And we'd be unwise to ignore today's unique circumstances that help drive it. In an intensely individualistic culture, absent a convincing moral purpose for their sexuality, many use sex in a callous and predatory way. For others, though, it can express a misplaced need for some form of deeper communion with another person and an antidote to loneliness they don't fully understand.

Whatever the motives, this puts young people at high risk of sexually transmitted diseases, now a national epidemic. It also creates the risk of unplanned pregnancy and the heavy social pressure to abort that always follows. The best moral convictions in the kindest heart can unravel in the face of a life-changing choice such as bearing an unplanned child, alone and unmarried.

All of which underscores a simple fact: The surest way to transform a culture is from the inside out. And the surest path to doing it isn't through reasoned debate (too tedious) or violence (too costly) but by colonizing and reshaping the culture's appetites and behaviors.

※

WE NEEDN'T LOOK FAR for examples. H. L. Mencken, the satirist (and anti-religious bigot), once described America's Puritan Christian legacy as "the haunting fear that someone, somewhere, may be happy." Today, applied to sex, the word "puritanism" conjures up a range of lurid images, from scarlet letters to boiling pots of healthy passion with their lids screwed down by moral repression. Modesty, virginity, celibacy, sexual restraint: These words are dust magnets in today's vocabulary, antibiotics past their expiration date.

But liberating sexual desire has had awkward side effects— among them, normalized pornography. Porn is one of those topics nobody likes to talk about. Doing so can seem slightly obsessive. After all, the taste for pornography isn't new. The walls of ancient Rome were alive with its graffiti. No society has ever been free of it. And really, isn't porn just a cheesy sideshow for sexual losers? Hardly the shaper of a nation's soul.

Maybe. But the profits involved say otherwise. Today is not like the past.

Today the porn business has massive scope and influence, easy access from anywhere, and the shield of domestic privacy. Americans will never return to a world without widespread, easily available porn. That kind of innocence is as lost as aspirin bottles without seals.

How did the sea change happen? Technology made the difference. Technology reimagined the industry's dinosaur marketing and distribution systems. New technologies helped the porn business to grow rapidly and reach globally while remaining a private addiction. And private addictions shared by enough people eventually become accepted public behavior.

Americans have a deep libertarian streak. Too many people see pornography as a matter of personal choice. Too many resist seeing its wider impact. And as an industry, it exerts influence because too many people also make money from it. Globally, annual porn revenues now approach $100 billion, with more than $13 billion of that in the United States.[3]

Those profiting include major corporations that donate to candidates and have lobbyists in Washington. Most major U.S. hotel chains make "adult" programming available to guests as part of their entertainment systems. In a different era, that might make them vulnerable to public pressure. Corporate boards are alert to boycotts and bad publicity (remember Indiana)— but shareholders tend to focus on profits, not what they see as moral fine print. And the fact is, no mass movement has yet managed to inflict the financial punishment against porn that would force big companies to listen.

Today, anyone on the Internet, anywhere, anytime, can get hard-core pornography for free. Even the most extreme content—no matter how abusive or strange, legal or illegal—can be had for a price. Determined appetites can find even child pornography, and the criminal risks of getting caught with it, while real and severe, deter very few. Many American boys encounter pornography by their early teen years. Millions of men, and many women, seek it out addictively. Users make scores of millions of porn Web searches every day. And up to 30 percent of all data transferred across the Internet is pornography-related.[4] Persons uneasy about their habit can easily hide it from others. Explicit content is now so mainstream that it runs on network television.

Clearly, pornography is not a fundamental factor in changing any country's character. It's typically the by-product of other, deeper forces. But it does have a formative effect on the appetites and interests of millions of citizens. Arguing otherwise is simply foolish. And, worse, pornography literally changes the brain.

The psychiatrist Norman Doidge describes the process in *The Brain That Changes Itself.* Porn impacts the part of the brain related to exciting pleasure, not satisfying it. In fact, *not* fully satisfying the appetite is part of pornography's power. "[Porn's] neurochemistry is largely dopamine-related, and it raises our tension level," he notes. "Pornography, by offering an endless harem of sexual objects, hyper-activates the appetitive system" and actually rewires the brain. It creates what he calls "maps" that the user wants to keep activated. Doidge compares men using pornography to rats in an experiment, pressing a bar to get another shot of dopamine. They've "been seduced into pornographic training sessions that [meet] all the conditions required for plastic change of brain maps."[5] Doidge also notes that in recent decades much of pornography has shifted from romantic eroticism to increasingly violent and humiliating sadomasochism.

Pornography hurts more than the user. It alienates spouses. It destroys real intimacy. It reduces people to objects. And those are just the immediate human costs. The social impact is much wider and more damaging. It's a major factor in divorce, infidelity, and broken families. And even more brutally, the porn industry also fuels and feeds on the exploitation of women and minors forced into "sex work."

Today is not like the past. In the America of today, pornography is part of a very different new normal. A lot can happen in fifty years.

IN A 1789 LETTER to James Madison, Thomas Jefferson wondered whether "one generation of men has a right to bind another." He concluded that the earth belongs to the living, "and the dead have neither powers nor rights over it" since, by the law of nature, "one generation is to another as one independent nation to another." He went on to argue that "every constitution, then, and every law, naturally expires" at the end of a generation. "If it be enforced longer, it is an act of force and not right."[6]

Jefferson's focus was narrow. At the time he wrote, he was worried about public debt. He feared the power of one generation to cripple future generations with a legacy of reckless spending. He did not repudiate the past, however. All the Founders, Jefferson included, worked with a keen respect for history and its lessons.

But ideas can have unforeseen results. More than two hundred years later, Jefferson's words seem prophetic in an unintended way. They perfectly capture the ruptures and discontinuity at the heart of our current culture. As a people, we Americans have steadily lost interest in the past, and we've steadily grown in our taste for self-invention. If the earth belongs to the living, then we—the living—can do with it as we please; which means our appetites are licensed to profoundly shape the future, against and in spite of the past.

Why is that important? The baby boomers of the 1960s—the happy agents of America's cultural revolution—had the benefit of rebelling against a society with a well-developed moral framework and coherent political memory, both of which they unconsciously borrowed from, even in revolt. They had children. Those children are now having children. And what those new young adults and teens think and do will make the next America.

And what will that "next America" look like? Plenty of data exist on the habits of today's young people and emerging adults. Much of it is already well known. The Notre Dame sociologist Christian Smith and his colleagues have done some of the best research. It's worth recalling parts of it here.

In 2011, speaking of Americans then aged eighteen to twenty-five, Smith wrote that, despite many good exceptions, large numbers of "emerging adults are oblivious to [spiritual truths, service to the well-being of others, and] other kinds of human goods . . . focusing almost exclusively on materialistic consumption and financial security as the guiding stars of their lives." Addictions and intoxications of all sorts are "a central part of emerging adult culture." And contrary to media reports and popular assumptions (e.g., regarding environmental activism), "most emerging adults today . . . have little care about, investment in or hope for the larger world around them."

As Smith notes, today's young adults are often "simply lost. They do not know the moral landscape of the real world that they inhabit. And they do not understand where they themselves stand in that real moral world." They've had withheld from them "something that every person deserves to have a chance to learn: how to think, speak, act well on matters of good and bad, right and wrong." And who did the withholding? For Smith and colleagues, "one way or another, adults and the adult world are almost always complicit in the troubles, suffering and misguided living of youth, if not the direct source of them."[7]

Roughly half of all American Catholic teens now lose their Catholic identity before they turn thirty. The reasons are varied. Today's mass media, both in entertainment and in news, offer a steady diet of congenial, practical atheism, highlighting religious hypocrisy and cultivating consumer appetite. As one study noted, many young adults assume that "science and logic are how we 'really' know things about our world, and religious faith either violates or falls short of the standards of scientific knowledge."[8] Others have been shaped by theories trickling down from universities through high schools into a vulgarized, "simple-minded ideology presupposing the cultural construction of everything" and fostering an uncritical moral relativism.[9]

But the example of parents remains a key factor—often the key factor—in shaping young adult beliefs. The family is the main transmitter of religious convictions. Disrupting the family disrupts an entire cultural ecology. Former Catholics tend to come from homes where parents were tepid, less engaged, and indifferent or skeptical in matters of faith. Divorce and single-parent households have furthered the problem. As families break up, fail to form, or simply lose interest in religious practice, the mental and moral universe of emerging adults becomes alienated from America's past. And if the mind of the young breaks fundamentally with the past, so, too, does that of the nation.

It's worth returning briefly to the impact of one particular technology. As Mary Eberstadt has argued, "the underlying and underappreciated quantum leap toward irreligiosity in the 1960s" owed most of its force to the birth control pill. It "[changed] relations between the sexes—that is to say, within the natural family—as never before."[10]

Just as Darwin's theory of evolution shook popular assumptions about human origins and identity, the pill "severed the cultural connection between Christian ethics and American common sense," inspiring a private revolution. The resulting disarray "extended well beyond the narrow issue of birth control to encompass the entirety of sexual ethics. Over the course of a decade or so, a large swath of America decided that two millennia of Christian teaching on marriage and sexuality were simply out of date."[11]

And not just out of date. The pill's impact rippled out in *political* ways:

> These changing attitudes led to the redefinition of the private sphere, in the courts and culture alike, and a widespread sense that issues like contraception, premarital cohabitation and divorce—and then, much more controversially abortion—were private matters where the government had no business interfering. The very idea of "morals legislation" became suspect, and Christian arguments about family law and public policy that might have been accepted even by secular audiences in the 1940s came to be regarded with suspicion as potential violations of the separation of Church and state.

At the same time, a more sweeping idea gained ground as well—the conceit that many of Christianity's stringent sexual prohibitions were not only unnecessary but perverse.[12]

It's tempting to shrug off this kind of worried analysis as yet another case of religious neurosis about the body, an exaggerated anxiety about sex. Many people do exactly that—it saves them the burden of thinking. But sex, as we'll see throughout these pages, is intimately linked to how we understand ourselves as human. And in that regard, we'd be wise to recall that our roots as a nation are not just Protestant. They're Protestant in a uniquely Puritan Calvinist way: restless, driven, and rigorous.

Calvinism is branded into our national character, even for unbelievers. And it's a mixed blessing. In the words of the Catholic political scholar Pierre Manent, early Calvinism made a "magnificent contribution . . . to modern political freedom." Why? Because in the Calvinist worldview, human power "is liberated or encouraged, but no human being, religious or secular, is above the law."[13]

Yet there's another side to the story. As the (also Christian) political philosopher George Grant put it, in North America, "The control of the passions in [Calvinist] Protestantism became more and more concentrated on the sexual . . . while the passions of greed and mastery were emancipated from traditional Christian restraints."[14] Translation: The peculiar frenzy for sex and acquisitiveness in today's American culture has oddly religious roots. The libertine sex is a reaction against (perceived) excessive sexual codes of the past. The consumer acquisitiveness is a celebration of material appetite and possibilities.

The great irony of the sixties' sexual revolution is this: In breaking down "bourgeois" morality—the covenantal bonds and sacred restrictions of Christian sexuality—it made all sex, and all relationships, a matter of *transaction,* a matter of consumption and disposal, between radically distinct individuals. The boomers, it turns out, were better free market capitalists than they knew. And their children even more so.

"NO MAN EVER STEPS into the same river twice, for it's not the same river and he's not the same man." It's a great proverb of simple wisdom, widely quoted on the Web. The words are probably a loose version of what the ancient Greek philosopher Heraclitus actually said—that's a matter of dispute—but they do capture the kernel of his thinking. Heraclitus was big on flux. He taught that all things change, all the time.

As with rivers and men, so, too, with nations. A simple example: In the seven years between 2007 and 2014, self-identifying Christians in the United States declined from 78.4 percent of the population to 70.6 percent. In the same period, Catholics dropped from 23.9 percent to 20.8 percent. As the Pew Research Center noted:

> The Christian share of the U.S. population is declining, while the number of U.S. adults who do not identify with any organized religion is growing . . . Moreover, these changes are taking place across the religious landscape, affecting all regions of the country and many demographic groups. While the drop in Christian affiliation is particularly pronounced among young adults, it is occurring among Americans of all ages. The same trends are seen among whites, blacks and Latinos; among both college graduates and adults with only a high school education; and among women as well as men.[15]

There's more:

Christians remain by far the largest religious group among legal U.S. immigrants, though their estimated share has decreased from 68 percent in 1992 to 61 percent in 2012. Over the past two decades, the U.S. has admitted an estimated 12.7 million Christian immigrants.

The second-largest religious category among legal immigrants is the unaffiliated, which includes atheists, agnostics and people who do not identify with any particular religion. In recent years, the share of immigrants who have no religious affiliation has held fairly stable, at about 14 percent. Since 1992, the U.S. has admitted an estimated 2.8 million religiously unaffiliated immigrants.

Over the same period, the estimated share of legal Muslim immigrants entering the U.S. each year has roughly doubled, from about 5 percent of legal immigrants in 1992 to about 10 percent in 2012. Since 1992, the U.S. has admitted an estimated total of about 1.7 million Muslim immigrants.[16]

According to Pew, of the roughly 11.1 million unauthorized immigrants living in the United States in 2011, some 9.2 million (83 percent) were Christians, mostly from Latin America. Many of the remaining 17 percent had no religious affiliation. Fewer than one in ten unauthorized immigrants were estimated to belong to non-Christian religious groups.[17]

Why mention any of this?

The American founding was a creature of the eighteenth century and one of its great political achievements. But demography matters, and the United States is a nation built on and by immigrants. Any such country constantly renews and rethinks itself as its demography changes. This is a good and healthy

thing, so long as a mechanism exists to ensure a basic continuity with the past, to blend the newly arrived immigrant into the
nation's basic vision of who man is and the nature of a good society. This in turn presumes that the nation's vision has some
positive meaning, some higher common purpose. "Every man
for himself" is poor soil for a shared identity.

Immigration has served the U.S. Catholic experience especially well. In recent decades, Latino immigrants have sustained
the Catholic Church as America's largest religious community,
second only to the country's collective evangelical churches.
Latinos account for a large percentage of the Church's growth
in America since 1960. They now make up between one-third
and 40 percent (depending on the survey) of the country's more
than 81 million self-identified Catholics.[18] They've brought with
them a lively faith, deep traditions, and a strong commitment
to family.

But unlike the past, the active engagement of newly arrived
immigrants in Church life is much weaker. Many drift away after
the first generation. Hosffman Ospino, of the Boston College
School of Theology and Ministry, notes that 61 percent of Latino
Catholics in the United States were born in this country. But
their future commitment to the Church can't be assumed. "The
secularization of Hispanics is the biggest threat to the future
of the Catholic Church in America," he notes. "Only 3 percent
of Hispanic Catholic children attend Catholic schools and fewer
and fewer Hispanics under 30 attend church. We run the risk
of losing a whole generation of Catholics. If we fail to address
the issues facing Hispanic Catholics and the parishes that serve
them, then the parish structure in America will experience a
dramatic decline as it did in Europe."[19]

Many Latino immigrants become evangelicals. In a narrow
sense, that's almost "good" news. The worse news is that many

others drop away from any religious affiliation. A Pew Forum on Religion and Public Life study showed that 43 percent of Latino evangelicals are former Catholics. "They come to a country where more than half the religious population changes religious affiliation at least once in their lifetime, and the majority of them change affiliation more than once," explained Luis Lugo, formerly with the Pew Research Center. "They come into a context where it is simply more acceptable to leave Catholicism for something else."[20]

Additionally—and ironically—Lugo noted that "Latino evangelicals are much more socially conservative than Latino Catholics . . . So when these people convert from Catholicism to evangelicalism, they actually come closer to the official views of the Roman Catholic Church on social issues."[21]

Again, why does any of this matter? The facts about immigrant faith, its fluidity and its decline, are important for a reason. Unlike the past, the formative spirit in today's American life is cool to religion and no longer broadly biblical. Thus, the newly arrived are now shaped very differently from the past by their experiences in this country. And what immigrants believe and practice (or don't) today will influence what the nation as a whole believes and practices (or doesn't) tomorrow.

Demography, of course, is only one of the many factors that combine to modify the nature of daily life. The ideals of a middle-class republic owned equally by everyone, along with every person's ability to improve his or her lot with hard work—these beliefs are still very much alive in the American imagination. The reality is more complex. Evidence is strong that, over the past half century, America's wealth has congealed in the top 1 percent of the country's population. The gulf between that elite and the rest of the country is deep and widening. Ordinary Americans still live well compared to much of the rest of the world. But the nation's top 1 percent in wealth is worth as much as 70 times the wealth of the lower classes. Its members own or control roughly 43 percent of the nation's total wealth. The next 4 percent owns or controls an additional 29 percent.[22]

Meanwhile, the cost of securing national office effectively excludes the vast majority of citizens and encourages the growth of a political class disproportionately peopled by the connected and privileged. During the 2016 presidential campaign, Donald Trump's wealth was valued at $4.5 billion, Hillary Clinton's at $45 million.[23] Both claimed to speak for an electorate whose 2013 median household net worth was $56,335.[24]

Social mobility for the remaining 95 percent of the nation is a more complicated picture. Some data, like those in a 2014 study by Harvard and UC Berkeley economists, suggest that "despite huge increases in inequality, America may be no less [socially] mobile a society than it was 40 years ago."[25] But in general, both major political parties agree that upward mobility has declined in recent decades.

America is also a nation of transients. American *geographic* mobility has decreased in recent decades, especially among persons of lower income.[26] Nonetheless, in U.S. Census Bureau figures for 2012–13, 12 percent of Americans (about 36 million persons at the time) moved their home within the twelve-month period surveyed. Most moved within their local county, but they moved out of their neighborhoods, away from schools, churches, clubs, and other local attachments. Starting at age eighteen, the average American may move nine times in his or her life. Even after he or she reaches age forty-five, another three moves are common.

Mobility can be a mark of economic success. People often move to provide more for their families. But it can also imply job loss and hardship. In both cases, this mobility—voluntary or forced—strains family life and interferes with the formation of stable long-term communities. Many people resist being "all in" for their community because it may not be their community for long. The sense of place, of rootedness, of having to engage other people because they'll be your neighbors for a long time, of staying with a neighborhood, a church, local schools, and civic associations: That experience has been lost to many Americans. They identify more with their work than with their neighborhood.

Technology may seem to ameliorate this. It abolishes distance in a virtual sense. It brings people together online whenever they want. But the unifying effect of online communities can be misleading. Life mediated through a screen of electrons or a telephone is very different from the flesh-and-blood experience of dealing with real people who can't be unplugged. In practice, despite its great value, the Internet isolates and masks as much as it connects and reveals. Working from a computer at home may sound blissfully domestic. But the long-term effect is that "home" becomes as virtual as the office that invades and colonizes it.

Technology has also played a big role—the decisive role—in disrupting and reinventing our economic lives. And it's also changed how we think. To put it another way: We use our tools, but our tools also use us. In half a century, the United States has gone from a manufacturing economy based on *production,* to a knowledge economy based on *consumption.* The impact on our imaginations and behaviors has been huge. Production is a joint affair. It requires guilds, unions, and corporations. It needs assembly lines, investment, heavy industry, and communities. Consumption is a private affair. It requires only the self.

This difference between production and consumption is what the philosopher Zygmunt Bauman calls the gulf between solid and liquid modern life. Older, "solid" societies based on production find their security in property ownership, delayed gratification, rational organization, methodical progress, and bulk power. "Liquid," consumer-based societies—children of the tech revolution and its rapid pace of change—feed on "incessant new beginnings" and experiences.

In liquid life, travel for its own sake "feels much safer and much more enchanting than the prospect of arrival: The joy is all in the shopping that gratifies, while the acquisition itself, with the vision of being burdened with its possibly clumsy and awkward effects and side-effects, portends a high likelihood of frustration, sorrow and regret." The biggest fear is "drag coefficient"—the weight of having to live with bad choices.

Thus, as Bauman notes, a society of consumers "is unthinkable without a thriving waste-disposal industry. Consumers are not expected to swear loyalty to the objects they obtain with the intention to consume." In fact, rapidly getting rid of past choices is the only way to make room for new ones. Inevitably, this approach to life shapes personal relations: Once the pattern "to reject and replace an object of consumption which no longer brings full satisfaction is extended to partnership relations, the partners are cast in the status of consumer objects."[27] In a very real sense, nothing is more liquid than no-fault divorce.

Bauman isn't alone in his thinking. More than a decade ago, in his book *The Age of Access*, the social theorist Jeremy Rifkin described American culture as increasingly a "paid-for experience" based on the commodification of passion, ideals, relationships, and even time. In a rapidly morphing, tech-driven economy, he warned, ownership of property would be seen as an albatross. Ownership would decline, replaced by a preference for access to rented goods and services, and designed experiences.

Today, millennials are proving both Bauman and Rifkin right with spending patterns that are "not quite a stampede from ownership, but it's close."[28]

As James Poulos writes, "Buying means responsibility and risk. Renting means never being stuck with what you don't want or can't afford . . . There's something powerfully convenient about the logic of choosing to access stuff instead of owning it." As a result, "from flashy metros like San Francisco to beleaguered cities like Pittsburgh, rising generations are . . . paying to access experiences instead of buying to own."

But there's a problem. It's this: Without "an organic and cohesive property tradition, freedom does not arise because it cannot even really be imagined." And it *can't* really be imagined because it's "the habits of experience developed by ownership that make freedom a concrete, incarnate reality."[29]

As the American Founders inconveniently saw more than two centuries ago, freedom requires maturity. Maturity depends on clear thinking and self-mastery. Property is real. And owning property makes demands. It anchors and disciplines the floating world of desire.

But the Founders have been gone a long time. And today is not like the past.

CHAPTER 4

THE TOPOGRAPHY OF FLATLAND

There's no place like home. There's no place like home. Readers my age will instantly know those words from the classic film *The Wizard of Oz*. Dorothy speaks them as she clicks her ruby slippers together, leaves Oz behind, and zips magically back to Kansas. It's a moment of triumph for Dorothy. The Wicked Witch is dead. The Lion has his courage. The Straw Man has a brain. The Tin Man has a heart. Her friends are happy. The Munchkins love her, and so does everyone else within a hundred miles of Emerald City. If she wanted the job, she could be a queen. And let's face it: Oz is a marvelously interesting place, vivid with wonders, especially compared to Kansas.

In the original Oz fairy tale, L. Frank Baum (the author), describes Kansas as a vast, flat skillet, a land baked and burnt, where "great whirlwinds arose, mighty enough to crush any buildings in [their] path." An immense prairie stretches away on every side. Dull and gray, the world is without a tree or house to break the "broad sweep of flat country that reached to the edge of the sky in all directions." The sky is gray. The grass is bleached. The houses are blistered. Even Aunt Em and Uncle Henry are gray and drained of joy.[1] For Dorothy, this is "home." Then a tornado hits and carries her off to an adventure. Which raises an obvious question: Why would she ever want to go back?

I know why. I was born and grew up in Kansas. And Baum— who created a fictional Kansas based on his experiences in South Dakota—imagined a world very different from the farms, hills, grasslands, towns, and rivers I knew. There's nothing dull or dead in the Kansas of my memory; only people and things that are precious to me, a sky grand in color and scope, and the beauty of nature filling even the empty spaces.

Home is more than a building. We are creatures of place, from the smell of the soil to the green of the spring. Human beings need change, difference and variety, all of which are fed by the seasons and our travels. But we also need familiarity, permanence, and roots. This is the essence of home. Home anchors us. It locates us in the world. It surrounds us with the safety of love. And so the old slogan that you can take the boy out of the country, but not the country out of the boy, is quite literally true. The world is mediated by our bodies. Place imprints itself on our senses and on our soul.

This is so wherever we are. In my years as a bishop in South Dakota, there was grandeur in the Badlands and Black Hills; then in Colorado, the Rocky Mountains and the Eastern Plains; and now in the rivers and woodlands of Pennsylvania. Humans have a hunger for beauty, and we find it first in nature. In the words of the naturalist John Muir, "everybody needs beauty as well as bread," and "God never made an ugly landscape. All that the sun shines on is beautiful, so long as it is wild."

Scripture confirms it. Genesis tells us, "And God saw everything he had made, and it was very good" (1:31). There's nothing
flat or dull about the created world for a heart fully awake.
Every life has heights and depths, fertility and volume; its cross-
beams are vertical as well as horizontal. God spoke to Moses in
fire *on a mountain*. Jesus was transfigured in light *on a mountain*. Human experience climbs from the lowest circle in Dante's
hell up the paths of Mount Purgatory to the ecstasy of the heavens. These things of eternity are not just pretty words or elegant metaphors. Every soul has a vivid foretaste of them in the
sufferings and joys, resentments and mercies, that we encounter here and now, because the world is a sacrament pointing
beyond itself—to greater realities and their Author.

Pope Benedict XVI wrote, "The environment is God's gift
to everyone . . . In nature, the believer recognizes the wonderful result of God's creative activity" because "nature expresses
a design of love and truth. It is prior to us, and it has been given
to us as the setting for our life. Nature speaks to us of the
Creator" and his love for humanity.[2]

Thus the farmer, far better than any engineer or technician,
understands the soul of the world and humanity's place in it. For
Benedict, "The farmer is . . . the model of a mentality which
unites faith and reason in a balanced way. For on the one hand
he knows the laws of nature and does his work well, and on the
other, he trusts to Providence, because certain fundamental
things are not in his hands but in the hands of God."[3] Or, in
the words of Pope Francis, "We were not meant to be inun-
dated by cement, asphalt, glass and metal, and deprived of
physical contact" with the beauty of creation or the God who
fashioned it.[4]

Christian teaching on nature is ancient and extensive, but

sometimes the best lessons about creation come from unexpected sources. C. S. Lewis and J. R. R. Tolkien both survived the technological savagery of the First World War, and both returned to write powerful fiction rich with implicit faith. In Lewis's *The Magician's Nephew,* one of the *Chronicles of Narnia* tales, the lion Aslan—a symbol of Jesus Christ—literally sings Narnia into existence out of nothing. Narnia isn't programmed or engineered but *loved* into life, for Aslan's song is a breathing-out of his spirit like a lover's sigh, full of meaning greater than its words.

In like manner, in Tolkien's *The Silmarillion*—the creation story of Middle-earth—Ilúvatar (God) calls the world into existence through music sung in exquisite harmony by the Ainur, his great angelic spirits:

> Then the voices of the Ainur, like unto harps and lutes, and pipes and trumpets and . . . countless choirs singing with words, began to fashion the theme of Ilúvatar to a great music; and a sound arose of endless interchanging melodies woven in harmony that passed beyond hearing into the depths and into the heights, and the places of the dwelling of Ilúvatar were filled to overflowing, and the music and the echo of the music went out into the Void, and it was not void.[5]

Even when the highest of the Ainur, Melkor (Satan), sows confusion with his own rebellious song, God reweaves the dissonance into his own creative symphony so that evil is "but a part of the whole and tributary to its glory."

For both Lewis and Tolkien, nothing about nature is supine or dead. It resonates with the love of its Author. Just as Aslan is a good lion, but not a tame one, so, too, the world he sings into being is good and beautiful, but not tame, and not lifeless. It demands reverence. It demands stewards, not exploiters.

The scholars Matthew Dickerson and Jonathan Evans outline the principles of Tolkien's (and by extension, Lewis's) thought this way:

1. The universe is a gift and the work of a divine Creator.
2. Creation is inherently good; beauty and dignity are part of its given nature.
3. Creation has meaning prior to any purely human plans; it has a purpose; it exists to bring pleasure to its Creator and to those who dwell in it.
4. The created order and its inhabitants are vulnerable to evil embodied in a cosmic enemy.
5. The mission of people dwelling in the world is to acknowledge the goodness of the earth, fulfill its purpose, and help in its restoration from evil.[6]

Love brought our world into being. And love, in its material form as undeserved beauty and unearned gift, disarms the intellect and touches the soul. But for a certain kind of modern thinking, this is not acceptable. Rather, it's the worst sort of insult to our vanity: Beauty makes us conscious of realities and truths we did not create and do not command. Therefore it reminds us that we are weak, so it cannot be trusted. It makes us dependent, and we prefer control. And control requires power. Power—even the modest power humans can imagine they deserve by right—is erotic; it's a drug for the ego, a faithless and demanding lover. And as in all toxic romances, the relationship always ends badly.

The bitter irony of a society built on the accumulation of

power is that most people are left relatively powerless, living lives handed over to systems or processes—bureaucracy, the economy, the demands of a networked world—that they do not govern, but instead which govern them. Thus, most people end up being moved not by greed or power but by necessity—what they think they *must* do—and therefore by fear.

It's worth remembering that in Baum's fairy tale, "Oz the Great and Terrible" turned out to be a squat little carnival huckster behind a curtain, using people for his own ends, his own safety, his own power. Not much of a wizard.

THE BLIND SEE. The lame walk. And while the dead don't yet rise, science is working on that problem. This is fact, not fiction—or it soon will be. Devices like eSight and the Argus II "bionic eye," among others, already replicate sight for many of the visually impaired, and sight technology is still in its infancy. In early 2016, the U.S. government approved a technology called Indego for public use—"a wearable robotic skeleton that supports, bends and moves the legs of people with spinal-cord injuries, multiple sclerosis and other types of lower body paralysis."[7] The Indego joins a similar exoskeleton already produced by Israel's ReWalk Robotics. And back in 2013, the tech giant Google started a biotech company—Calico—with the goal of "curing death" by defeating the aging process.[8]

The Google/Calico effort was inspired in part by Ray Kurzweil, the futurist author. Kurzweil talks openly "about his ambition to achieve eternal life, even speculating that it might be possible to bring his dead father back from the grave in the process," and for the rest of us to escape the shabby wetware we call bodies.

Americans are technology addicts, and boosterism shapes

much of the media coverage of today's tech developments. In the two-month period from November 2015 through January 2016, the *Wall Street Journal* carried stories with headlines like "Life with your digital model. Within a decade our online alter egos will go on interviews and find deals. Millions of copies of your model could roam the Internet, doing all the things you'd do if only you had the time."

And: "You will speak every language. Coming soon: earpieces that offer real-time translations." And: "A robotics scientist aims to build models that speak to human emotions." And: "How technology will transform retirement. Get ready for a new array of devices and services that will make it easier to work, stay healthy, live at home and remain connected to friends and family."

It sounds great. In a sense, it is. These are dazzling ideas. And they're not a surprise. More than forty years ago, the writer Arthur C. Clarke hinted at the future in his famous "Clarke's laws": First, when a distinguished but elderly scientist states that something is possible, he is almost certainly right. When he states that something is impossible, he is very probably wrong. Second, the only way of discovering the limits of the possible is to venture a little way past them into the impossible. Third, any sufficiently advanced technology is indistinguishable from magic.

Science and technology have made life rich in massive ways. When they serve real human development—as they often do in medicine and food production—the Church welcomes their results. As Benedict XVI wrote, "Technology, in this sense [of serving human dignity], is a response to God's command to till and keep the land (see Gen 2:15)."[9] And in *Laudato Si*, Pope Francis noted that "Human creativity cannot be suppressed. If an artist cannot be stopped from using his or her creativity, neither should those who possess particular gifts for the advancement of science and technology be prevented from using their God-given talents for the service of others."[10]

This makes sense because the Western idea of progress has theological roots. Christianity is a restless faith. It points us beyond this life, but also seeks to remake the world in holiness. Christians honor the past as part of salvation history. The past sets the stage for our own small parts in God's story. But the Gospel can't be satisfied with the world as it was, or is. Rather, the disciple serves God in "renewing the face of the earth." Thus, the modern secular urge to improve the world and break away from the past is often a kind of Christian faith scrubbed of its supernatural content. The almost "religious" zeal in some progressive political movements has the same roots.

The problem with progress is how we define it.

For the Church, "Man is not a lost atom in a random universe," and "authentic human development concerns the whole of the person in every single dimension." For a Christian, material progress alone is not enough. It may in fact kill the good in a culture. In *Caritas in Veritate*, Benedict stressed that "[genuine] development requires a transcendent vision of the person, it needs God: Without him, development is either denied, or entrusted exclusively to man, who falls into the trap of thinking he can bring about his own salvation." And this ends by making creation (in the words of Pope Francis) a vast trash heap. As Benedict wrote:

> The technical worldview . . . is now so dominant that truth has come to be seen as coinciding with the possible. But when the sole criterion of truth is efficiency and utility, development is automatically denied. True development does not consist in "doing" . . . Even when we work through satellites

or through remote electronic impulses, our actions always remain human, an expression of our responsible freedom. Technology is highly attractive because it draws us out of our physical limitations and broadens our horizon. *But human freedom is authentic only when it responds to the fascination of technology with decisions that are the fruit of moral responsibility* (emphasis in original).[11]

In the 1600s, the scholar Francis Bacon promoted early modern science as a way to ease human life and end suffering. The words he used could be oddly brutal. He spoke of "torturing" nature—putting her on the rack—to force her to give up her secrets. But Bacon was also a great lawyer and salesman. In a time of conflict—the Reformation was very recent—he used his skills to argue that scientific thinkers had "minds washed clean of opinions." They were men of courage. Men of intellect. They dealt only with facts. In Bacon's words, scientists stood above the petty bickering of the day. They worked from reason, not emotion or religious passion.

Bacon's lobbying helped science thrive in a badly divided era. But in reality, science is anything but neutral. Working on the frontiers of knowledge, "science is all about arguments and opinions." And scientists are not purely objective creatures moved by disinterested investigation, but creatures also moved by ego, ambition, funding competition, and personal and group bias. Scientists also tend to speak with a "priestly voice" of expert knowledge that—innocently or otherwise—can discourage unwelcome questions and criticism from the general public.[12] This has been clear for years in America's bioethical disputes.

None of this denies the good done by today's science and technology. But it also doesn't free us from questioning their approach to nature. Our words "awe" and "wonder" come from the Old English and Norse terms for dread, great reverence, and the miraculous. Applied to nature, they suggest the presence of the holy. We feel awe when we meet something in creation much greater than human, something transcendent that commands our respect.

Not so in modern thought. A scientist may feel "awe" as a person when he looks at the night sky. But science as a discipline allows no such category. Science is about collecting and analyzing measurable data. Technology is about organizing nature into a "standing reserve" of raw material for human use. Things not measurable or useful are not relevant. In a sense, they're not even real. That includes beauty. Beauty (so the reasoning goes) is an idea stamped on physical data by a person's emotions and the conditions of culture. Beauty can't "dwell" in the thing described as beautiful, because it doesn't exist outside the mind of the observer.

Modern technology thus tends to cause deep changes in our relationship with nature. Creation is no longer a sacrament. In fact, the word "creation" is seen as misleading since it implies a Creator. Rather, nature is just *there*—dead material waiting for the human will to give it meaning. And technology's inner logic is a self-directing juggernaut. To put it another way: In a Christian culture, life moves toward the goal of eventual rest in God. In a Marxist culture, the goal is different, but similar: Life moves toward eventual rest here on earth when the state withers away and men finally live as brothers.

But in a technocratic culture—what the media scholar Neil Postman called a "technopoly"—technology is its own justification. It's the driving force of life. The essence of technology's spirit is *becoming,* not arriving; restlessness as a destiny. No end point. No rest. No peace. Only more speed, more change, more new appetites and experiences, more intensities of discarding the past, outgrowing the present, and grasping for the fabulous future . . . always just out of reach.

⚜

WHY DOES ANY OF this matter in daily life? It matters because if we understand the inner logic of our culture, we can try to change it. And a central fact of modern American life is idolatry.

Which sounds outlandish. But check the evidence.

We're a nation held together by respect for the law. The seminal law in our civilization comes from the experience of Moses on Mount Sinai—which is why Moses (inconveniently for unbelievers) shows up on so many of our public buildings. Until recent decades the Ten Commandments were so widely memorized and revered that almost any citizen could recite them by rote. And note their arrangement. The first three speak to our relationship with God. The last seven speak to our relationship with other persons. The God of Israel does not mince words:

1. I am the Lord your God; you shall not place foreign gods before me.
2. You shall not take the name of the Lord your God in vain.
3. Remember to keep holy the Sabbath.

Now here's a simple test. How many public figures, or even personal friends, do you know who genuinely place God first in their thinking? How much of God do you find in American public life? How many times in a day are the words "Jesus Christ" abused at work, on the street, in our public entertainment? How many malls close, how many people take a break from work, and how many families disconnect from media, sports, and shopping in order to spend time together, without distractions, on an average Sunday? And how much time do any of us make for silence—the kind of silence that allows God to speak, and us to listen?

For most of us, the answers aren't pretty. American life is a river of noise and pressure, a teeming mass of consumer appetites. It's profoundly ordered *away* from the first three commandments, even when we pay them lip service. And ignoring the first three inevitably undercuts the other seven. The dignity of others is an empty piety, subject to editing as we find useful, *unless* it's guaranteed by Someone greater than us, to whom we owe our fidelity. Without that Someone, the rights of other people are no more solid than our moods.

To borrow the words of Jean-Marie Lustiger, the great French churchman, "[How] can we claim to be Christian when we continue to live like pagans?"[13] But we're often worse than pagans. True pagans had a reverence for nature and the gods. Today we worship ourselves and our tools. That sin defaces the world. It also kills our ability to see things as they really are. Simple blades of grass in heaven cause the visiting souls from hell so much pain in C. S. Lewis's *The Great Divorce* because they're too real to bear for creatures made unreal by their own delusions. Consumer culture—the world we live in every day— is deeply anti-Christian not just in its gluttony and its exclusion of the needs of others, but also in its damage to the mature, clear-thinking self.

As Americans, we're uniquely prone to an idolatry of progress. The reason is our history. Nobody saw this more clearly than the writer George Grant. The United States is an invented nation. It was carved out of the wild with a "conquering relation to place [that] has left its mark within us . . . Even our cities have been encampments on the road to economic mastery."[14]

Our religious roots have stamped America with an appetite for results and a distrust of contemplation. Early Calvinism gave us "a practical optimism which had discarded awe [and so produced] those crisp, rationalized managers who are the first necessity of the kingdom of man. Those uncontemplative and unflinching wills without which technological society cannot exist, were shaped from the crucible" of pioneering Puritanism.[15]

Our roots have withered. But their effect remains: "What makes the [American] drive to technology so strong is that it is carried on by men who still identify what they are doing with the liberation of mankind."[16] And that project is going strong. God may be gone, but our belief in progress endures.

But progress, it turns out, takes its revenge in unintended consequences.

At home, the tech revolution means more comforts for everyone. It means easier communication, education, transportation, and work. Technology equalizes opportunity in important ways. Much of this is good. But it also fuels a cult of efficiency, a fetish for tools, and a lopsided focus on the future. It fosters boredom with the past. It feeds self-interest. It transfers huge wealth to a new, highly secular leadership class. It punishes many workers in traditional industries. It renders, or seems to render, the "supernatural" obsolete. And with its power to manipulate and propagandize, it reshapes our political life. As citizens are swarmed by ads, noise, and political messaging, people's sense of powerlessness grows. So does their anger at the privileged. So does their skepticism about the democratic process.

And abroad? Overseas, technology has helped millions of people in formerly "underdeveloped" countries. As Thomas Friedman wrote in *The World Is Flat* (2005), the tech revolution has globalized the world economy by "flattening" the playing field for emerging nations. But the same technologies have often hurt the environment. They've also damaged traditional cultures. And terrorists have used them with brutal effect.

The proverb remains true: "For the man with a hammer, every problem is a nail." Our tools come with a bias to use them on nature and on people without fully understanding either. And in the process, we change ourselves. In Tolkien's *Lord of the Rings* trilogy, the wizard Saruman turns from wisdom to rapacity in his taste for power. He rips out the ancient trees and flattens the land to make room for the industries of war. The lesson is simple: All technology, along with its blessings, also carries a temptation—an appetite for control, a willingness to flatten the world (if needed) to make space for the human will.

And that flattening instinct, which sees the whole world as raw material, comes with an enmity for those things technology can't fix—including imperfect human beings. So we—all of us—inevitably become the targets of our own tools.

In denying any higher purpose to nature, science (or, better, "scientism"—the materialist philosophy that feeds off science) undercuts any special status for humanity, any natural rights inherent to being human, any firm grounding for justice. All these things are flexible. All are subject to change by whoever has power.

Cleaned up from the Nazi era and now with better marketing, eugenics is back. Genetic screening for fetal flaws is common. So is trafficking in the body parts of aborted children. As early as 2005, the ethicist Leon Kass, M.D., described our "peculiar moral crisis" this way:

> We are in turbulent seas without a landmark, precisely because we adhere . . . to a view of human life that both gives us enormous power and that, *at the same time*, denies every possibility of non-arbitrary standards for guiding its use.

Though well-equipped, we know not who we are or where
we are going. We triumph over nature's unpredictabilities
only to subject ourselves, tragically, to the still greater unpre-
dictability of our capricious wills and fickle opinions. Engineering the engineer as well as the engine, we race our
train we know not where . . . That we do not recognize our
predicament is itself a tribute to the depth of our infatua-
tion with scientific progress and our naïve faith in the suffi-
ciency of our humanitarian impulses.[17]

Kass, a former chair of the President's Council on Bioethics,
offered those words at Washington's Holocaust Memorial
Museum. At the time, he dismissed as "a few zealots" the
"immortalists [and] bionics boosters . . . trying to build a super-
man or a post-human being."

But less than two decades later, transhumanism—the quest
through genetics and technology for a new kind of humanity
that transcends the jail cell of the purely human brain and
flesh—is a new research frontier spearheaded by leading biotech
companies.

⚜

WE HOLD THESE TRUTHS to be self-evident: All men are created equal. They are endowed by their Creator with certain
unalienable rights. These rights include life, liberty, and the
pursuit of happiness.

These are wonderful words. Most Americans know them,
or at least once learned them. As a national creed, these beliefs
from the Declaration of Independence have enduring character and beauty. They're imprinted on our national memory. And
rightly so.

Too bad they're not true. Or, more accurately, they're true, but only in a particular biblical sense. One of the facts of life is that people are *not* equal in intelligence, beauty, wealth, social skills, athletic ability, physical health, family influence, potential earnings, or access to the best schools. The list of life's inequities is long, and always part of the human experience. Life isn't fair. And this is so even in revolutionary societies based on egalitarian ideals. The old ruling class may end up without their heads. But new hierarchies always take their place.

This isn't news. Most people know that differences and inequalities are inevitable in the real world. So they sort themselves, or get sorted by events or other people, into categories of merit and influence. Whether these distinctions are formal and obvious, or invisible and officially denied, is irrelevant. Life doesn't treat people equally. The poor and infirm are living witnesses. And in a utilitarian world, the natural-rights sentiments (including equality) that moved the nation's Founders in 1776— as great as those beliefs still are—"appear false and meaningless or superstitious" to many of the leading minds that now shape our political imagination.[18]

When key scientists and scholars argue, as some now do, for human cloning, or the legitimacy of killing disabled newborns, or breeding children for spare parts on a mass scale, these proposals may be morally vile. But in a world with no higher purpose, they're not illogical or inconsistent.[19]

People are equal in one sense only, but it's a decisive sense deeper than any simple equations of worth. Think of it this way: Does a mother really love each irreplaceable child she bears "equally"—or in some much more profound and intimate way? Can a good father really weigh the "comparative value" of the young lives that come from his own flesh and blood? Our dignity is rooted in the God who made us. His love, shared in every parent's experience, is infinite and unique for each of us

as individual persons—because each son and daughter is an
unrepeatable miracle. Only God's love guarantees our worth.
And therein lies our real equality. In him, our inequalities
become not cruelties of fate, but openings that lead us to love,
support, and "complete" each other in his name.

For the Christian, human beings are not sovereign individuals. Not interchangeable reasoning and consuming units. Not
variables in a math equation. Our differences invite us to depend
on and to help one another. And this fact should shape every
aspect of our lives.

A skeptic might call this sort of thinking an alibi for living
with chronic evils. Not so. Nothing absolves Christians from the
duties of justice. In the political realm, equal treatment under
the law is vital to a decent society. In matters of economy, the
poor may always be with us, as Scripture says. But that doesn't
excuse us from working as hard as we can to make our country
a worthy home for all our citizens. The Gospel should move us
to change the world for the better, not bless it as it is.

That Christian restlessness, or leaven, is the engine of the
civilization we call the West. Christianity *invented* the idea of
the "individual." And the world shifted because of it:

> Christianity changed the ground of human identity . . . By
> emphasizing the moral equality of humans, quite apart from
> any social roles they might occupy . . . [t]he New Testament
> stands out against the primary thrust of the ancient world
> with its dominant assumption of "natural" inequality . . .
> The Christian conception of God provided the foundation
> for what became an unprecedented form of human society.
> Christian moral beliefs emerge as the ultimate source of the
> social revolution that has made the West what it is.[20]

This is why even the harshest critics of biblical faith often see liberal democracies as a form of secularized Christianity. Humanitarian compassion, embodied in the welfare state, is the virtue of charity drained of its God content. At its best, democracy works from a biblically derived belief in every person's value.

But if the people are the only source of power and moral authority, and the people are venal and corrupt, then so is the state. If the state's economic life feeds venality and corruption, the problems get worse. Moreover, in its purest instincts, democracy distrusts any material form of inequality. And as those inequalities seem to disappear, democracy grows more hostile to any remaining inequalities. Its leveling effect on all institutions and relationships gets stronger as differences and distinctions weaken.

As we've already seen, religion checks these tendencies only when people actually believe and practice what their faith teaches. And if new orthodoxies of unbelief attack inherited faith, if scientism and a cult of technology lower our eyes to the gadgets in our hands, the effect ripples across a culture's soul. In the words of David Gelernter, the Yale computer scientist,

> Scientists have acquired the power to impress and intimidate every time they open their mouths, and it is their responsibility to keep this power in mind no matter what they say or do. Too many have forgotten their obligation to approach with due respect the scholarly, artistic, religious, *humanistic* work that has always been mankind's spiritual support. Scientists are (on average) no more likely to understand this work than the man on the street is to understand quantum physics. But science used to know enough to approach

cautiously and admire from the outside, and to build its own work on a deep belief in human dignity. No longer.[21]

Thus it's no surprise that colleagues of the (atheist) philosopher Thomas Nagel publicly savaged him some years ago for claiming that "the materialist new-Darwinian conception of nature is almost certainly false."[22] His sin? Heresy. He doubted a new orthodoxy and got a taste of the new intolerance.

It's also no surprise, as a *Wall Street Journal* essay said after the death of Steve Jobs in 2011, that the "most singular quality [of the Apple founder] was his ability to articulate a perfectly secular form of hope . . . He believed so sincerely in the 'magical, revolutionary' promise of Apple" and its technology "precisely because he believed in no higher power."[23]

"This is the gospel of the secular age," said the *Journal* piece, and for "people of a secular age, Steve Jobs' gospel may seem like all the good news we need. But people of another age would have considered it a set of beautifully polished empty promises, notwithstanding all its magical results. Indeed, they would have been suspicious of it precisely because of its magical results."

A POSTSCRIPT

More than 130 years ago, an Anglican priest named Edwin Abbot wrote a curious little novel called *Flatland*.[24] The story imagines a world of intelligent two-dimensional figures. These creatures are straight lines, triangles, squares, and polygons, led by a priestly class of circles. The circles oversee all science, business, engineering, art, and trade.

Flatland is a complex society guided by the creed of Configuration. For Flatlanders, all of reality consists in width and length. State doctrine condemns "those ancient heresies which led men to waste energy and sympathy in the vain belief that conduct depends upon will, effort, training, encouragement, praise or anything else but Configuration." And what is Configuration? It's the belief that all misconduct, all crime, comes from some deviation in Regularity of line or angle. Those who are Irregular end up in hospitals. Or prisons. Or executed.

One night the narrator, an urbane and orthodox Square (an attorney), is visited by a Sphere. The Sphere lifts him out of his Flatland universe. It shows him the glory of three dimensions and proves that Flatland is only part of a much larger reality. Then it sends the eager narrator back to his own world as an apostle of the Gospel of the Three Dimensions. Where he's promptly locked up for mental illness and heresy.

Popular wisdom holds that *Flatland* was a satire of the conventionalism of the Victorian era. But we might find better parallels closer to our own land, in the scientism of our own time.

CHAPTER 5

LOVE AMONG THE ELOI

What *is* it about the French? They're an exhilarating paradox.

Also exasperating. A blend of northern and Mediterranean Europe; faith and atheism; romance, passion, and reason. And France itself is unique: a land of great saints (Louis IX, Thérèse of Lisieux), great artists (Gauguin, Monet), great murderers (Robespierre), great writers (Claudel, Bernanos, Péguy), great warriors (Jeanne d'Arc, Bonaparte), great scholars (Pascal, Descartes, and, yes, Tocqueville), great Churchmen (Jean-Marie Lustiger), and great libertines (de Sade).

The French have a genius for grasping the heart of a new idea or historical moment early, then driving it to its logical, and sometimes unpleasant, conclusion. What begins at the Bastille ends at the guillotine.

All of which might be interesting for another book. But what's it got to do with *us*? Just this: France has produced some of the sharpest critics of the globalized culture Europeans and

Americans now share. And among the most skilled of those critics is Pascal Bruckner—penetrating, funny, and thoroughly cynical. Bruckner is no friend of Christianity. Just the opposite. He's happy to blame Christians for "[overdramatizing] our existence by subjecting it to the alternative between hell and paradise. The life of a believer is a trial that takes place entirely before the divine Judge . . . The hope of redemption is thus inseparable from a fundamental worry."

Christian faith (in Bruckner's view) can be summed up in a single question: "Why should we cling to a few instants of joy on Earth at the risk of frying forever in Satan's realm?"[1]

And so on. Nothing new there.

But what sets Bruckner apart is this: He's just as fierce in describing the contradictions and self-indulgence of modern *secular* life. A few samples:

On the 1960s, and the generation of Peter Pan fathers and mothers they fostered: "Beer-bellied, balding and near-sighted, the children of the baby-boom, often having become well-established and cleaned up, remain riveted to their dreams; little hellions until the day they die, side by side with decrepit young people who age prematurely, aware that their parents, by refusing to grow up, stole their youth from them."

On "It's all about me": "[Today's] individualism . . . swings like a metronome" between two extremes, "a proclamation of self-sufficiency . . . and the giddiness of total plagiarism that makes each person into a weather vane."

On "I deserve it": "No concept is richer and more likely to get us on our feet than the 'right to' something . . . The relationship between infantilism and victimization resides in this: Both are founded on the same ideas of *rejecting obligations*, denying duty and feeling certain of having an infinite amount of credit with one's contemporaries."

On our biggest legal narcotic: Television demands of the viewer "only one act of courage—but one that is superhuman— that is, to turn it off . . . TV is the continuation of apathy by other means."

On today's victim culture and its "holy family of victims": "If all it takes to win [disputes or concessions] is to be recognized as a victim, then . . . being a victim will become a vocation, a full time job."[2]

Finally, and most usefully for our purposes here and now, *on Eros*:

Eros has the peculiarity of making love calculable and sub- jecting it to the power of mathematics; in the seclusion of the bedroom, [today's] lovers take the exam of happiness and ask themselves: Are we up to snuff? It is from their sexual- ity, that new oracle, that they are asking tangible proofs of their passion. Combinations of the academic and gastro- nomic models: following a good recipe gets a good grade. From caresses to positions, from perversions to thrills, they test their marriage or their relationship, draw up balance sheets of orgasm, compete with other couples in noisy dem- onstrations, exhibitionist confessions, give themselves prizes or honorable mentions, and try in this way to reassure them- selves as to the state of their feelings. Erotic pleasure is not only an old audacity that the liberalization of mores has transformed into a commonplace . . . it is the only thing on which people can count and that allows them to convert into memorable quantities the fleeting emotions passing through them. Thus they use the magic of numbers to evaluate the harmony of their relationships and check to be sure that the yield in pleasure is adequate.[3]

Bruckner's countryman Michel Houellebecq captures the hollowed-out shell of a person that results from this kind of hypersexualized life in his novel *Platform*. It's the portrait of a man for whom sex has gone from casual to compulsive to the bored scratching of a physical itch.[4]

But of course, we Americans are much more sensible than the French. Much more grounded and pragmatic. The French have always been slightly unhinged on matters involving sex. And everybody knows that Europeans are past their prime and wallowing in decadence. On our side of the Atlantic, we're still pretty religious. On our side of the Atlantic, we do things differently. Or so we like to think. And it's a happy thought, because it confirms how much healthier we are than everybody else. Except we're not.

It's helpful to remember that more than a million people took to the streets protesting "gay marriage" in *Paris* (2012), not in Washington. Americans marry more but also divorce more than do people in any European nation. Americans experience single parenthood and repartnering more frequently. In the United States, 10 percent of women will have had three husbands or live-in partners by the age of thirty-five. In France, the number is fewer than 2 percent.

Americans marry and cohabit at a younger age than in Europe. And their relationships are much more tenuous. More than half of cohabiting American couples will break up within five years, a much higher rate than in Europe. And one-fifth of all Americans who marry will divorce or separate in the same five-year time frame. That's more than double the number in Europe. Children in the United States live through more parental breakups, and they have more new adults moving in with the biological parent who cares for them, than children in any

Western European country. As a result, American family life involves more upheavals and transitions than anywhere in Western Europe, with negative impact on the young.[5]

Plenty of data confirm that Americans who actively practice their religious faith, and who attend religious services regularly, have more stable marriages and families. And as the social researcher Andrew Cherlin notes, it's quite true that Americans are more religious than Europeans. But while American religion, shaped by the Reformation and its aftermath, has a communitarian surface, it also has a strongly individualist undercurrent. As Cherlin notes, this can actually encourage marriage breakup rather than slowing it down.[6] It's worth understanding why.

Prior to the mid-nineteenth century, romance had little to do with the choice of marital partner. Arranged marriages among the elite were common. For everyone else, reality set the demands. In agrarian societies like the early United States, farming needed two dependable workers, a husband and wife. It also needed children to help with the labor and pass along ownership. In the cities, families needed a reliable mother in the home to raise children and a reliable father in the work force to earn what the family required. Sexual attraction and emotional fulfillment were factors. They always have been. But for the serious work of marriage and family, they weren't the main ingredients.

The movement of industry from the home to the factory during the industrial revolution reduced the need for large families. Educating young people to be economically competitive became more costly. Parents had fewer children. Thus, throughout the twentieth century, marriage shifted to a more "companionate" and individualized model. Romance, sexual satisfaction, and personal fulfillment took on greater importance.

American religion (with its individualist focus) inadvertently fueled the shift from marriage as an objective institution that serves the common good to a subjective relationship that pleases and rewards each of the partners. And this intensified a basic tension in the American character: a hunger for the moral ideal of marriage versus a right to pursue one's individual happiness *right now.*

The point is this: Today's pressures for sexual liberation didn't happen in a vacuum. They fit comfortably with trends in American culture that go back many decades, even before the 1960s. As evidence, it's useful to revisit Wilhelm Reich's book from 1936, *The Sexual Revolution.* Reich, an Austrian psychoanalyst, argued that a really fundamental revolution in human affairs can only be made at the level of sexual freedom. And it needs to begin by wiping away institutions like marriage, family, and traditional sexual morality.

What's interesting about Reich's work is that, eighty years ago, he saw the United States as the most promising place for that kind of revolution to happen, despite its rigorous Puritan history.[7] And again, the reason is simple. Americans have a deep streak of individualism, a distrust of authority, and a big appetite for self-invention. As religion loses its hold on people's behavior, all of these instincts accelerate. The trouble is that the sexual revolution is not just about personal sexual morality or the sociological health of American family life—though it obviously impacts both. Rather, as Michael Hanby notes, "the sexual revolution is, at bottom, the *technological* revolution and its perpetual war against natural limits applied externally to the body, and internally to our self-understanding" (emphasis added).[8]

Just as modern feminism depends on the technological conquest of the female body—the suppression of fertility—so, too,

Hanby argues, same-sex marriage depends on the technological mastery of procreation. Surrogacy and artificial reproductive technologies can now provide same-sex couples with the offspring to reinforce their claims of equality with natural marriage. And if the state recognizes the legal equality of same-sex and natural marriages, then denying the traditional financial and political privileges of marriage to same-sex unions is clearly a form of bigotry.

Once the genie is out of the bottle, sexual freedom goes in directions and takes on shapes that nobody imagined. And ultimately it leads to questions about who a person is and what it means to be human.

FOR ANYONE WANTING FOOD for thought in today's "new normal," we now live in an orchard of low-hanging fruit. A brief sampling of the menu:

Tinder and similar phone apps for young-adult sex hookups. High school mobile sexting. Websites for the married but adulterous (online dating for cheaters). The rapid rise of "postnups"—they're like prenuptial agreements, but signed *after* the wedding, often after one of the spouses has already tripped up and been caught cheating (see adultery websites). Pet bereavement leave for (often childless) dog and cat owners. Cost-benefit sex on campus (sex yes, relationship no—negative yield on time and emotional investment).[9] And so on. It's a long list.

These bite-size nuggets of confusion are a meal for future anthropologists. But they're more than curiosities. They're expressions of sexual trending with deep implications. The advent of phenomena like same-sex marriage hasn't ended the frictions of sexual politics. It's kicked them into high gear. The debate over same-sex and transgender rights disguises a much more basic struggle over truth. The meaning of words like "mother" and "father" can't be changed without also subtly changing the meaning of "child." More specifically, is there *any* higher truth determining what a human person is, and how human beings should live, beyond what we ourselves make or choose to describe as human?

It's an unwelcome question to ask. And anyone who poses it can expect blowback.

As the scholar Augusto Del Noce observed decades ago, the sexual revolution, for all its talk of freedom, has a distinctly totalitarian undercurrent. Classic virtues like modesty can't be ignored; they must be recast as abnormal.[10] If the goal is uprooting millennia of traditional sexual morality, a need exists for the means and the ruthlessness to enforce the uprooting. The process doesn't need to be vulgar or brutish. But it does need to be thorough—and in an advanced media culture, that can be achieved by reshaping public perceptions. And so what we face now is what the *Wall Street Journal* described as "the new intolerance." As the *Journal* editors note, "even as America has become more tolerant of gays, many activists and liberals have become ever more intolerant of anyone who might hold more traditional cultural or religious views."[11]

This should surprise no one. Sex is profoundly connected to human identity. Same-sex activists can therefore never be satisfied with mere tolerance or acceptance. They need vindication— which means the hounding of contrary beliefs. And this is exactly the course of events in places where efforts to ensure religious liberty by law have been attacked as "anti-gay." This is rich in irony. Sexual expression, which has no mention or standing in the Constitution, now routinely seems to trump religious practice and teaching, which are explicitly protected under the First Amendment.

The collapse of clear reasoning on same-sex unions has also fueled support for the far frontiers of gender ideology. Media coverage of transgender issues has been lavish and lopsidedly positive. It has also been based on science that is at best inadequate and at worst gravely flawed.[12] An entire reporting franchise has sprung up around stories with titles like "Trans Rights Behind Bars," "Helping the Young with Gender Transitions," "Opening a Bathroom Door to Make All Feel Welcome," and "Heather Has Two Genders."[13] This, too, should surprise no one. A new ideology of sex and gender needs new archetypes to shape the young and re-form public thought.

The "Heather Has Two Genders" story tracks a recent publishing boom in children's books with transgender themes. As Meghan Cox Gurdon, the article's author, notes:

> "I have a girl brain but a boy body," says a young child in *I Am Jazz*, a picture book by Jessica Herthel and Jazz Jennings that came out [in 2014]. In Shelagh McNicholas's sherbet-hued illustrations, Jazz looks like a typical girlie-girl who likes to dance and play princess dress-up with her friends. She is also genetically male . . . [We] are entering a miniboom in children's books about a particular type of sexual identity, or misidentity. It will surprise no one that these books refrain from skepticism about the transgender condition, or . . . the appropriateness of adolescents undergoing genital surgeries and powerful hormone treatments.

These new children's books, says Cox, are designed to "nudge the needle of the culture." And woe unto them who doubt the new orthodoxy. Writing in Britain's *Spectator* magazine early in 2016, Melanie Phillips noted that

The enemy on this particular battlefield [of gender identity and fluidity] is anyone who maintains that there are men and there are women, and that the difference between them is fundamental. This "binary" distinction is accepted by the vast majority of the human race. No matter. It is now being categorized as a form of bigotry. Utterly bizarre? Scoff at your peril. It's fast becoming an enforceable orthodoxy, with children and young people particularly in the frame for attitude adjustment ... The intention is to break down children's sense of what sex they are and also to wipe away from their minds any notion of gender norms.[14]

It's worth pausing here for a moment to recognize that at least one good has emerged from today's gender-identity wars. The disputes remind us that real persons and real families are struggling with a wide range of difficult sexual issues. Every man and woman dealing with same-sex or transgender impulses is a child of God. Each has an inherent dignity. That dignity demands our respect. It precludes any intentional mistreatment or unjust discrimination.

But all rights are also conditioned by simultaneous duties to the common good. And that's where the battles get ugly. There's an oddly fierce kind of moralizing in gender ideology. It's a Puritanism without the religious baggage; a revolt against biology itself—and it's not without its own peculiar form of bullying. It seeks to push liberation past any limits, whether people want it or not. And if details like the democratic process get in the way: *too bad.*

To recall just one example: Oklahoma attorney general Scott Pruitt, along with ten other state attorneys general, sued the federal government in May 2016. The reason? The Education Department of the outgoing Obama White House issued a

"Dear Colleague" letter. The letter insisted that students should be free to use bathrooms and similar facilities based on their self-chosen gender identity rather than biological sex. To the average person, the idea might have sounded invasive and outlandish. But not so in Washington. The implied price of not complying: loss of all federal funds should they violate federal regulations that ban sex-based discrimination.

As Pruitt wrote at the time, "People of good will may disagree about the course American society should take, but we should all agree that we decide that course through the democratic system, which starts at the local level and allows for communities to shape themselves in different ways." It's not for any remote authority "to decide this issue—or any issue—through a bureaucratic cram-down in the last days of [a] presidency."[15] Strong words and true. But of course, by 2016, we'd already had decades of the "democratic system" being evaded or overturned by courts, regulations, and executive action, along with plenty of mass media emotional conditioning.

We might assume that academic freedom ensures a more open and honest discussion of sex and gender issues on many Catholic-inspired campuses. And we can hope it's so. But it's also worth noting this, from the (tenured) professor of theology Mickey Mattox:

> The new [higher education] gender regime rides on the strong currents of celebrity culture, while Washington's "soft power" deters resistance. Grants or certification necessary to receive federal subsidies require conformity to the government's priorities, which now include promoting the LGBTQ agenda. At [my university], a Title IX training program required for all employees includes warnings that the wrong kind of talk about sexual morality—meaning talk

based on traditional moral judgments—should be avoided in the workplace if one does not want to face charges of harassment or discrimination. Thus the paradox: We are repeatedly warned against talking about sex, even though the rule-makers seem to talk of little else.

Resistance to this new regime seems futile—and likely to get you into trouble. Even tenured faculty members hesitate, worried about official repercussions, formal or informal.[16]

The takeaway is this: What's at stake in current sex and gender-identity struggles is not just the ability of Catholic ministries and schools to serve unhampered in the public square. The freedom of Catholic families to raise their children according to Christian beliefs is also, in everyday practice, becoming more difficult. Most Catholic children attend public schools, whose curricula are often beyond parental control. The volume of noise advancing transgender and same-sex rights is strong at every level of our culture, and it distracts us from the most obvious and unsettling dimension of the gender-ideology debate.

In decoupling gender from biology and denying any given or "natural" meaning to male and female sexuality, gender ideology directly repudiates reality. People don't need to be "religious" to notice that men and women are different. The evidence is obvious. And the only way to ignore it is through a kind of intellectual self-hypnosis. Gender ideology rejects any human experience or knowledge that conflicts with its own flawed premises; it's the imperialism of bad science on steroids. For Christians, it also attacks the heart of our faith: the *Creation* ("male and female he created them"); the *Incarnation*—God taking the flesh of a man; and the *Redemption*—God dying on the cross and then rising in glorified bodily form. The Catholic faith, more than any of its Protestant cousins, is a religion not just of the mind and will but also of the bodily senses. And while the senses can make mistakes, when it comes to sexuality, they ground us firmly in the real.

The human body, complementary in its male and female forms, is precious, not simply as a pious ideal but as an organic reality. The body reveals who we are as human beings. Sexual difference expresses the manner in which we're called to love in the world. Thus the body is our rootedness in nature. It's a gift. It engages us with creation as part of creation. It has meaning. It's integral to who we are and fundamental to the whole Christian message. But for American culture—in its exhibitionism, and in its endless appetite to reveal every intimate aspect and detour of human sexual behavior to a global audience—the body is now little more than animated modeling clay.

GEORGE ORWELL WAS THE better writer and thinker. But when it comes to "negative utopias," Aldous Huxley was the shrewder prophet. Orwell's novels *Animal Farm* and *1984*, written in the turmoil of the 1940s, are still brilliantly scary. But in a postmodern world long on amnesia and short on historical curiosity, they seem dated. Implausible. Between mass marketing, the mass media, behavioral psychologists, and special interest lobbies, Orwell's brutal Thought Police are out of a job—they were too heavy-handed.

Huxley's *Brave New World*, written in 1932, is quite another matter. From state-run baby hatcheries that replace live births, to mood-lifting *soma* drugs, to ubiquitous sex, plenty of comforts and universal contraceptives, to mandatory happiness conditioning and "feelies" as entertainment: Yes, it's science fiction. But increasingly, it's more science than fiction. Rereading *Brave New World* can feel just a bit too familiar.

As noted earlier in these pages, those of us who were around in the 1960s will recall that the birth control pill was originally marketed as an aid to marriages and families. But detaching sex from fertility leads in unintended directions. One of them is artificial reproductive technology. It's worth remembering that in Huxley's novel, the words "mother" and "father" were vulgarisms—literally, dirty words. Today, in modern practice, babies have no necessary link to sexual intimacy and romance. They can be created in a lab almost as easily as the old-fashioned way.

But there are problems. Relocating conception from the embrace of a husband and wife to a petri dish—though it's often innocently intended by couples desperate for a child—nonetheless alters the nature of the experience. The child is still beautiful. Still sacred. His or her inherent dignity is undiminished. But the process has been sterilized and commodified. In effect, the new life is *manufactured*. The natural conceiving and bearing of a child are marked by physical self-giving (each spouse to the other, in the presence of God), intimacy, and passion. The lab is marked by calculation, transaction, and control. Something human—about ourselves, not the child—is lost in the bringing forth of a new life.

Sexual intimacy, rightly understood, is about the total coming together of persons, body and spirit, two becoming one in a uniquely potent way. It's a vulnerable act, physically and emotionally. It involves risk. Therefore it requires trust. But in giving ourselves totally to a spouse, we take part in God's creative, deeply fertile love. This is the genesis of the family, the first human community. The nature of marital love is to bear fruit in new life. Obviously there are wonderful married couples who desire but can't have children. Other couples, for various good reasons, must delay or refrain from bearing children. But these difficult cases aren't the norm. Nor do they change the basic nature of marriage: a vocation of intimate unity and bringing new life into the world.

What happens when a resistance to bearing children takes hold of a culture? The result is always the same: a slow and subtle unraveling of bonds, an aging of the spirit, a fatigue with the world, and ultimately a loss of purpose and hope. The fertility of sexual intimacy is the seal and ennobler of male-female relationships. It creates the future. It orients the couple, and indirectly the whole community, toward the next generation.

Contraceptive intimacy, in contrast, is finally not "intimacy" at all. It makes every sexual contact a disconnected point in time and an event without a future—two people using each other as instruments for their own relief. They may like each other a lot. They may be decent persons in a thousand other ways. But their sexual contact is neither intimate nor fertile, nor really mutual in any sense.

The consequences of today's sexual confusion go well beyond individuals and couples. Sterilized of a future, reflecting whatever a nation of sovereign consumers wants *right now*, modern sexuality celebrates the individual and inevitably undermines the humility, fidelity, and sense of obligation that family life requires. Thus it's no surprise that the health of our families and communities over the past fifty years has been in historic decline.

Consistent with the research of Andrew Cherlin, American children are less likely to be raised by their married, natural parents than at any time in our history. Whether it's through single motherhood, divorce, or the growing cohort of same-sex parents, many children no longer receive the benefit of being raised in a stable, organic family.

In his groundbreaking book *Coming Apart*, the sociologist Charles Murray notes that young people, on average, do best when raised by their married, natural parents. "I know of no other set of important findings," he writes, "that are as broadly accepted by social scientists . . . and yet are so resolutely ignored by network news programs, editorial writers for the major newspapers, and politicians of both major political parties."[17]

Why the reluctance to focus on family breakdown? Some of it's deliberate: glee from those on the cultural left who are delighted by the end of imagined boogeymen like patriarchy, hetero-normalcy, and sexually repressive institutions. But more common is a sense that we've reached a critical mass of broken families. We can't speak candidly about this disaster for fear of hurting the collaterally damaged innocent or aggravating the guilt of culpable parties. In any small group, let alone a big room, it's likely that at least one person has been wounded by family turmoil.

One activist who has publicly tackled "family fragmentation" is Mitch Pearlstein, a think tank founder in Minnesota. In his book on the issue, *Broken Bonds*, Pearlstein records his conversations with dozens of experts from several fields. A recurring theme in the book is the interplay between family dysfunction and broader social disintegration. The former trend is both a product and a driver of the latter. One of Pearlstein's sources, a county judge in Minnesota who deals on a daily basis with the bitter debris of family breakdown, placed the blame on the idiosyncrasies of American democratic life: "We have a rugged individualistic society where self-interested people strive for personal fulfillment. We have a throwaway culture: Meet my needs, and if the product or person doesn't, I'll look elsewhere."[18]

The term "throwaway culture" echoes Pope Francis, who uses the same words to describe advanced consumerist societies. The alternative, according to Francis, is a "culture of encounter"—that is, a culture where people meet and treat one another as full persons, not as means of personal advancement, political achievement, or economic efficiency. It's a culture in which we get to know our neighbors (or our spouse) in such a way that we can authentically fulfill our duties in love to them.

The family is where such a culture must be nurtured. We first learn how to love our neighbor in the home. We learn how to go out into the world by first watching those closest to us. When the family is torn by divorce or deception, it becomes a victim of the throwaway culture rather than a counterweight. In *Broken Bonds*, a leader of the Minnesota Catholic Conference tells Pearlstein: "It is hard to develop a sense of solidarity when one parent [has] walked out of the family, or your parents have decided *they* would be happier if they went their separate ways. Children are forced to embrace a distorted, but understandable, sense of independence just to survive emotionally."[19]

WHEN ALEXIS DE TOCQUEVILLE toured America in the early nineteenth century, he saw that its social and political institutions forged a kind of solidarity. All classes were clearly felt to be dependent on one another.[20] He noted that "in the United States the more opulent citizens take much care not to isolate themselves from the people; on the contrary, they constantly come close to them, they gladly listen to them and speak to them every day."[21] Tocqueville described this cross-class interaction largely in terms of mutual self-interest. But the intermingling also made fertile space for a culture of encounter.

The data-driven thesis of Charles Murray's *Coming Apart*, however, is quite different. As Murray sees it, American socioeconomic classes have been diverging culturally, economically, and geographically for the past fifty years. (Murray focuses on white Americans to avoid the confusion of confounding variables, but his analysis is also broadly applicable to Americans of color.) Murray identifies two archetypal neighborhoods: Boston's upscale Belmont suburb stands in for college-educated professionals, and Philadelphia's Fishtown area stands in for non-college-educated blue-collar workers. He then tracks five decades of relative stability in comfortable Belmont, and decline in less privileged Fishtown.

Half a century ago, people from Belmont and Fishtown lived in roughly similar neighborhoods. Their children went to the same kinds of schools and played in the same kinds of parks. But as Murray quotes the researcher Douglas Massey, "During the late 20th century . . . the well-educated and the affluent increasingly segmented themselves off from the rest of American society."[22] Along with this geographical separation came a cultural separation, especially in family life.

Based on every metric—marriage rates, divorce rates, nonmarital childbearing, happiness with marriages—the Fishtown cohort went from comparable to the Belmont cohort in 1960 to being radically deficient in comparison by 2010. We needn't dwell on the numbers, but one set of figures may be useful. In 1960, more than 95 percent of children in both Fishtown and Belmont lived with both natural parents when the mother was forty years old. In 2004, this was still true for 90 percent of the Belmont cohort. But in that same year, fewer than 30 percent of Fishtown children were living with both natural parents. Murray argues that the Fishtown figure "is so low that it calls into question the viability of white working-class communities as a place for socializing the next generation."[23]

In Murray's view, Americans are raising a wave of young citizens seriously unprepared for the demands of self-government.

And most persons from the Belmont cohort who do continue to model family stability have abandoned the solidarity across class lines that previous generations saw as a duty.

Unsurprisingly, Murray sees a sharp drop in "social capital"— participation in community life through associations—in Fishtown, but not in Belmont (though the latter's prosperity doesn't necessarily translate into moral integrity).[24] When the family is hurting, it gets very difficult for other communities to form properly. And when local communities can't form, as Tocqueville notes and we've already seen, the state steps in to fill the void.

Successful democracy requires a delicate balance of social cohesion and personal liberation. The late distinguished sociologist Robert Nisbet, following Tocqueville, argued that when the forces of personal liberation are dominant in a culture, the result is not maximal liberty, but the absorption of liberty by government. In reflecting on the history of liberal democracy, he noted the importance of family and the flesh-and-blood bonds of kinship in shaping viable citizens. He wrote that in a genuinely free society, "freedom has rested neither upon release nor upon collectivization but upon the *diversification* and the decentralization of power" (emphasis Nisbet's).[25] Stable and fruitful families and associations—including and especially religious associations—form the substance of those competing poles of authority. Their decline is not a form of liberation for individuals, but exactly the opposite.

Again: The erosion of religious liberty in America is more than a misunderstanding about the importance of religious belief in public discourse. It's the playing out of the Nisbet-Tocqueville theory: The disintegration of marriages, families, and communities (and the meaning of all three) leads to a less human, less forgiving, and less intimate form of authority filling the empty spaces they leave behind. It's thus perfectly logical that the most acute threats to our religious freedom come not from some Orwellian gang of bullyboys in bad uniforms, but from gender theorists and sex-rights activists (and businesses happy to support them) who push "liberation" and who are very well suited to life in a brave new world.

To borrow a thought from C. S. Lewis, the human person is a kind of "amphibian"—a creature made by God for both this world and the next, a fusion of spirit and flesh that gives the body special dignity. The rightly ordered joy of our senses in this world—the scent of spring, warm rain in the summer, the music of Mozart or Beethoven, the face of a beloved—is a foretaste of the glory God made for all of us to share, when we one day stand in his presence.

The crime of the modern sexual regime is that it robs Eros of its meaning and love of its grandeur. It's a lie. It's a theft. It makes us small and ignoble. A young adult friend of mine complained recently that many of her age-cohort peers don't have romances, passions, or lovers. They have *relationships.* Lewis's devil Screwtape would probably feel her pain. He yearned for the taste of a really great adulterer—a Renaissance libertine of character and spirit, capable of sinning heroically—instead of the cramped souls of the modern age, almost too insubstantial and pathetic to be worth damning.

The point of course is to be a great saint, to love greatly, rightly, and with passion, until we burn ourselves up in service to God and to others. Our wholeness, our integrity, depends on the health of our friendship with God. It was he who fashioned us from the dust. It was he who breathed his life into our bodies. So when we ignore God's Word, we violate our own identity.

Pornography, cohabiting, adultery—all these things push us away from God. They also inflict on us a kind of self-mutilation, as we sever what we do with our bodies from our true selves.

And what about chastity? It's a basic truth of Christian discipleship. And it does not mean, "Sorry, no sex for you." Rather, God asks us to live our sexuality virtuously according to our calling. For some this means celibacy, setting aside marriage for love of the larger family of the Church and a different form of fertility in service. For most people, though, in most times, it means sexual intimacy within marriage.

As the philosopher Roger Scruton puts it, "A society based on *agape* [selfless love] alone is all very well, but it will not reproduce itself: nor will it produce the crucial relation—that between parent and child—which is the basis on which we can begin to understand our relation to God. Hence, the redemption of the erotic lies at the heart of every viable social order."[26] Of course, very few couples—at least the ones I know—fall in love to redeem the erotic or build a viable social order. They have other motives. But the end result is the same: By its nature, human erotic love is ordered to creating and raising new life, and to the mutual joy and support of a man and woman vowed in a covenant of love.

But what do words like "vow" and "covenant of love" actually mean beyond routine expressions of piety?

Again, from Scruton: "[A] vow is a self-dedication, a gift of oneself"—open-ended in its commitment to a shared destiny between parties. "A vow of marriage creates an existential tie, not a set of specifiable obligations." And it's these irreversible ties, which can't be revoked, that hold marriages, families, communities, and societies together over time. They're the sinews of a genuinely human world, connecting the past with the present, and the present with the future. Thus they're different *in kind*, not merely in degree, from a contract or a negotiated deal. "[The] world of vows is a world of sacred things, in which holy and indefeasible obligations stand athwart our lives and command us along certain paths," whether we find it convenient at the moment or not.[27]

The paradox of Christian faith is this: It affirms the importance of every individual, no matter how weak or disabled. God loves each of us uniquely and infinitely. But our faith also binds us in a network of mutual obligations to others. God made us not just for ourselves. He also made us for others.

In this, our beliefs directly oppose a growing dimension of American economic life. The nature of that life, says the Lutheran theologian Daniel M. Bell Jr., may be disguised by its remaining biblical residue. But in practice, it "encourages us to view others in terms of how they can serve our self-interested projects." Other people "become commodities themselves—mere bodies to be exploited and consumed, and then discarded":

> As a consequence, marriages are viewed as (short-term) contracts subject to a cost/benefit analysis, children become consumer goods or accessories, family bonds are weakened and our bodies are treated like so many raw materials to be mined and exploited for manufacture and pleasure. Those individuals rendered worthless as producers and commodities by obsolescence—the old and infirm—are discarded (warehoused or euthanized) and the nonproductive poor (the homeless, the unemployed, the irresponsible, the incompetent) are viewed as a threat.[28]

In current American experience, true to Bell's words, marriage often resembles a real estate transaction. Two autonomous individuals enter into a limited liability partnership that can

easily be dissolved. Children serve as the various shared properties. And in such a world, an unplanned, unwanted unborn
child is clearly the most annoying kind of drain on the emotional profits.

A friend with a taste for the moral wisdom of fairy tales likes
to remind me, these days, of H. G. Wells's great fable *The Time
Machine.* The story is simple. A man invents a time machine. He
rides it eight hundred thousand years into the future. He finds
an astonishing world of peace, plenty, and perfectly manicured
luxury. The resident humans—the beautiful (if somewhat brainless) Eloi—spend their days in eating, chattering, playing, and
having innocent sex.

When the sun goes down, a different agenda applies. From
the tunnels under the earth come the once-human managers
of this paradise, the Morlocks. They're ugly. They're hungry.
And they have a special fondness for Eloi.

We can draw whatever lessons we like. It's just a story. But
what we do in the world, how we live and how we love (or misuse love)—these things always have consequences. And they
always emerge from the past to pay a visit. Choices don't stay
buried.

CHAPTER 6

NOTHING BUT THE TRUTH

True illness of the mind and spirit sets in when a
man no longer cherishes the truth but despises it,
when he uses it as a means to his own ends, when
in the depths of his soul, truth ceases to be to him
the primary, the most important concern.

—ROMANO GUARDINI

In 2015, writing in the *New York Times*, Justin
McBrayer—a philosophy professor—noted an odd trend in
public schools. Current standards in his local school district
required students to know the difference between facts and
opinions. But in checking his second-grade son's homework, he
realized that every moral or ethical premise his child encountered was treated as an opinion as opposed to a fact. "All men
are created equal." "Copying homework assignments is wrong."
"Cursing in school is inappropriate behavior." All these things
were being taught as opinions, not facts.[1]

In his essay, McBrayer argued that such a curriculum "sets
up our children for doublethink."[2] Students learn standards of
conduct and mutual respect in school as part of growing up.
That's always been the case. But today they're also taught that
those same standards are, in essence, elegant-sounding opinions.

In practice, students learn that the only concepts worthy of the term "truth" are those that can be empirically proven. Moral truths accessible to human reason, such as those in the Ten Commandments, don't really qualify as *true*. "Our public schools," McBrayer wrote, "teach students that . . . there are no moral facts. And if there are no moral facts, then there are no moral truths." In effect, truth becomes a social convention that humans themselves invent. Thus it can change from culture to culture.

That's a problem for two reasons. First, in losing a fixed definition of truth, we also lose a sense of goodness and beauty. Why? Because belief in objective truth, and the framework of moral right and wrong that naturally grows from it, is the "bone structure" of a society. It supports every other virtue and roadmap to meaning that can help people build a decent common life. There's nothing really "shared" in a public arena that invents its own ground rules on the fly—nothing, that is, except a Darwinian struggle for dominance. Second, the damage done to a child's moral reasoning doesn't stop with the individual student. It inflicts itself on the wider culture as he or she grows and engages with others.

In recent decades, Americans have grown more and more allergic to claiming that any behavior (especially sexual behavior) is right or wrong, always and everywhere. This is so in public and often in private. "Truth" is a big word in a rapidly changing world, with a lot of intrusive power. And nobody wants to judge—or rather, to be *seen* to judge—because nobody wants to *be* judged.

It's easy to blame this new reality on the power of the mass media and social science scholarship. Each tends to have a corrosive effect on traditional certainties and patterns of life. And each surely deserves some of the blame. But we should also look for culprits closer to home, starting with the mirror. After all, as Tocqueville said, "I do not know any country where, in general, less independence of mind and genuine freedom of discussion reign than in America."[3]

That sounds odd, though. Didn't Tocqueville also claim that individual liberties are better guaranteed in America than anywhere else in the world?

He did. But for Tocqueville, democracy, left to itself, doesn't encourage strong characters. It creates self-absorbed ones. Democratic man depends heavily on public opinion as the source of his own convictions. Public opinion is the proof (or the disproof) of any institution's or belief's legitimacy. In effect, a legitimate opinion exists only because it's widely held. And it's through public opinion that "in democratic republics, tyranny does not proceed [through violence and physical coercion]. It leaves the body [unharmed] and goes straight to the soul."[4]

It follows that shaping public opinion can shape the course of the culture. Creating and enforcing a new "truth" is simply a matter of mobilizing enough public opinion to make it so. Today's social media have a massive and almost instantaneous ability to bring the pressure to conform on any selected target. If an end is seen as "good," justifying the means to achieve it is simply a matter of marketing. And this invites a subtle, chronic kind of lying—the editing and massaging of information—to get the results claimed to be needed.

This is why polling, including which questions get asked and how they're framed, plays such a key role in American public life. The power of public opinion explains the size of the lobbying and public relations industries. It explains our addiction to survey data. It explains the increasingly explicit editorial bias in the nation's flagship news organizations. It explains how lawmaking and social science research can literally, if subtly, be molded, and why public views on issues like same-sex marriage can change so rapidly and sharply over just twenty years. All of these trends are thoroughly "democratic"—but only because they emerge naturally from the weaknesses, rather than the strengths, in democracy's internal logic. Public opinion is not simply spontaneous. It can be formed and re-formed.

These problems are the outward signs of deeper issues that implicate us as citizens. The weakness of the individual citizen is only partly coerced by democracy's structure. It's also freely chosen, because we find it convenient. It allows us to assign blame to others and escape our own responsibility. It's easier to accept lies by invoking a misguided alibi of tolerance and mutual respect than to live outside the cone of public approval. This is clear in every recent national debate over abortion, marriage, family, sexuality, and rights in general. Many of us are happy to live with half-truths and ambiguity rather than risk being cut out of the herd. The culture of lies thrives on our own complicity, lack of courage, and self-deception.

The point is this: Everyone's grasp of truth rests to some degree on authority. No one is really autonomous. We can't know everything on our own. We need to trust others for guidance. This is normal. But who and what we trust matter greatly. In American life, democracy and capitalism, despite their advantages, tend to erode the place of traditional authorities (families, religious faith, and other institutions), while putting new authorities (public opinion and market forces) in their stead. And that has consequences.

As we've already seen, Augustine teaches that no government can offer perfect peace and harmony. Sin prevents it. The mirage of perfectibility through political action is seductive, but it's also dangerous. To bring about utopia, modern leaders have done monstrous things. They've built whole societies on innocent people sacrificed to lies.

As citizens, we live with certain tensions in creating a decent society. A delicate balance exists between personal liberty and our duty to others, and democracy depends on it. The destabilizing effect of today's attitudes toward sex, as we've already seen, upsets that balance.

Something similar occurs with truth. Democracy tends to unmoor society from the idea of permanent truths. Placing the law, which ideally reflects right and wrong, under the power of elections can seem to put truth itself on the ballot, because most people tend to equate the legal with the acceptable or good. On the one hand, truth becomes relative and contingent on popular whim. But on the other, it becomes radically privatized by the individual citizen.

This dynamic of forceful self-assertion and a simultaneous fear of being out of step with majority opinion is one of the central contradictions of American life. As always, Tocqueville's thoughts are useful. Just fifty years into America's independence, he saw the young nation's character clearly.

Tocqueville said of Americans that they "are constantly led back toward their own reason as the most visible and closest source of truth."[5] The thirst for equality, key to our political and cultural life, tends to make us resentful of anyone else's intellectual authority. We've all heard the words "Who are *you* to impose your morality on *me*?"

But that's not the whole story. As Tocqueville noted, European regimes of his time lacked America's formal free speech protections. Yet appearances could be misleading. There were always spaces in those older European societies where nearly any opinion could be voiced, and shelter for the nonconforming could be found. In America, by contrast:

> The majority draws a formidable circle around thought. Inside those limits, the writer is free; but unhappiness awaits him if he dares to leave them. It is not that he has to fear an auto-da-fé [forced public penance and execution], but he is the butt of mortifications of all kinds and of persecutions every day. A political career is closed to him; he has offended the only power that has the capacity to open it up.[6]

As with the writer, so with the private individual. One of the worst fates in American public life is being tarred as "out of the mainstream." The great fear of the average voter is to be seen as extreme. As citizens, most of us urgently want to be inside the constantly shifting range of acceptable opinions. And that yearning creates a chronic, low-grade unease. It also blinds us to the fact that Christian faith, by its nature, is very often "out of the mainstream."

This weakness in the American system was constrained for a long time by a widely shared biblical moral framework among the people. In the mid-nineteenth century, as Tocqueville wrote, "Americans, having accepted the principal dogmas of the Christian religion," typically also accept the "moral truths that flow from them and depend on them." Hence the behavior of individuals was channeled "within narrow limits."[7]

Times have changed. Culture precedes and informs politics. And American culture has moved miles from the assumptions of the Founders.

There's also a factor Tocqueville could not have foreseen: a very powerful market economy. The real soul of modern American life is the market. We work in the market to earn a living.

We buy our necessities and luxuries in the market. We're colonized and shaped by the market everywhere we go, from newspapers to television to computers to smartphones. It's the elevator music of daily life. And while the market serves our well-being in many ways, and has lifted great numbers of people out of poverty, its "religion" is money and profit. For the market, truth is not a category unless consumers make it so. Which is exactly what the spirit of the market—its relentless pressures and distractions—works against.

As with democratic politics, the market is a mass of individuals making discrete choices within a framework shaped by larger forces, over which they have limited control. It falls to individuals, then, to make truth the primary value in the choices they make.

And we can only begin to do that by placing truth first in our own lives, and demanding it of others.

OBVIOUSLY, THE POWER OF public opinion has limits. People don't automatically adopt the ideas that win power in any given election. Inertia, both for good and for bad, is a powerful factor in human behavior. Rather, the process that degrades our appetite for truth in politics seems to work in two ways.

First, many of us are tempted to affirm whatever our favorite political tribe affirms, and deny whatever it denies. Nobody likes to risk losing friends and allies over a policy issue. So we're subtly pressed to believe what we're expected to believe as a good "conservative" or a good "liberal." Anything outside our narrow channel is hostile terrain. But exactly this kind of tribalism subordinates the common good (and often the truth) to party loyalties. And party agendas can be cavalier, short-sighted, and destructive.

The second way we lose the habit of truth is by refusing to think clearly when damaging cultural trends become political orthodoxies. The last thing too many people want is to be seen as retrograde in their views when the cost may be social exile. The same-sex marriage debate was, and remains, a classic case. No one wants to be left behind by the herd. This fear of exclusion sustains an entire therapeutic industry—in effect, a new clergy—of social experts. One of their main expert functions is to enable and excuse the outsourcing of personal moral reasoning. Dubious choices always sound better when they're blessed by, or at least can be blamed on, a specialist.

Obviously, counselors and experts can also play a vital healing role. Many do. The point is this: When we no longer have the courage to live by the truth ourselves, when we no longer really hunger for it, then we no longer insist on it from others. The result is a culture of evasive unreality, a nation of alibis. And we come to accept more dishonesty and less integrity in our politics as unavoidable rules of the road.

The same applies to the market. We expect to be hustled as part of the market's liturgy of goods and services. Inflated advertising, sweetened with humor or sex or hints of product-induced ecstasy, is the fuel that runs the consumer economy. We laugh at it. But it works.

Aristotle taught (and experience confirms) that character is formed through habits. As we consciously perform good deeds, we get accustomed to goodness. We start to do good without thinking twice. This is virtue; in the words of the *Catechism of the Catholic Church*, the "habitual and firm disposition to do the good." As we do good, our relationship with God also grows. So does the grace he sends to help us to continue doing good.

But the process also works in reverse. As we habitually

choose against the good, we grow numb both to the beauty of goodness and to the ugliness of evil. We starve and eventually kill our relationship with God, denying ourselves the help of his grace.

Everything true about growing in goodness is also true about growing in truth. We grow to love the truth by seeking it out and living by it. Conversely, the beauty of truth fades from memory as we edit it out of our lives. Eventually we no longer know truth when we see it. We put our minds to the task of excuse making and rationalizing, and these become truth's reasonable (or at least reasonable enough) facsimiles. We end up believing our own self-deceptions and the lies we tell to others, because we've made truth into a product of our own manufacture.

The effect of untruth on the mind and the soul is confirmed in M. Scott Peck's classic book *People of the Lie*. Dr. Peck was a noted psychiatrist and author. He was also a committed Christian. His writings ably combine the science of mental health with moral sensibilities, while respecting both.

Over the course of decades, Peck met patients who didn't fit a standard diagnosis but had certain recurring traits. These persons showed chronic disregard for the good of others to the point of causing grave psychological harm. They were subtly but pervasively self-centered. Their symptoms were broader than narcissistic personality disorder, but they weren't sociopaths. They knew right from wrong.

But their main shared trait was the habit of lying. They all lied constantly and effortlessly about everything—especially about themselves, to themselves. As such, they were opaque even to highly trained therapists. More important, they were opaque to themselves. For Peck, the "layer upon layer of self-deception" that "people of the lie" build up insulates them so thoroughly from truth that they no longer recognize it. Their own irreproachability is their only truth.

Peck didn't mince words. He calls such persons evil.[8] While he fleshes out his use of that word in his book, he never backs away from it. Peck's "evil" people erect so many defenses against self-examination and repentance that these become almost impossible without a miracle of grace.

"People of the lie" embody Aristotle's teachings on the formation of character. They don't wake up one morning and decide to be cruel. Rather, they accumulate years of decisions to ignore the true good in favor of their own apparent good, until they fully identify their own will with what's genuinely good.

As Peck notes, this reveals itself as a preoccupation with appearances: "While they seem to lack any motivation to *be* good, they intensely desire to appear good. Their 'goodness' is all on a level of pretense. *It is, in effect, a lie*" (emphasis added).[9] The evasion of truth soon makes their entire lives little more than an intricate ruse.

For these morally crippled creatures, the pretense of goodness salves the scars of conscience that do exist, but that have been routinely ignored and abused. "The central defect of the evil [person] is not the sin but the refusal to acknowledge it."[10] We all sin, of course, but the unwillingness to take any responsibility for our sins implies a more deeply damaged spirit. And so the evil person doubles down on his or her lies by cultivating false appearances and scapegoating the innocent.

As Peck puts it, "We become evil by attempting to hide from ourselves. The wickedness of the evil is not committed directly, but indirectly as part of [the] cover-up process. Evil originates not in the absence of guilt but in the effort to escape it."[11]

One of the most striking case studies in *People of the Lie* is that of a wealthy couple whose teenage son suffers from depression. As Peck probed the cause of the son's depression with the boy and his parents, the adults avoided even a hint of responsibility for his mental state. They ignored both their son's needs and Peck's advice, and then shifted the burden for their own self-serving decisions back onto the boy and his doctor. After the son acted out by taking part in a petty theft at school, his parents pressed to have him diagnosed as a genetically predisposed and thus incurable criminal.

The story ends with a letter from the boy's mother informing Peck that they had followed his kind advice and sent their son to a military boarding school. The punchline: This was exactly the opposite of Peck's counsel. The parents had washed their hands of responsibility for their own son. Any problems would henceforward be the fault of the school or the doctor, but never them. Rather than face their self-deception and damage the illusion of their own goodness, they lied to Peck and further harmed their son.

"People of the lie" don't reject the idea of all sin—only their own. They're quite willing to condemn others. In fact, as Peck points out, scapegoating is one of the universal traits of "people of the lie." They project their own guilt, which they feel but won't accept, onto others. "Rather than blissfully lacking a sense of morality like the psychopath, they are continually engaged in sweeping the evidence of their evil under the rug of their own consciousness."[12]

A person wrapped in deception does not blind himself to sin. He blinds himself to the possibility of forgiveness. In refusing any obligations to truth outside of himself, he closes himself off to the mercy of God. Dr. Peck puts in psychological terms what believers know by faith: "Mental health requires that the human will submit itself to something higher than itself. To function decently in the world, we must submit ourselves to some principle that takes precedence over what we might want at any given moment. For [religious persons] this principle is God, and so they will say, 'Thy will, not mine, be done.' "[13]

We typically think of this submission as an act of obedience to God's will, as Peck mentions. But it's actually a submission to God's love and mercy. This requires, of course, admitting our own sinfulness. The spurning of forgiveness is the most self-poisoning symptom of the "people of the lie," and the source of their despair.

IN DISCUSSING *PEOPLE OF THE LIE*, it's easy to use the words "they" and "them." But what's bracing about Scott Peck's work is that it implicates all of us and our wider culture. The pretense of goodness, the perversely moralistic scapegoating, the self-deception—these aren't just the sins of "evil" people. They're qualities rooted in our fallen nature and pandemic in a society based on license. We're all, to some degree, "people of the lie."

Dr. Peck wrote about extreme cases, but we should see them as warnings to heed, not specimens to gawk at. The feckless parents discussed above weren't born with a resentment of the truth. Rather, they nourished it with thousands of little untruths. They developed alibis and habits of deception, especially self-deception, that over many years formed their character. Every one of us is prone to the same process. It's up to us to see and arrest it before it begins.

That's not so simple. We live in a culture eager to make truth a boutique experience as malleable as our personal tastes require. As the moral philosopher Harry Frankfurt writes, a vast and congenial river of baloney, humbug, and mumbo-jumbo flows through American culture that has its source in "various forms of skepticism which deny that we can have any reliable access to an objective reality, and which therefore reject the possibility of knowing how things truly are."[14] But we need to remember what—or rather who—comprises the culture. Things we can't control do often impact our personal decisions. But the fact remains that "the culture" is little more than the sum of the choices, habits, and dispositions of the people who live in a particular place at a particular time. We can't simply blame "the culture." We *are* the culture.

Failing to cultivate a taste for truth, then, is an abdication of our duties not just to God, but also to one another. By contributing to a culture that seeks to invent its own truth, we make it harder for others to find the real thing. The results are deeply damaging. Subcultures of deceit emerge in places within our society where honesty is most important.

The United States military is one of the nation's most trusted institutions, even as other key institutions have fallen into disrepute. A report in an army academic journal suggests, however, that even the military today struggles with a culture of untruths. The report is strikingly similar to Scott Peck's concerns:

Untruthfulness is surprisingly common in the U.S. military even though members of the profession are loath to admit it. Further, much of the deception and dishonesty that occurs in the profession of arms is actually encouraged and sanctioned by the military institution. The end result is a profession whose members often hold and propagate a false sense of integrity that prevents the profession from addressing— or even acknowledging—the duplicity and deceit throughout the formation.[15]

The report's authors find a culture within the military "where it is literally impossible to execute to standard all that is required. At the same time, reporting noncompliance with the requirements is seldom a viable option."[16] Rather than risk one's reputation, officers routinely sign off on substandard and incomplete tasks. "As a result, an officer's signature and word have become tools to maneuver through the Army bureaucracy rather than being symbols of integrity and honesty."[17]

The pattern is not unique to the military. The Church in her institutional forms has her own long list of problems. But the report does show the way a culture of deception metastasizes from individual compromises with the truth to infect an entire institution—any institution, even one explicitly built on honor. Truth becomes secondary to careerism and the façade of perfection.

A similar issue occurs in education, where a parade of cheating and grade-boosting scandals in recent years has shown that, for many students and even their teachers, the truth is important only if it serves the goal of advancement. Students have cheated for millennia. There's nothing new about it. But these days in America, 75 percent of high school students admit to cheating on their academic work.[18] And the problem goes well beyond high school.

The curious thing about today's academic cheating is the shift from cheating out of desperation to cheating to stay on top. The archetypical school-age cheater is thought to be a struggling student who peeks at the smart kid's test answers. But with the proliferation of cheating and the rising stakes of academic performance, the new "typical" cheater is a successful student anxious to remain at the head of the class for college or professional placement.[19]

A California high school student captures not just the cheating mentality, but a core fact of current American life: "There's so much pressure to get a good job, and to get a good job you have to get into a good school, and to get into a good school you have to get good grades, and to get good grades you have to cheat." Note the words "have to." The student ignores her own agency and blames a culture that requires her to cheat. It's a plausible kind of lie, pitched both to the interviewer and to herself. But it's still a lie. The culture of deception is, in part, the free choice of students who *decided* to cheat.

It would be foolish, though, to blame academic cheating mainly on young people. Fierce academic competition—or at least the competition to get into the "right" schools—places huge pressure on persons just emerging from childhood. The combination of high stakes and the implicit message that honesty can be set aside for a while to serve a sufficiently vital goal like long-term financial success almost guarantees a culture of lying.

The pressure often starts within the family. Evidence suggests that a great deal of cheating is done to please parents.[20] In many U.S. households the family culture—not the big, bad, soulless society "out there," but the values passed down from parents to their children—places achievement above honesty. And when parents are, for example, " 'diagnosis shopping' to get a doctor to say [their children] have [attention deficit disorder] so they can have extra time to complete their SAT test," it's not hard to see how that message is being sent.[21]

The banking industry, corporate life, the mass media, religious ministries, athletics, law schools: Each has its scandals. In nearly every case the pattern is similar: Truth is adjusted or "interpreted," ignored or justified away, to get seemingly urgent results. And deceit then spreads and takes root like a weed.

❧

CARING FOR LANGUAGE, WROTE Marilyn Chandler McEntyre, is a moral issue. "Caring for one another is not entirely separable from caring for words. Words are entrusted to us as equipment for our life together, to help us survive, guide and nourish one another."[22] This is why honesty in a leader always ranks among the qualities most admired by colleagues. No one wants to hear bad news or criticism. But people consistently prefer the truth to soothing lies that end in bad surprises.

For McEntyre, language is a life-sustaining resource. And like any other resource, it "can be depleted, polluted, contaminated, eroded and filled with artificial stimulants. Like any other resource, it needs the protection of those who recognize its value and commit themselves to good stewardship."[23]

It's useful to keep this in mind in answering Pontius Pilate's very modern, perfectly cynical question, *What is truth?* (Jn 18:38). The word "truth" (*veritas* in Latin) comes from the Old English *triewth* or *treowth,* meaning faithfulness, constancy, trustworthiness. It may ultimately derive from the Indo-European base word for wood or tree, "the semantic link being the firmness or steadfastness of oaks and such trees."[24] The idea that "true" means something "consistent with fact" dates back a very long way and took on the added meanings of real, genuine, accurate, and correct over the centuries.

For Christians, of course, truth is a Person. As Jesus says, "I am the way, and the truth and the life" (Jn 14:6), the incarnate Word of God. And God, the source and sustainer of everything real, can't lie. This is the substance of our faith.

But in an everyday sense, "truth" means the conformity of what we say and hear with things that are real—"real" being more than just material, measurable data but never excluding them. When we tell the truth, we're faithful to the facts as we know them, whether we like them or not. We can never escape our point of view, but we're truthful when we make an honest effort to present the facts fairly and accurately, respecting the rights of the people who will hear them—whether we like *them* or not. That's telling the truth. Therefore words are precious because they can serve or subvert this important task.

It's been a bad century for words. Language has "rectified" borders, "neutralized" antisocial elements, "pacified" villages, "liquidated" enemies of the people, "resettled" Jews, "cleansed" religious and ethnic minorities, and regretted the "collateral damage" of combat—all on an industrial scale.

Laundered words and empty slogans, as George Orwell suggested, are the political obscenities of the age. Evasion and understatement mislead the hearer. They also corrupt the user. Dishonest language not only reflects a lying spirit, it also feeds it, leading to more mendacious thinking, more lies, and more corrupt action. And the result? "In our time," Orwell famously said, "political speech and writing are largely the defense of the indefensible . . . When there is a gap between one's real and one's declared aims," one turns to "long words and exhausted idioms, like a cuttlefish squirting out ink."[25]

Orwell fought as a socialist in the Spanish Civil War and was a bitter critic of the Catholic Church. But in many ways, he was an honest man. He saw and despised the duplicity of Soviet "aid" to the Spanish Republic firsthand, much of which consisted in crippling or murdering other noncommunist forces on the left.

What Orwell didn't see but would have equally despised were politically engaged American reporters like Martha Gellhorn and Ernest Hemingway, and photographers like Robert Capa, who covered the war as they preferred to imagine it, with or without the truth, and who "were prepared to manipulate the reality of what they witnessed to produce something—a photograph, a film, a journalistic dispatch—that they hoped would further the cause they believed in . . . the finer points of truth could be set aside without conscience."[26]

Later, at the height of the Cold War and its systematic degrading of truth by ideology, the philosopher and critic George Steiner wrote:

> Languages have great reserves of life. They can absorb masses of hysteria, illiteracy and cheapness . . . But there comes a breaking point. Use a language to conceive, organize and justify Belsen; use it to make out specifications for gas ovens; use it to dehumanize man during 12 years of calculated bestiality. Something will happen to it . . . Something of the lies and sadism will settle in the marrow of the language.[27]

Lying comes in many forms, some of them appealing, some of them omissions of inconvenient sources or facts, but all of them a kind of violence. The Catholic philosopher Josef Pieper summed it up when he said that "the abuse of political power is fundamentally connected with the sophistic abuse of the word." And the degradation of man by man, and the systematic *physical* violence against human beings, have their beginnings "when the word loses its dignity" because "through the word is accomplished what no other means can accomplish, namely, communication based on reality."[28]

"Communication based on reality" brings us to the news industry, and there, too, the record is less than sterling. Overt lying certainly can and does happen in America's news industry. Jayson Blair at the *New York Times*, Stephen Glass at the *New Republic*, and Janet Cooke at the *Washington Post* are merely the most high-profile cases in recent memory—along with NBC's former news anchor Brian Williams and his factual "mistakes."

But much more common is a chronic newsroom prejudice in the shaping of certain kinds of news. Planned Parenthood is assumed good, while critics who secretly film its cynicism, profiteering, and barbarism are assumed bad, to cite only one of many examples. And the language of "abortion rights," common in most newsrooms, has the familiar Orwellian ring of avoiding an unpleasant reality (killing a child in utero) by calling it something else.

Thus does the magic of words rework the sinews of the universe.

And as in the news media, so, too, in politics. The White House elected to power in November 2008 campaigned on compelling promises of hope, change, and bringing the nation together. The reality it delivered for eight years was rather different: a brand of leadership that was narcissistic, aggressively secular, ideologically divisive, resistant to compromise, unwilling to accept responsibility for its failures, and generous in spreading blame.

As the prophet Jeremiah noted even longer ago than Orwell, Steiner, and Pieper, every one of us, given the right combination of pressure and temptation, has a heart that can be "deceitful above all things and desperately corrupt" (17:9). Too often in the real world, as one scholar observed, quoting Pascal, "We 'hate the truth, and people hide it from us; we want to be flattered, and people flatter us; we like being deceived, and we are deceived.' The deceptions we particularly seem to want are those that comfort, insulate, legitimate and provide ready excuses for inaction."[29]

Every deceit is a trip to unreality, and unreality can be a pleasant place to visit. But it's a narcotic that always wears off with an ugly hangover. For an individual, a taste for it is tragic. For a people, it's lethal.

You will know the truth, and the truth will make you free. So says the Gospel of John (8:32). There is no justice, no beauty, no goodness, without truth, because truth is the voice of God's authentic reality. Truth is the measure of reality itself; and without it, "justice" is a human equation based on power and arbitrary will. We were meant for something higher. We were made to be the kind of creatures who share in the glory of God himself. Freedom is the self-mastery to know and to do what's right, and thus to have the capacity to stand upright in the presence of God's judgment and love.

And this is why the great American Catholic writer Flannery O'Connor said that the truth will not only make you free, it will also make you odd. In a world of hyperbole, duplicity, factual disfigurement, and spin, speaking plainly and living honestly in obedience to Jesus Christ is an abnormal behavior. And the cost of that discipleship (but also its rewards) can be high.

CHAPTER 7

DARKNESS AT NOON

And God said, "Let there be light," and there was
light. And God saw that the light was good; and
God separated the light from the darkness.

—Gen 1:3–4

L IGHT IS THE BEGINNING OF CREATION. LIGHT GROWS OUR
food. Light helps us see. Light warms our faces in the
summer.

Dark is a very different matter. In Scripture, the "outer darkness" is a place we want to avoid. The dark, even when it's thick
with silence and scents and romance, can also be thick with car-
nivores—a fact that imprinted itself very early on our species'
memory. Put simply: Light is good. Dark is not. Thus, moderns
speak of the Dark Ages and the Enlightenment, the light of
reason and the darkness of ignorance. It's hard to imagine anyone confusing the two. But given the right circumstances, odd
things can happen.

Here's an example. It's night. We're walking down a corridor. The lights are intense, so we squint. Then they suddenly go
black—all of them. For a few moments, we're blind. After all,
it's dark. But just as our eyes adjust to the dark, the lights snap

back on. And now we're squinting again. The jolt from bright to pitch black to bright again is a vividly conscious experience.

Now imagine we're walking down the same hallway. This time, the lights dim slowly. This time, we hardly notice. By corridor's end, the dark is so deep we can barely see the signage on the walls. But the change has been subtle, the fading of the light gradual, and we humans are adaptable. We can adjust. In fact, we can survive in the dark a long time if we need to or choose to. We can even learn to prefer it. Rather like the Morlocks.

That, arguably, is the story of our past three hundred years— not a history of the whole world, but a history of *our* world, the singular Western world that shaped the modern era, the world we call our own. Consider the following:

In his masterwork *After Virtue*, the philosopher Alasdair MacIntyre starts with a thought experiment. It goes like this. Picture a world where a massive, unforeseen disaster has wrecked the environment. The survivors blame science. Mobs lynch physicists. Books are burned. Instruments are trashed. Labs and computer networks are torn to pieces. Teaching and practicing science are banned. Even the memory of science is attacked, and where possible, stamped out.

Time passes. Eventually, enlightened minds try to resurrect science. But all they have to work with are pieces; the half-memories, partial theories, and fragments of a much larger (but lost) organic body of knowledge. The new scientists forge ahead anyway. They speak confidently and get some fine results. They use many of the same words crucial to the old science—neutrino, mass, velocity, and so on—but without fully understanding them. They also push competing and incompatible ideas about what the old science was and meant, and how science should be conducted. They share a common vocabulary. But the same words mean different things. The result is disorder—a disorder no one can heal or even adequately recognize, because no one possesses the older body of knowledge that has been lost.

For MacIntyre, the point of the fairy tale is simple. Today, "in the actual world we inhabit," he writes, "the language of morality is in the same state of grave disorder as the language of natural science" in the fantasy world he describes. "We continue to use many of the key expressions" of traditional morality, but "we have—very largely, if not entirely—lost our comprehension, both theoretical and practical, of morality."[1] In effect, "the language and the appearances of morality persist, even though the integral substance of morality has to a large degree been fragmented and then in part destroyed."[2]

What that means is this: The moral conflicts that permeate our public policy debates are endless and irresolvable because our culture no longer has a rational, mutually accepted way of getting to moral agreement. The answer of the liberal state (including our own) to these stubborn disputes is to remove morality to the private sphere. But that course of government is itself a value judgment, a morally loaded act disguised as neutrality. All law and all public policy embody someone's idea of what we ought to do, including the notion that we "ought" to keep personal moral beliefs out of public debates.

The underlying assumption of our public discourse today is that facts and values are radically distinct. "The plane crashed" is a statement of *fact*, and therefore "real." Crash evidence is tangible. Nobody can argue with debris. On the other hand, "Don't kill the disabled" is a statement of *value*. It's an expression of opinion and sentiment—so the logic goes—and therefore not "real" or "true" in the same solid sense. For example, the importance of protecting disabled persons is an admirable and widely shared view; surely that's obvious. But some people might disagree. Some people might argue quite sincerely that disabled persons are a waste of precious resources, and we'd be better off without them. Some people did argue that way in Germany in the last century, with great effect.

Of course, for most of us, murdering the disabled, starving the poor, or deliberately targeting innocent civilians in war is an appalling idea, a crime against humanity. But apparently sucking the brains out of unborn children, or trading in their body parts, is not so appalling. It may even be "good," because we already do it. We not only do it, but we also build a fortress of pious-sounding chatter about reproductive rights to surround and bless it.

This is the kind of obscenity that comes from reducing a nation's politics to a clash of allegedly equal values. What it masks is a transfer of power from proven traditions of moral wisdom to whoever can best lobby the media, the courts, Congress, and the White House. It's the reason MacIntyre warned that today's barbarians "are not waiting beyond the frontiers; they have already been governing us for quite some time. And it is our lack of consciousness of this that constitutes part of our predicament."[3]

AFTER VIRTUE IS A challenging work. It's not for the casual reader. But if we want to understand ourselves as a nation, some of its key ideas are worth noting. As we've already seen, America is a child of both biblical and Enlightenment spirits. Its roots are therefore tangled. And they go back a long way.

The medieval Europe that preceded modern times was the product of classical and Christian thought. Aristotle, the ancient Greek philosopher, played a large role in shaping it. For Aristotle everything, including man, has an inherent nature or purpose. A man lives a good life when he acts in accord with that nature. In Aristotle, "the relationship of 'man' to 'living well' is analogous to that of 'harpist' to 'playing the harp.'"[4] As the harpist disciplines herself through practice to play the harp more beautifully, so also man cultivates the virtues—courage, justice, mercy, humility, and so on—to become more truly human.

Moreover, in the classical tradition, to be a human being involves fulfilling certain roles, each with its own distinct purpose: husband, wife, father, mother, soldier, philosopher, citizen, servant of God. And it "is only when 'man' is thought of as an individual, *prior to* and *apart from* all roles," that the idea of "man" ceases to be a meaningful, purpose-filled concept (emphasis added).[5] In other words, for Aristotle, what it means to be human is not a matter of self-invention; it depends on our network of human connections and responsibilities.

Aristotle gave Thomas Aquinas the tools for articulating a medieval Christian civilization that combined both reason and biblical faith. For Christians, man does indeed have a purpose. Scripture reveals that purpose and provides the foundation on which human reason builds. We were made to know, love, and serve God in this world. We're also meant to be happy with him in the next, to show love to others, and to care for the world placed in our keeping. God is the Author and sustainer of creation. Thus all things in nature are a gift. They have a God-given meaning prior to any human involvement.

Man is part of creation but endowed with special dignity. Every man is a free moral agent, responsible for his personal choices and actions. But no man exists in isolation. Every man is also an actor in a much larger divine story, and he's shaped by his social relationships and duties to others. Thus the purpose of knowledge is to understand, revere, and steward the world, and to ennoble the people who share it—and thereby to glorify God.

As *After Virtue* notes, the Enlightenment thinkers of the

eighteenth century were diverse. Generalizing about their beliefs can be dangerous. But most wanted to keep a Christian-like morality, purified of "superstition" and based on reason. They also wanted to discard any approach to nature based on Aristotle or Aquinas. For the Enlightenment, nature is simply raw material. It has no higher purpose. Man alone gives it meaning by using it for human improvement. Thus the goal of knowledge is to get practical results. And man is not a bit player in some divine Larger Story. He's a sovereign individual who creates his own story.

As MacIntyre shows, the Enlightenment tried to keep the moral content of Christianity while eliminating its religious base. But it doesn't work. The biblical grounding can't be cut away without undermining the whole moral system. Every attempt to build a substitute system has suffered from incoherence, no matter how reasonable sounding. And bad ideas have consequences. The resulting moral confusion has trickled into every corner of our daily life.

Simply put, once a higher purpose and standard of human behavior are lost, moral judgments are nothing but personal opinions. In a nation of sovereign individuals, nobody's opinion is inherently better than anyone else's. All moral disagreements become rationally irresolvable because no commonly held first principles exist.

This post-Christian confusion—MacIntyre calls it "emotivism"—now shapes American public life. In such an environment, the purpose of moral discourse, he writes, "[becomes] the attempt of one will to align the attitudes, feelings, preferences and choices of another with its own." Other people become instruments to be dominated and used. They're means to achieve our ends, not ends in themselves.[6] As a result, most of our moral debates about public policy never get near the truth of an issue. They're exercises in manipulation. In MacIntyre's words:

> [Each] of us is taught to see himself or herself as an autonomous moral agent; but each of us also becomes engaged by modes of practice, aesthetic or bureaucratic, which involve us in manipulative relationships. Seeking to protect the autonomy that we have learned to prize, we aspire ourselves not to be manipulated by others; seeking to incarnate our own principles and standpoint in the world of practice, we find no way open to us to do so except by directing toward others those very manipulative modes of relationship which each of us aspires to resist in our own case. The incoherence of our attitudes and our experiences arises from the incoherent [Enlightenment-born] conceptual scheme which we have inherited.[7]

For MacIntyre, this incoherence explains three chronic patterns in our public life: the appeal to rights, the eagerness to protest, and the appetite for unmasking. Aggrieved parties demand their *rights*, which are allegedly self-evident (despite the absence of any agreed-upon grounding for rights). They *protest* the attack on those rights by oppressive structures and rival parties. And they seek to *unmask* the wicked designs of their opponents. All of which feeds a spirit of indignation and victimhood across the culture.

In a world of bickering individuals, the job of government becomes managing conflict. And since, in a seemingly "value-neutral" state, no higher moral authority can be appealed to, government becomes the ultimate referee of personal appetites and liberties and justifies itself by its effectiveness. Effectiveness demands a managerial class of experts, as MacIntyre notes:

Government insists more and more that its civil servants themselves have the kind of education that will qualify them as experts. It more and more recruits those who claim to be experts into its civil service . . . Government becomes a hierarchy of bureaucratic managers, and the major justification advanced for the intervention of government in society is the contention that government has resources of competence which most citizens do not possess.[8]

Never mind that many of the government's expert managers are in practice incompetent. Bureaucracy by its labyrinthine size interferes with its own accountability. The politics of modern societies swings between extremes of personal license and "forms of collectivist control designed only to limit the anarchy of self-interest . . . Thus the society in which [Americans, among others] live is one in which bureaucracy and individualism are partners as well as antagonists." They're locked in a permanent embrace. "And it is in the cultural climate of this bureaucratic individualism that the emotivist self is naturally at home."[9]

Running a society of warring, emotivist selves, of course, requires two things from political leaders: the *claim* of value neutrality and the *reality* of manipulative skill.[10]

THE WORLD OF *AFTER VIRTUE* shows itself in at least five major features of current American culture. They reinforce one another. And they have a big impact on the course of our shared life.

The first feature is the role of the social sciences (demography, anthropology, political science, and similar disciplines). Parents often complain that America's education establishment abuses the classroom and misuses their children by preaching new moral orthodoxies on a whole range of issues like gender identity. The courts and legal profession then enforce those new orthodoxies. But it's the social sciences that actually help create them. Among scientists, social scientists tend to be the least religious. Exceptions do exist. Christian Smith and Mark Regnerus, both of them distinguished social researchers, are committed Christians. So are many others. But as a group of disciplines, the social sciences tend to reflect agnostic or atheist thought committed to a particular brand of social reform.

This should surprise no one. By their nature, the social sciences objectify the human person. They make man a specimen of study and desacralize him in the process. They seek to identify and apply scientific laws to human behavior, the better to understand (and control) it, and they assume that such laws exist. It's no accident that the gambling industry has used behavioral psychology to sharply increase its profits. Casinos and a new generation of electronic gaming machines are deliberately crafted to produce "addiction by design" in the gamblers who use them— an economic model now spreading to other industries.[11]

The social sciences also tend to dismiss religion as a manmade illusion, a projection of purely human hopes and needs. This is clearly the case with Freudian psychology. The same is true in the work of Auguste Comte, the father of sociology.

Sociology is a useful example. As Christian Smith writes, "Sociologists today are disproportionately not religious compared to all Americans . . . And a great deal of sociology is devoted to showing that the ordinary world of everyday life as it *seems* to most people is not *really* what is going on—in short, to debunking appearances" (emphasis in original).[12]

In the words of Smith,

American sociology as a collective enterprise is at heart committed to the visionary project of *realizing the emancipation,*

*equality and moral affirmation of all human beings as autono-
mous, self-directing, individual agents [who should be] out to
live their lives as they personally so desire, by constructing their
own favored identities, entering and exiting relationships as
they choose, and equally enjoying the gratification of experi-
ential material and bodily pleasures* (emphasis in original).[13]

In practice, many different forces shape American sociology.
They range from Enlightenment liberalism to the Marxist tradition. They include the progressive social reform movement of
the early twentieth century and John Dewey's pragmatism. They
also include the lessons of therapeutic culture, the civil rights
struggle, community organizing, the 1960s sexual revolution,
and LGBT activism.[14]

But why does any of this matter? It matters because the
social sciences, especially psychology and sociology, work in secular society as a new kind of priesthood.[15] As critics like to argue,
the social sciences are really a disguised form of storytelling, not
science. They lack the rigor and credibility of natural sciences
such as physics and chemistry. But they do bring a set of tools
to social problems that produce useful statistics. And their data,
in skilled hands, can seem to have moral weight and prove some
otherwise dubious things.

In their effect, as Alasdair MacIntyre saw, the social sciences
serve as a means of social control "to sustain bureaucratic authority."[16] And as a result of their influence, as the historian Christopher Lasch said, "Today the state controls not merely the
individual's body, but as much of his spirit as it can preempt;
not merely his outer but his inner life as well; not merely the
public realm but the darkest corners of private life, formerly
inaccessible to political domination."[17]

A second key feature of current American culture is the role of education. A friend of mine is a well-known economist at a leading American university. He's also the gatekeeper for an elite doctoral program in his field. Asked once what he valued most in candidates for his program, he said, "an undergraduate degree in Classics." Homer and Virgil, of course, have very little to do with things like debt-deflation theory. But my friend's reasoning is, in fact, quite shrewd.

Since economics is a human (i.e., social) science, its practitioners should first know how to be actual human beings before learning their specialized skills. A formation in the classics or any of the other humanities is an immersion in beauty and knowledge. It has no utility other than enlarging the soul. But that achievement—the ennobling of a soul, the enlarging of the human spirit to revere the heritage of human excellence and to love things outside itself—is something no technical skill can accomplish.

As Leo Strauss once wrote, "liberal education is concerned with the souls of men, and therefore has little or no use for machines . . . [it] consists in learning to listen to still and small voices and therefore in becoming deaf to loudspeakers."[18] A liberal education—a balanced experience of the humanities, art, music, mathematics, and the natural sciences—is designed to form a mature "liberal" adult; liberal in the original sense, meaning free as opposed to slave. Thus for Strauss, "liberal education is the counter-poison . . . to the corroding effects of mass culture, to its inherent tendency to produce nothing" but specialists without vision or heart.[19]

Scholars like Anthony Esolen, Allan Bloom, Neil Postman, Matthew Crawford, and Alasdair MacIntyre, each in his own way and for different reasons, have all said similar things. For all of them, the point of a truly good education, from pre-K to graduate school, is to form students to think and act as fully rounded, mature, and engaged human beings. In other words, as adult persons of character.

As Matthew Crawford puts it, "Education requires a certain capacity for asceticism, but more fundamentally it is erotic. Only beautiful things lead us out [of our addictive self-focus] to join the world beyond our heads."[20] But the dilemma of postmodern life is that we can't agree on what a fully rounded, mature "human being" is—or should be. The fragmentation in American culture runs too deep. Recent battles over imposing gender ideology in school curricula and rewriting and politicizing civics and American history textbooks simply prove the point. So does the "progressive" intellectual conformism in so many of our university faculties.

Meanwhile, as American student skills decline in global comparisons, more and more stress is placed on developing STEM (science, technology, engineering, and math) competence at earlier student ages. There's nothing wrong with this in principle. Technical skills are an important part of modern life. But as we've already seen, American trust in the promise of technology is robust and naive to the point of being a character flaw. And a real education involves more profound life lessons than training workers and managers to be cogs in an advanced economy.

We tend to forget that "everything that human beings are doing to make it easier to operate computer networks is at the same time, but for different reasons, making it easier for computer networks to operate human beings."[21] We also tend to forget that our political system, including its liberties, requires a particular kind of literate, engaged citizen—a kind that predates the computer keyboard.

A third feature of our common life is the role of the law, the courts, and the legal profession. As we've already seen, America is an invented nation, a legal contract. Americans are bound together by neither blood nor ancestry. We're a "people" only in the sense that we share allegiance to a fundamental law—the Constitution—and the public institutions and procedures it prescribes. This makes our lawmakers, courts, and the legal profession arbiters of justice. It also makes our political allegiance more tentative and less organic. And in the world of *After Virtue*, it also makes all of us warriors in an ongoing guerrilla conflict over what "justice" is, and who gets it, and when and how.

"The strangeness of our day," notes the political scientist Robert Kraynak, "consists in a strong moral passion for the virtue of justice sitting alongside a loss of confidence in the very foundations of justice, and even an eagerness to undermine them" by leading secular thinkers.[22] Kraynak goes on:

> [T]he crucial requirement for human equality is a conception of human dignity, which views human beings as having a special moral status in the universe, and individuals as having unique moral worth entailing claims of justice.
>
> What is so strange about our age is that demands for justice are increasing even as the foundations for those demands are disappearing. In particular, beliefs in man as a creature made in the image of God, or an animal with a rational soul, are being replaced by a scientific materialism that undermines what is noble and special about man, and by doctrines of relativism that deny the objective morality required to undergird human dignity.[23]

In effect, secular thinkers live off the capital of religious beliefs they reject. "The 'faith' of these modern thinkers in human dignity," says Kraynak, is actually a convenient, parasitic laziness. It "enables them to have respectable moral commitments while avoiding the hard work of actually establishing foundations for them, whether in the moral order of nature or the revealed knowledge of God."[24]

The problem with a justice-related idea like equality is that, divorced from other public virtues and networks of obligation, it acts like a bulldozer. It flattens everything in its path. When it infects Supreme Court decisions, it licenses an official bigotry like Justice Anthony Kennedy's opinion in *United States v. Windsor*. In striking down the federal Defense of Marriage Act (DOMA), Kennedy argued in *Windsor* that by passing a law rooted in centuries of moral tradition, Congress had acted with a "bare desire to harm" motivated by malice.

So much for the will of the people and their elected representatives.

But disregard for "the will of the people and their elected representatives" is hardly limited to the courts. Administrative law and especially executive orders were the preferred tools of the Obama administration and others before it. And they embody a kind of government absolutism with roots in European monarchy. In the words of Philip Hamburger, the distinguished Columbia Law School scholar,

> Administrative adjudication evades almost all of the procedural rights guaranteed under the Constitution. It subjects Americans to adjudication without real judges, without juries, without grand juries, without full protection against self-incrimination, and so forth . . . [A]dministrative courts substitute inquisitorial process for the due process of law—and that's not just an abstract accusation; much early administrative procedure appears to have been modeled on civilian-derived inquisitorial process. Administrative adjudication thus becomes an open avenue for evasion of the Bill of Rights . . .

Rather than speak of administrative law, we should speak
of administrative power—indeed, of absolute power or more
concretely extra-legal . . . power. Then we at least can begin
to recognize the danger.[25]

A fourth feature of our current culture is the character
of our emerging young adult leadership. Writing in April
2001, David Brooks offered a portrait of Ivy League students as
America's "meritocratic elite." He focused on young people at
Princeton, but he saw the same pattern at other leading universities. These elite millennials were very different from their
boomer parents. They were disciplined, hardworking, and
courteous. They had little interest in politics. They respected
authority. They were generous in their community service,
upbeat about the future, and intensely driven to achieve.[26]

Children of privilege from the start, they lived at a unique
moment. They had no memory of Vietnam. No memory of deep
social conflict. The Cold War was over. We had won it. Prosperity was growing. The United States was the world's only great
power. The possibilities for personal success were bright. Brooks
found these students open, sensible, and deeply likable. It's
what he didn't find that bothered him.

The students he met lacked the basics of what earlier Ivy
League generations would have learned as a matter of course.
Things more vital even than material success. Things like a sense
of moral gravity and duty, a distrust of luxury, "a concrete and
articulated moral system," and some understanding that "life is
a noble mission and a perpetual war against sin, that the choices
we make have consequences not just in getting a job or a law
school admission but in some grand battle between lightness
and dark."[27]

Five months after the Brooks article, the Twin Towers were

attacked. Wars in Iraq and Afghanistan followed. In 2008, so did a global financial meltdown. The world changed. And harsher times led to a very different environment.

What we have now at elite universities, according to one former Yale scholar, is a "system [that] manufactures students who are smart and talented and driven, yes, but also anxious, timid and lost, with little intellectual curiosity and a stunted sense of purpose: trapped in a bubble of privilege, heading meekly in the same direction, great at what they're doing but with no idea why they're doing it."[28]

And what about students outside the Ivy elite? Comparing his own talented students to the ones David Brooks had encountered thirteen years before, the Villanova scholar Mark Shiffman was struck not by their lack of curiosity, but by their *fear*:

> When the kid at the next desk might out-compete me, edging me out of the path to economic security, then the hope that we may prevail together gives way to the fear that I will be the one who fails. When the specter of shrinking prosperity increases competition for scarce opportunities and engenders doubt that I will do as well as my parents, that fear intensifies . . . Our fear has become a pathological condition, a desperate need to bring the future under control. And we seek therapy from colleges and universities, the therapy of cumulative achievement along clearly marked pathways to success.[29]

College isn't cheap. As costs rise and the college success-therapy model fails, the fear of many young adults goes deeper. That fear, fused with the lack of a demanding, morally coherent vision for university life, helps drive the confusion, anger, hypersensitivity, and spirit of entitlement that now too commonly mark student life.

And that leads to a fifth and final feature of our current national life. But first some background.

※

WRITING ABOUT THE PREVALENCE of scientific fraud in 2016, William Wilson, a Bay Area software engineer, noted that "When a formerly ascetic discipline suddenly attains a measure of [policymaking] influence, it is bound to be flooded by opportunists and charlatans, whether it's the National Academy of Science or the monastery of Cluny."

In practice, earnest-sounding junk thought from opportunists can infect every element of society, not just science. And junk thought—from rewriting history, to inventing new narratives of oppression, to sex and gender studies that claim to prove the implausible—is the human intellect weaponized to serve political goals. Especially the goal of silencing different views.

Culture warriors come in all shades of opinion, including the most ostentatiously tolerant, progressive, and forward-thinking. In fact, to borrow a warning from the great French writer Charles Péguy, we may never fully know the acts of deceit and cowardice that "have been motivated by the fear of looking insufficiently progressive."[30]

So this is the fifth key feature of our common national life today: malice wrapped in the language of tolerance, sensitivity, and rights. It consists in an appetite to use power not simply to prevail in political debate, but to humiliate and erase dissent, and even its memory, in reworking the cell structure of society.

Examples range from the strange to the bitter. They include efforts to scrub Confederate public monuments from the South, and "progressive" academic attacks on American Founder Alexander Hamilton (of *Hamilton* Broadway musical fame). They include companies like Apple and Salesforce.com that attack religious liberty legislation in states nationwide and "use economic threats to exercise more power over public policy than the voters who use the democratic process." And they include selective shaping of the Advanced Placement U.S. history framework by the College Board, controversial efforts to "fix" democracy by major philanthropies, and bitter posthumous attacks on "unprogressive" public leaders.[31]

There's more. In 2011, the Obama administration stripped funds from the U.S. bishops' Migrant and Refugee Services anti-human-trafficking program. MRS was a highly regarded leader in its help to victims of sex trafficking. But it was defunded because the bishops declined to provide abortion and contraceptives as part of MRS services. The money was reassigned to groups ranked lower in quality, but more ideologically compliant, by the same White House.

The same intolerance marked the administration's fight to coerce abortion and contraceptive services as part of national health care. It tenaciously refused reasonable compromise on exemptions for religiously affiliated providers and organizations and deliberately sought to break any opposition—prompting a sardonic *Wall Street Journal* editorial renaming the Little Sisters of the Poor "the Little Sisters of the Government."[32]

The pattern of a White House calling for compromise and national unity, and then making both impossible, is hardly the sin of any one party. Nor is it new. But the scope and the nature of the damage today *are*. Because unlike fifty years ago, and many other serious moments of national confusion, the country's character is now fundamentally different.

For many Americans today, the life of the nation has become

something remote. It offers too little sense of a shared history or national purpose; too little reasoned debate; too little civility (despite endless calls for it); too little moral gravity or continuity with the past; too little value to warrant personal engagement; and too few reasons for anyone to risk his or her life in defending through military service what many see as the public-square equivalent of a big-box discount store.

It takes an extraordinary faith in democracy and the integrity of higher education to share in America's tradition of optimism when, day after day, the most distinguished national newspaper of record offers stories like "Colleges Show Their Lobbying Might" in the same pages as "The Rise of the College Crybullies," "A Campus Mayhem Syllabus," "I Was Disinvited on Campus," "Speechless on Campus," "Tolerance, Free Speech Collide on Campus," "A Campus Crusade Against the Constitution," "Bonfire of the Academy," "Whatever Happened to Religious Freedom," "The First Amendment Needs Your Prayers," "When the College Madness Came to My Campus," "Radical Parents, Despotic Children," "The Climate Police Escalate," and "Yale's Little Robespierres."[33]

As Greg Lukianoff and Jonathan Haidt wrote in 2015, "A movement is arising, undirected and driven largely by students, to scrub campuses clean of words, ideas and subjects that might cause discomfort or give offense." Faculties and administrators— adults who should know better but, lacking a moral center of gravity, don't—have often buckled under the pressure. And how does that fit with the genuine greatness of the American experiment? Thomas Jefferson answered it best at the founding of the University of Virginia: "This institution will be based on the illimitable freedom of the human mind. For here we are not afraid to follow truth wherever it may lead, nor to tolerate error so long as reason is left free to combat it."[34]

We've come to the end of a long, dimming corridor. And as we do, we might remember some lessons from the last century.

In 1935, Sinclair Lewis wrote *It Can't Happen Here*, the tale of a populist candidate who runs for president on a platform of patriotism, deep economic and political reform, and traditional values. Once elected, he imposes a homegrown American fascism.

Five years later, in 1940, Arthur Koestler told the story of Rubashov, one of the original "Old Bolsheviks," a man arrested and condemned to death by the communist revolution he spent his life fighting for. Koestler's *Darkness at Noon* is one of the great novels of the twentieth century. And it has one of the era's greatest themes:

> Rubashov wandered through his cell. It was quiet and nearly dark. It could not be long before they came to fetch him. There was an error somewhere in the equation . . . It was a mistake in the system; perhaps it lay in the precept that until now he had held to be incontestable, in whose name he had sacrificed others and was himself being sacrificed, in the precept that the end justifies the means. It was this sentence that had killed the great fraternity of the Revolution and made them all run amuck. What had he once written in his diary? "We have thrown overboard all conventions; our sole guiding principle is that of consequent logic; we are sailing without ethical ballast."
>
> Perhaps the heart of the evil lay there. Perhaps it did not suit mankind to sail without ballast. And perhaps reason alone was a defective compass, which led one on such a winding, twisted course that the goal finally disappeared in the mist. Perhaps now would come the time of great darkness.[35]

Fascism, communism, complicated ideologies of every shape and sort: Today in pragmatic, postmodern America, these clumsy, antique systems of thought are museum pieces. Misshapen children of the Enlightenment. Words from a dark time, long past. They clearly don't belong in any sane discussion of advanced liberal democracies. They can't happen here. And it's quite true: They really *can't* happen here.

But there's more than one way to skin a cat, as Tocqueville saw long ago. The peculiar despotism innate to democracy

> extends its arms over society as a whole; it covers its surface with a network of small, complicated, painstaking, uniform rules through which the most original minds and the most vigorous souls cannot clear a way to surpass the crowd; it does not break wills but it softens them, bends them, and directs them . . . it does not tyrannize, it hinders; compromises, enervates, extinguishes, dazes, and finally reduces each nation to being nothing more than a herd of timid and industrious animals, of which the government is shepherd.[36]

To put it another way: The Enlightenment's crippled children have a gentler, more successful, and far more congenial sibling. Us.

CHAPTER 8

HOPE AND ITS DAUGHTERS

Again Jesus spoke to them saying, "I am the light of the world; he who follows me will not walk in darkness, but will have the light of life."

—Jn 8:12

[A]nd hope does not disappoint us, because God's love has been poured into our hearts through the Holy Spirit who has been given to us.

—Rom 5:5

W E'VE SPOKEN FRANKLY SO FAR ABOUT THE AMERICAN landscape as we now know it. Some of the words have been difficult. But candor is not an enemy of love. And real hope begins in honesty.

The current spirit of our country inclines us to be troubled. It's a sensible temptation. How can any one person or small group of people make a difference? How can we change and renew things so that our children grow up in a better world? We come back to a question suggested at the start of this book: How can we live in joy, and serve the common good as leaven, in a culture that no longer shares what we believe?

The answer to that question springs from a simple historical fact: On a quiet Sunday morning two thousand years ago,

God raised Jesus of Nazareth from the dead. This small moment, unseen by any human eye, turned the world upside down and changed history forever. It confirmed Jesus' victory over death and evil. It liberated those living and dead who lay in bondage to their sins. An anonymous ancient homily for Holy Saturday, speaking in the voice of Jesus Christ, reminds us of the full import of his resurrection:

> I am your God, who for your sake [has] become your son. Out of love for you and for your descendants, I now by my own authority command all who are held in bondage to come forth, all who are in darkness to be enlightened, all who are sleeping to arise. I order you, O sleeper, to awake. I did not create you to be held a prisoner in hell. Rise from the dead, for I am the life of the dead. Rise up, work of my hands, you who were created in my image. Rise, let us leave this place, for you are in me and I am in you; together we form only one person and we cannot be separated.

Jesus rose from the dead so that we could be joined to him and his victory. Believers know that Jesus was not only victorious then, in Jerusalem. He'll also come in royal glory at the end of time, when he will judge the living and the dead. At Christ's second coming, his kingdom will fully arrive. His reign will be complete. The time in which we find ourselves is an interim one. We may struggle as we seek to follow Jesus, but we also remember the great victories of our King: the victory in the past and the victory certain to come. And those victories give us hope.

Hope is how we as a Church, and as individual Christians, continue along our journey on earth when we face obstacles and our own shortcomings. But many of us don't really understand

hope. We talk about "hoping" to get a certain gift or a promo-
tion. We think of hope as a good feeling, or a kind of optimism.
But real Christian hope is the fruit of faith and the seed of charity.
It's also a breath of life from the Holy Spirit that fills our lungs
to *sustain* both our faith and our love. We're at a point, then,
when we need to look at what hope is and what it isn't. We need
to reflect on the traditional sins against hope: presumption and
despair. Finally, we need to take a closer look at that common
secular cousin of hope—faith in the inevitability of progress—
in contrast with the Christian understanding of God's providence. Reminding ourselves of hope's nature is important
because it keeps us focused on God. True hope depends not
on our own efforts, but on the grace of a loving Creator, on
whom we must rely if we seek to serve him and build his kingdom in our time.

So, what exactly is hope? The *Catechism of the Catholic
Church* describes it as "the theological virtue by which we
desire the kingdom of heaven and eternal life as our happiness, placing our trust in Christ's promises and relying not
on our own strength, but on the help of the grace of the Holy
Spirit."[1]

Let's unpack that step by step. First, hope is a virtue. That
means that it's not just a feeling, nor is it optimism. As the late
priest and scholar Richard John Neuhaus put it, "Optimism is
simply a matter of optics, of seeing what we want to see and not
seeing what we don't want to see. Hope is only hope when it is
hope with eyes wide open to all that challenges hope."[2] Upbeat
feelings are fickle. They don't last long if we look hard at the
problems in our own lives and the world around us.

Rather, hope is like a muscle or a skill that, with practice,
lets us throw a fastball or play the piano. Moreover, it's a *theological* virtue, a gift from the Holy Spirit that enables us to do

what we couldn't do on our own. So while we're correct in saying that hope is something we cling to, we also need to remember that hope is something we first receive as God's gift. It can't be founded on our own striving. It rests on God's strength and the truth about Jesus Christ.

This gift of hope creates in us a desire for heaven and eternal life as our happiness. It's an act of trust in God's future. In other words, it points our lives in the right direction. Hope refocuses our gaze away from passing pleasures, money, power, fame, and possessions, and toward living with God forever. It shows us what makes us truly happy, and it helps us to want that deeper happiness instead of the many other things that society tells us—and we too often think—will make us happy.

The *Catechism* explains this more fully: "The virtue of hope responds to the aspiration to happiness which God has placed in the heart of every man; it takes up the hopes that inspire men's activities and purifies them so as to order them to the kingdom of heaven; it keeps man from discouragement; it sustains him during times of abandonment; it opens up his heart in expectation of eternal beatitude. Buoyed up by hope, he is preserved from selfishness and led to the happiness that flows from charity."[3]

When we hope, therefore, we align our wants and our wills as God intended. We're able to love the things of the world rightly instead of clinging to them selfishly. We're able to work for the kingdom of God and not our own glory, because we're confident that our final happiness lies in union with God, and that this union will come about through the power of the Holy Spirit and Jesus Christ, the conqueror of death. In 1 John 3:2–3, we read: "Beloved, we are God's children now; it does not yet appear what we shall be, but we know that when he appears we shall be like him, for we shall see him as he is. And everyone who thus hopes in him purifies himself as he is pure." Believing that God loves us and has made us his children, and hoping to see him as he is, purifies our hearts and minds.

We also start to see here how hope connects to the other theological virtues, faith and charity. As Romanus Cessario, O.P., notes, faith, hope, and charity represent the order of actual development in the life of a mature Christian.[4]

First we believe in Jesus Christ and the truth about him, what he did for us, and the happiness he promises us in union with God. Then we come to desire Christ and union with God. Finally, God gives us his own charity, which allows us to take part in that union even now.[5] In the words of the twelfth-century monk William of St. Thierry, faith posits the existence of God, whom we love. Hope promises us that because God is merciful, he will allow that love to come to fruition.

Or, as Father Neuhaus put it, "hope is faith directed to the future."[6] To oversimplify, faith is a matter of the head. Hope is a matter of the heart. Charity is the pledge of the love we believe in and hope for. In that sense, charity is like an engagement ring. It's the first act whereby God begins sharing his life with us now, an act that begins the full sharing of the divine life that we will know in heaven.

Because God is a trustworthy bridegroom, we can have hope in the promise that he will bring us to perfect union with him in heaven.[7] As Paul says in Romans 5, we can rejoice in suffering because suffering produces character, character produces hope, "and hope does not disappoint us, because God's love has been poured into our hearts through the Holy Spirit who has been given to us." In this way, Romanus Cessario notes, the virtue of hope allows us to take part now in the salvation that is to come. It's a confident movement toward the future, a preparation for receiving the love of God fully, but it also allows us to receive that love right here, right now.[8]

In his great encyclical *Spe Salvi* (*Saved by Hope*), Pope Benedict XVI expands on this theme. He writes that faith is not merely a matter of reaching out to something absent, but it gives us "even now something of the reality we are waiting for, and this present reality constitutes for us a 'proof' of the things that are still unseen. Faith draws the future into the present, so that it is no longer simply a 'not yet.' The fact that this future exists changes the present; the present is touched by the future reality, and thus the things of the future spill over into those of the present and those of the present into those of the future."[9] And because faith and hope allow our future happiness to break into our present moment, Benedict writes, we can spend our lives generously and fearlessly for God.

Benedict tells us that early Christians did not find their security in possessions or their ability to support themselves. They had confidence in God not because their beliefs shaped the culture around them, nor because they were able to win elections, nor because people thought they were wise or important. In fact, none of those things were true. Early Christians were despised and persecuted. Because they loved Jesus, people confiscated their possessions and tortured them. Those who remained faithful had to have a more secure substance by which they lived. Their lives had to be founded on Jesus Christ, whom they claimed in faith and hope.

Furthermore, those who founded their life on Christ in faith and hope experienced a new freedom. The more they relied on Jesus, the more they were able to live joyfully and follow him. We see this in the lives of saints like Francis of Assisi, who stripped himself of all possessions except for the Lord. We see it in women and men who consecrate themselves to Christ under religious vows, and in couples whose radical generosity leaves them rich in love even if their bank accounts are small. In the eyes of the world, these men and women love foolishly. By the calculus of the world, they often seem crazy. But the eyes of faith and hope make perfect sense of their sacrifice.

These men and women live in the assurance of what they hope for; they're filled with the conviction of what they don't yet see (see Heb 11:1). They understand that, as Blessed John Henry Newman put it, "our duty as Christians lies in this, in making ventures for eternal life without the absolute certainty of success."[10]

Faith, Newman continues, "is in its very essence the making present [of] what is unseen; the acting upon the mere prospect of it, as if it really were possessed; the venturing upon it, the staking present ease, happiness, or other good, upon the chance of the future."[11] Believers understand that the Christian life can be an adventure embarked on with joy because faith, hope, and love hold us close to Christ. They see clearly that a genuinely Christian life involves risks, that if we are in fact wrong about Jesus, and our hope in him is false, "we are of all men most to be pitied" (1 Cor 15:19).

So the Christian life is a dangerous wager. But as believers, we know it's a wager worth making. Because we've received the love of God, because Jesus *did* rise from the dead, and because he wants us to live with him now and forever in heaven, our hope won't be disappointed. So it is that hope enables us to risk what we have for Jesus, even in a world that grows more hostile by the day. We don't do this rashly or lightly, Newman says, but "in a noble, generous way." We don't fully know what we will lose or what we will gain. Rather, we walk forward "uncertain about our reward, uncertain about our extent of sacrifice, in all respects leaning, waiting upon him, trusting in him to fulfil his promise, trusting in him to enable us to fulfil our own vows, and so in all respects proceeding without carefulness or anxiety about the future."[12]

The men and women who do this glow white-hot with the Spirit. They live to the full what Richard John Neuhaus called "the high adventure of Christian discipleship." Their lives are hard. Living the Christian life requires sacrifice and self-denial. But those sacrifices lead to greater love and joy than many in the world have ever known.

﹏

OF COURSE, THERE ARE other paths we can take instead of hope: despair and presumption. Whereas hope is rooted in faith and gives birth to love, despair and presumption are rooted in pride.[13] When we hope, we trust in God. When we despair or presume, we choose to trust ourselves instead. In a way, despair seems to make sense. It's a logical response to the problems in the world and in us, and to our inability to fix either on our own. It sees, quite clearly, that the things of this world can never fully satisfy us. But despair makes sense only if God is not merciful and Jesus did not rise from the dead. That's why despair is a denial of the mercy and the justice of God and of the possibility of redemption. If hope says that our true and final happiness lies in heaven, then despair says that there is no New Jerusalem. It says that this world is all that we have, and that we can never attain true peace and happiness.[14]

In a striking insight of psychology, Thomas Aquinas names spiritual sloth and unchastity as the most common causes of despair.[15] Since living the Christian life—especially a chaste Christian life—seems to get harder by the year, it's no surprise that we can feel inclined to despair. But this is a trick of the Evil

One. We can't surrender to our discouragement. We can't become a people of cynicism and inaction.

If the temptation of some Christians is to fall away from the faith when it becomes difficult, the temptation of many other Christians is to grow angry or bitter. We complain about how sexualized the media are, but do we pay attention to how *angry* they are as well? We can readily worry about sexual content in the media and how it excites the unwary, but what about that special and delicious rush *we* get from being outraged? Neither rage nor inaction acknowledges that Jesus Christ is Lord. Neither relies on his power to help us, or his desire to save us. Neither remembers that Jesus will ultimately be victorious, in his own time and on his own terms.

Moreover, we can see what despair looks like when we look at our wider culture. We've become a nation of despair in our flight from the real problems all around us. So often, when faced by violence abroad, division in our own country, and the breakdown of families and neighborhoods, our response is to turn inward. Most of us can't afford gated communities, but we put up fences around our hearts.

Instead of helping the poor, we go shopping. Instead of spending meaningful time with our families and friends, we look for videos on the Internet. We cocoon ourselves in a web of narcotics, from entertainment to self-help gurus to chemicals. We wrap ourselves in cheap comforts and empty slogans, and because there are never enough of them, we constantly look for more. We enjoy getting angry about problems that we can't solve, and we overlook the child who wants us to watch her dance, or the woman on the street corner asking for food.

We need to break out of ourselves. Augustine famously described someone caught in sin as curved in on himself. We need to ask God to hammer us straight so that we can look at him, and at the world he created around us, in the light of his truth. We need to hope in God and in heaven not as heartwarming pieties but as our real and final home. When we do, we'll see that there's no more room for despair, no time for sloth, but an open vista of joy before us.

If despair anticipates the failure of hope, then presumption anticipates its fulfillment in an equally perverse way. Presumption says that the open vista of joy comes without a cost. If despair says, "I can never get better," presumption says, "I'm pretty good just the way I am." Both of these mistakes are deadly. Like despair, presumption comes from relying on ourselves and not having faith in God.[16] It thinks that the path to heaven is a first class flight where we can just sit back and relax. We can get to heaven on our own because, all things considered, we're already good enough. We can sin as much as we want because God is always there to dispense forgiveness.[17]

We can see presumption alive and well in our own churches. How many of our homilies and hymns subtly stroke our vanity? How many of our prayers say, in effect, "God, thank you for making us the swell people you've made us to be. Help us to become even better than we already are"? And we see presumption alive and well in our country's naive optimism that a certain leader or a certain group of people can finally bring us what amounts to salvation. "We're the ones we've been waiting for," we're told. We can bring about a more or less just society based on our own power and performance.

The truth is that while we're often good and just in our actions, we're also selfish, mean, and greedy. We can't make heaven here on earth because, given the people we are now, "heaven" would be a long way from pleasant, let alone perfect. We have to trust that God will bring about his kingdom in our hearts and in the world in his own time, and we have to remember that this will require sacrifice if we're going to serve his plan. Furthermore, we can, in fact, fall away from the path to heaven and end up unhappy forever. We tend to forget about it, but hope is both "the confident expectation of divine blessing and the beatific vision of God," as the *Catechism* puts it, *and* "the fear of offending God's love and of incurring punishment."[18]

That's not to say that we should ever be afraid that God might turn against us, or that he's eager to find reasons to punish us. No loving human father would act that way, so how could a loving God? But holy awe is a healthy thing. It recognizes that God is Lord and we're not. "Fear of the Lord"—a gift of the Holy Spirit—involves a prudent respect for his justice. If he were less than just, if the gulf between good and evil in our actions made no final difference, then God would not really be God, and his word could never serve as a sure foundation of our hope.

Despair and presumption, in their equal evasions of God, are the subtle and very peculiar parents of the secularized religion we call progress—a kind of Christianity without Christ. The great Harvard historian Christopher Dawson noted that progress is the "working faith of our civilization."[19] And the historian Christopher Lasch described that faith

> not [as] the promise of a secular utopia that would bring history to a happy ending, but the promise of steady improvement with no foreseeable ending at all. The expectation of indefinite, open-ended improvement, even more than the insistence that improvement can come only through human effort, provides the solution to the puzzle that is otherwise so baffling—the resilience of progressive ideology in the face of discouraging events that have shattered the illusion of utopia.[20]

Americans talk about progress with an odd kind of reverence. Progress is the unstoppable force pushing human affairs forward. And it's a religion with a simple premise: Except for the random detour, civilization instinctively changes for the better. And it's up to us to get on board or get out of the way; to be part of the change or to get run over by history if we try to obstruct it. Hence we Catholics are routinely warned that we're on the wrong side of history. Critics tell us that our view of human nature, especially human sexuality, will one day be treated with the same enlightened scorn as the so-called scientific racial theories of a century ago.

Of course, such voices tend to gloss over the fact that it was "progressives" who pushed those racial theories—theories that led to massive suffering abroad and vulgar bigotry here at home. In the name of progress, activists like Margaret Sanger vigorously promoted contraception and eugenics. In order for the world to improve, their logic went, we need the wrong kind of people—people from the wrong kinds of races—to stop having babies. Sound familiar?

This idea of progress does have its appeal. As the economist Sidney Pollard put it: "The world today believes in progress because the only alternative to the belief in progress would be total despair."[21] We might go a step further: Clinging to a belief in progress is actually a *product* of despair, generously seasoned by sloth. History is cruel, social change is difficult, and a relationship with God involves a lot of unpleasant truth-telling—especially about ourselves. Better to just shift the burden of living in a flawed world at an imperfect time onto some positive force that will bring about the change we want "some" day.

It's a heartwarming delusion. But that's all it is: a delusion. A brief glance at the twentieth century destroys the myth. In

just a few decades, "progressive" regimes and ideas produced
two savage world wars, multiple murder ideologies, and the
highest body count in history. And yet, as Christopher Lasch
noted, people still cling to the religion of progress long after
the evidence wrecks their dream.

The cult of progress is the child not only of despair, but also
of presumption. It's a kind of Pelagianism, the early Christian
heresy that presumed human beings could attain salvation by
their own efforts without the constant help of grace. Hence the
philosopher Hans Blumenberg says that what separates the
progressive idea of history from the Christian one is "the asser-
tion that the principle of historical change comes from within
history and not from on high, and that man can achieve a better
life 'by the exertion of his own powers' instead of counting on
divine grace."[22]

While we can and should work for social improvement—
an obviously worthy goal—we're too riddled with sin to ever
build paradise on earth. As Benedict XVI put it, authentic progress doesn't come automatically. In every age, human freedom
must be weaned over to the good.[23] And because our freedom
can be used for good or evil, progress is always ambiguous:

> Without doubt, it offers new possibilities for good, but it also
> opens up appalling possibilities for evil—possibilities that
> formerly did not exist. We have all witnessed the way in
> which progress, in the wrong hands, can become and has
> indeed become a terrifying progress in evil. If technical pro-
> gress is not matched by corresponding progress in man's
> ethical formation, in man's inner growth (see Eph 3:16 and 2
> Cor 4:16), then it is not progress at all, but a threat for man
> and for the world.[24]

Ironically, it's the religious subtext of progress that makes it so attractive. Again, as Friedrich Nietzsche and many others observed, progress is a kind of Christianity without Jesus and all the awkward baggage that he brings. The Protestant theologian Reinhold Niebuhr saw this years ago when he wrote that "the idea of progress is possible only upon the ground of a Christian culture. It is a secularized version of Biblical apocalypse and of the Hebraic sense of a meaningful history, in contrast to the meaningless history of the Greeks."[25]

This contrast is crucial. Ancient peoples like the Greeks and Babylonians had a far darker view of history than Christians do. They saw humanity as controlled by fate, whose dictates could not be resisted. Greeks and Romans also had little hope of heaven. Many ancients believed that at death, human life ended. Hence the emperor Hadrian, one of Rome's most cultivated and humane rulers, would write of his soul: *"Poor ghost, my body's friend and guest / Erewhile, thou leav'st thy home; / To what uncertain place of rest / A wanderer dost thou roam? / Pale, cold, and naked, henceforth to forgo / Thy jests among the sullen shades below."*

One of Christianity's key contributions to Western civilization was to give men and women a sense of freedom from the whims of fate, a hope for life after death because of the victory of Jesus Christ. And over the centuries, that confidence in life beyond the grave has taken vivid form in the here and now.

THE CASTEL SANT'ANGELO IN Rome, the old papal fortress near the Vatican, is also the tomb of Hadrian. Visitors can find Hadrian's poem about his soul on the wall. But walking eastward in Rome, the pilgrim will come to a very different meditation on death. The Capuchin Franciscans have an ordinary-looking church on the Via Veneto. But its crypt contains a series of rooms decorated with human bones—thousands of them.

The ceilings look like those of a baroque palace, except that they're made of vertebrae. There's a clock built of arm and finger bones. Skulls and femurs create decorative arches and columns. Through unbelieving eyes, it can easily seem ghoulish. It's certainly a sobering encounter with our mortality. But it's also very Franciscan. It takes death, that thing we fear most, and literally plays with it. And that couldn't happen without a firm faith that Jesus Christ had crushed death, turning it from our ancient foe into what Saint Francis called "Sister Death," the gateway to eternal life with God. The Capuchin bone crypt is uniquely Christian because beneath its somber appearance, it offers— for those who believe—a firm and joyful hope about what we find in Christ.

The Christian alternative to the cult of progress is not only hope, but the idea of providence. Providence is the understanding that God has a plan for each of our lives and for the whole world, and that for each of us, his plan is good. As Paul writes in Romans 8:28, "We know that in everything God works for good with those who love him, who are called according to his purpose." Whereas progress might claim that history has an inevitable arc, faith in providence has confidence that the Lord of history will one day make all things right. A healthy understanding of providence and a lively hope should be united to a thirst for justice, and to the assurance that God will provide justice on the Last Day.

What about those who blame God for the injustices of the world? Our failed attempts at doing good show us that only God can create justice. Faith gives us the certainty that he does so. A world without God, Benedict XVI writes, would be a world without hope.[26] This is why faith in the Last Judgment is an integral part of hope.[27] One day God will judge the world justly. Wrong will be made right. The wicked will answer for their crimes and be punished, and those whom Christ has redeemed will be led to eternal life. Without a final vindication of right and wrong—and without a just judge to do the vindicating—we would live in a world where good and evil have no meaning.

As Christians, we believe that Jesus Christ is that just judge. He's not only the guide of history, but its focal point. He makes sense of history and frames the story of the world.[28] Paul tells the Ephesians that God "has made known to us in all wisdom and insight the mystery of his will, according to his purpose which he set forth in Christ as a plan for the fullness of time, to unite all things in him, things in heaven and things on earth" (Eph 1:9–10). This unity in Christ of all things in heaven and on earth is one of the truths we mean when we talk about the kingdom of God. And as members of the body of Christ, we Catholics are called to work for that reign of Christ even now.

We know how the story ends, and that it ends well. And because we have confidence in our future with Christ, we should live differently. By faith and hope, we're given new life.[29] Longing for heaven doesn't make us lose interest in bringing Christ's love into this world. We're called to work for progress understood in the light of Christ, which means, as Neuhaus put it, that we are "free agents who are capable of participating in the transcendent purpose that, being immanent in history, holds the certain promise of vindicating all that is true, good, and beautiful."[30]

That may sound complicated, but it means that Jesus' promise of bringing justice at the end of time is present even now in our own time. Christ's kingdom doesn't come because of an inexorable, impersonal force. It comes because God builds it with our hands. Christian hope compels us to be faithful to our spouses and care for our children, to feed the hungry and welcome immigrants, to visit prisoners and sit by the dying *right now*. Augustine is often quoted as saying, "Hope has two beautiful daughters. Their names are anger and courage; anger at the way things are, *and courage to see that they do not remain the way they are.*" The words are apocryphal. There's no real evidence that Augustine ever wrote them. But their content is clearly true and worth remembering as a guide to Christian discipleship.

That doesn't mean we'll succeed in our efforts. And it doesn't mean our work will be easy. But even in the face of failure and hardship we maintain our hope because it's founded on Jesus Christ, not ourselves. As Pope Benedict so beautifully said:

> It is important to know that I can always continue to hope, even if in my own life, or the historical period in which I am living, there seems to be nothing left to hope for. Only the great certitude of hope that my own life and history in general, despite all failures, are held firm by the indestructible power of Love, and that this gives them their meaning and importance, only this kind of hope can then give the courage to act and to persevere. Certainly we cannot "build" the kingdom of God by our own efforts—what we build will always be the kingdom of man with all the limitations proper to our human nature. The kingdom of God is a gift, and precisely because of this, it is great and beautiful, and constitutes the response to our hope. And we cannot—to use the classical expression—"merit" heaven through our works. Heaven is always more than we could merit, just as being loved is never something "merited," but always a gift.[31]

Our action and cooperation are essential, but Benedict is right: The kingdom of God, such as we can advance it now and when it comes fully in heaven, is ultimately a gift. It's not our project; it belongs to the Lord. And that should be an immense source of consolation.

A hundred years ago, the French poet Charles Péguy penned a book-length poem called *The Portal of the Mystery of Hope*. It's a haunting meditation. Péguy writes that hope is the most difficult of the theological virtues. Faith sees what is, and charity loves what is, but hope sees and loves what will be.[32] In our "carnal" and "vagrant" hearts, he writes, we are called to preserve the word of Christ so that it does not fall silent.[33] He envisions men and women passing held water from hand to hand and says that likewise, we must hand on God and hope.[34]

That, in the end, is our calling as Christians: to make Christ known in the world. To hand on the hope that fills our hearts. To work for God's justice in our nation, honoring all that remains beautiful and good in it. And always to do so knowing that we're on a journey to our final homeland. Longing for that life inspires us along the way. It's hard to imagine what eternal life with God would be like, and maybe that's why it can sometimes be so hard to hope in it.

Heaven certainly won't be boring or a series of humdrum days. Benedict XVI imagines what it will be: "something more like the supreme moment of satisfaction, in which totality embraces us and we embrace totality—this we can only attempt. It would be like plunging into the ocean of infinite love, a moment in which time—the before and after—no longer exists. We can only attempt to grasp the idea that such a moment is life in the full sense, a plunging ever anew into the vastness of being, in which we are simply overwhelmed with joy."[35]

That's the end goal of the Christian life. *That's* the gift that Jesus Christ offers us and makes it possible for us to attain. And that is our greatest reason for hope.

CHAPTER 9

RULES FOR RADICALS

E VERYONE LOVES A STORY. SO HERE'S "A TALE OF TWO
Rulebooks." It goes like this:

In 1971 Saul Alinsky published *Rules for Radicals*, his
famous guide to community organizing. On the dedication page
he wrote: "Lest we forget at least an over-the-shoulder acknow-
ledgment to the very first radical: from all our legends, mythol-
ogy, and history . . . the first radical known to man who rebelled
against the establishment and did it so effectively that he at least
won his own kingdom—Lucifer."[1]

Alinsky didn't believe in anything so primitive (in his view)
as the devil. So his words are ironic and mainly for shock value.
But his book is very useful for understanding recent American
politics and national leadership. And they make a good comparison with another, rather different set of rules.

Rules for Radicals echoes Machiavelli and the Marxist
thinker Antonio Gramsci as a shrewd map to seeking power. But
Alinsky sees himself as going beyond Machiavelli. Instead of

teaching rulers how to hold power, he will instruct the have-nots on how to take it away: "The ego of the organizer is stronger and more monumental than the ego of the leader . . . The organizer is in a true sense reaching for the highest level for which man can reach—to create, to be a 'great creator,' to play God."[2] *Rules* seeks to create a just and happy world through strong-willed, and sometimes ruthless, action to fix it. For Alinsky, activists are in a war against the establishment, and in war, the ends justify almost any means.[3]

Alinsky is blunt about this: "You have to do what you can with what you have, and clothe it with moral arguments."[4] It makes sense, then, that Alinsky prescribes tactics that rely on manipulation, lying, and demonizing opponents. Make your enemies insecure, he teaches. Ridicule them. Don't attack institutions; attack people. None of these ugly tactics is new to American public life, of course. What *is* new is the systematic nature of their application—an organized vindictiveness and addiction to power in today's politics that barely bothers to hide itself behind a veil of sloganeering.

The word "radical" comes from the Latin *radix*, which means "root." Radical ideas speak to the root nature of things. And in that sense, the core sin of *Rules for Radicals* is that it's not nearly radical enough. Rather, it's the familiar human appetite for power dressed up in progressive-left language. And it stands in sharp contrast to the kind of true radicalism demanded by a Christian life.

Over the centuries men and women have served the poor and fought injustice by another set of rules. These rules long predate Alinsky's. They've influenced far more people. And their founder knew no worldly success. He healed the sick, but he didn't abolish sickness. He "fought the power," and when the powerful murdered him, he forgave them. His rules are radical because they turn our human ideas of power upside down. That radical, of course, is Jesus of Nazareth. And we know his rules as the Beatitudes.

At first glance, the Beatitudes seem impossibly idealistic. They seem to pull us farther away from the realities of modern life the harder we try to live them. In fact, we can't ever live them perfectly. So maybe they're not for ordinary Christians—people who live in the world of mortgages, tough jobs, and complaining children.

But not so. The Beatitudes are meant for all Christians in the routines of their daily lives. They're meant for plumbers and doctors, teachers and salesmen, mothers and fathers. And their purpose is to help us live in a way that speaks the truth in love. We can find the Beatitudes in Matthew 5:1–12 and Luke 6:20–22. But we'll use Matthew's version:

Seeing the crowds, he went up on the mountain, and when he sat down his disciples came to him. And he opened his mouth and taught them, saying:

> "Blessed are the poor in spirit, for theirs is the
> kingdom of heaven.
> "Blessed are those who mourn, for they shall be
> comforted.
> "Blessed are the meek, for they shall inherit the
> earth.
> "Blessed are those who hunger and thirst for
> righteousness, for they shall be satisfied.
> "Blessed are the merciful, for they shall obtain
> mercy.
> "Blessed are the pure in heart, for they shall see
> God.

*"Blessed are the peacemakers, for they shall be
    called sons of God.
"Blessed are those who are persecuted for
    righteousness' sake, for theirs is the kingdom
    of heaven.
"Blessed are you when men revile you and persecute
    you and utter all kinds of evil against you falsely
    on my account.
"Rejoice and be glad, for your reward is great in
    heaven, for so men persecuted the prophets who
    were before you."*

Jesus plays various roles in the Gospels. Here he's the teacher. Typical of rabbis of his time, he sits down with his disciples and starts to instruct them.[5] If we study what Jesus says, we'll notice something surprising: The Beatitudes aren't actually "rules." We might expect this young teacher to give us a new set of laws, but he doesn't really do that. Instead of giving commands, Jesus makes promises.[6] This is because the New Law of the covenant that Jesus brings isn't burned onto tablets of stone. It isn't a new Ten Commandments. Rather, it's the love of God inscribed on our hearts through faith in Christ.[7]

The Beatitudes, then, are promises that show what God will accomplish in those who belong to him. As the Old Law constituted the Jews as a people under God, the Beatitudes constitute the kingdom of Jesus Christ. The Beatitudes don't supersede the Old Covenant—God can never go back on his word—but they do transcend it. They gather the promises God made about the Promised Land and point them to the kingdom of heaven. They show a new Israel (the Church) what her life with God will look like.[8]

They also show us that just as God came to his people on

Mount Sinai in thunder, he now comes to his people more intimately, as one man to another. God came in violent majesty then.
Now God comes to suffer violence himself.[9] And just as the Old
Law revealed the love and justice of God, so the Beatitudes
reveal the tenderness of God's heart.[10] They show us the One
who loves us, but they also offer us a challenge and invitation.
Do we really want our hearts to look like the heart of Jesus? And
if so, are we really willing to live as he did?

The Christian life involves hardship and action. The Beatitudes sugarcoat none of the challenges. But note the main
word they use to describe life in the Spirit: *Blessed.* In New Testament Greek the word is *makarioi,* which means "blessed" or
"happy." The Latin word is *beati,* which means the same, and
it's where we get the name *Beatitudes.* So the first thing that the
Beatitudes teach us about the life of Jesus is that he was happy.
Countless sages have offered their answers to the great human
question "How can I be happy?" Here on the mount, Jesus
gives God's response.[11]

The *Catechism* notes that our desire for happiness is part of
human nature, and that "God has placed it in the human heart
in order to draw man to the One who alone can fulfill it."[12] We
see this most famously, perhaps, in the *Confessions* of Augustine.[13] As Augustine put it, our hearts are restless until they rest
in God.[14] After trying so many other options, Augustine concludes that we best live the happy life by rejoicing over God. Joy
in the truth *is* the happy life, and that means joy in God.[15] The
Beatitudes show us what a life that rejoices in God looks like.
They give us a portrait of the kind of happiness that Jesus knew.

But what a seemingly paradoxical happiness. The Beatitudes
speak not of wealth, prosperity, and safety, but of poverty, hunger, and persecution. If the words of Jesus are a map, they seem
to point to things we're trying our best to escape. The Beatitudes

involve suffering not because suffering is good, but because suffering always accompanies love. Love is a risk because it can always be misused or rejected. The rewards are immense, but the costs can be heavy. Thus Jesus' life was one of great love—and also great risk and suffering for the sake of that love. Being a disciple of Christ means having a life that looks like his.

The Beatitudes tell us that if we follow Christ, we'll suffer. But we'll also find that mysterious joy that comes from choosing the way to eternal life. There's a reason we call eternal happiness with God "beatitude." That's what we were made for, as the *Catechism* reminds us: to become "partakers of the divine nature" and enter into the joy of the Trinitarian life.[16] The paths to that life lie along the road shown to us by the Ten Commandments, the parables of Jesus, the teaching of the apostles, and especially the Beatitudes. "Sustained by the grace of the Holy Spirit, we tread [those paths], step by step, by everyday acts. By the working of the Word of Christ, we slowly bear fruit in the Church to the glory of God."[17]

The Beatitudes, then, are intimately connected to the idea of hope. They promise us blessing amid our sorrows. They direct our eyes to the promise of happiness in heaven, even as they name the trials we'll inevitably encounter—trials in which Jesus walks with us every step of the way.[18]

IT'S WORTH PAUSING TO reflect on each of the Beatitudes. And with the moral theologian Servais Pinckaers, O.P., as our guide, we can start to think about how we might live them in our own lives. So let's begin.

Blessed are the poor in spirit, for theirs is the kingdom of heaven.

The first Beatitude reminds us of one of the strongest themes

of Scripture: God's love for the poor, the weak, and the vulnerable. We see this in the Old Covenant, in which God instructs
the people of Israel to care for the poor and the alien in their
midst. He tells the Israelites not to harvest every speck of grain
in their fields, but to leave some for the poor and the stranger
who have no food of their own (Lev 19:9–10). He also commands
them to set aside every fiftieth year as a Jubilee. In that year,
property that was bought or sold must be returned to its original owners (Lev 25:8–28).

Through the prophets God rebukes those who violate the
spirit of these commands: "Therefore because you trample upon
the poor and take from him exactions of wheat, you have built
houses of hewn stone, but you shall not dwell in them; you have
planted pleasant vineyards, but you shall not drink their wine.
For I know how many are your transgressions, and how great
are your sins—you who afflict the righteous, who take a bribe,
and turn aside the needy in the gate" (Amos 5:11–12).

Later Jesus says that, in fulfillment of Isaiah's prophecy, he
is the one on whom the Spirit of the Lord rests, the one whom
the Lord has anointed to preach good news to the poor (Lk
4:16–21).[19] In our own time we tend to distinguish between spiritual and material poverty. But in the Bible, these concepts are
tightly linked. The rich have wealth, but they become overly
proud and ignore or oppress others. They use their money to
buy influence and exploit the needy. They forget their dependence on God. The poor man, by contrast, is always reminded
of his dependence. He will be humble and trust in the Lord.[20]

We see this clearly in Jesus' parable of Lazarus and the rich
man. The rich man had elegant clothes and ate sumptuously. But
he ignored Lazarus, who sat right at his gate, covered in sores
that the dogs licked. Every time he entered or left his house the

rich man would pass Lazarus, yet he did nothing to ease his needs. When the rich man died, he ended up in Hades. Now he suffered, while Lazarus sat in the bosom of Abraham.

The story underscores a simple fact: If we don't love the poor, *we will go to hell.* If we let our possessions blind us to our dependence on God, *we will go to hell.* If we let food and clothes and all the other distractions of modern life keep us from seeing the needs of our neighbors, *we will go to hell.*

We might assume that Scripture condemns the wealthy. But that's not the case. As the early Church Fathers noted, the Lazarus parable is really a tale of two rich men: an unnamed callous one, and the patriarch Abraham. Abraham was a rich man who never forgot his dependence on God. Whereas the wealthy sinner let Lazarus wallow in squalor, Abraham welcomed the three strangers in the Old Testament who visited him, and he fed them with rich food. Abraham was generous and shared his abundance, always remembering that everything he owned was a gift from God. The lesson is obvious: Possession is really about service. When it's not, we become slaves to our goods instead of living in a culture of interior freedom.[21]

Poverty comes in many forms, and Father Pinckaers names some that are familiar: illness, loneliness, age, failure, ignorance, and sin. All of these come back to the poverty at the heart of our very being: We didn't create ourselves, and someday everything we have will be taken away by death. Even our body will turn to dust. Our poverty, in turn, puts us at a crossroads. We can either rebel against God, or let ourselves be shaped by suffering and become more open to God and others.

For believers, then, the poverty we experience purifies us. It keeps us from getting weighed down by excess baggage on the road to heaven. The first Beatitude is addressed to all of us.[22]

It asks us how we will respond to the blessings and sufferings of life. Even if we don't embrace the complete poverty of a Dorothy Day, the principle of her life still speaks to us. In giving away our treasure and our very selves, we find life and freedom. Only if our hearts are open can we receive the kingdom of heaven, which is the richest gift of all.

Blessed are the meek, for they shall inherit the earth.

Let's put aside the second Beatitude for just a moment and focus on this one, the third, because it relates intimately to the first. For too many of us, this Beatitude will conjure up a sanitized Jesus with rosy cheeks and soft blond hair. He's gentle and sweet. In order to follow him, we need to make ourselves precious or emasculated. We start to wonder if Nietzsche was right in his contempt for Christianity as a slave religion, a cult of the weak trying to dominate the strong.

But this is remote from real meekness. Meekness is the poverty and self-mastery of Jesus, the king who rode a donkey instead of a war charger into Jerusalem.[23] Remember that Aslan—C. S. Lewis's great Narnia figure for Jesus—was a meek lion, but very far from a soft or weak one. Real meekness is the quiet self-discipline and courage with which Jesus opposed the Pharisees and Sadducees. Think of a mother who commands her children's respect not by raising her voice, but by her quiet authority. That's meekness. The meek person is strong and gentle because he's filled with the confidence of God's wisdom and love.[24] Far from any hint of weakness, Pinckaers writes, meekness is "the outcome of a long struggle against the disordered violence of our feelings, failings and fears. In such instances meekness implies tremendous inner strength."[25]

Meekness meets injustice and suffering with the endurance that comes from Jesus Christ and the mercy of God the Father.[26] And, as Jesus teaches, the meek will inherit the earth. In the Old

Testament, God promises land to Abraham and Israel. Here he promises that those who follow in his footsteps of meekness will inherit a new land, the kingdom of heaven.[27] The meek person is able to live out the Beatitudes from the strength he or she has in Christ. That's why we can meet violence with charity. That's why we can be peacemakers. In a sense, the meek person is already living the life of heaven now.

Blessed are those who mourn, for they shall be comforted.

When we think of mourning, we usually recall someone who has just died and the feelings of loss he or she leaves behind. We've all seen photos of a mother weeping over the death of a child. Her heart aches. Her body responds with tears. The life she birthed and nurtured is gone. Nothing, it seems, can ease her grief. Yet Jesus promises that she—and the countless more like her—will be comforted. Mourning is a universal experience because death comes to us all. Mourning honors the unrepeatable beauty of a life that has passed away. But life in this world is not where the story of each person ends. Jesus will dry our tears. And he knows the pain of those tears because Jesus himself mourned. Scripture says he mourned over Jerusalem (Lk 19:41) and wept over the death of his friend Lazarus (Jn 11:35).

Isaiah describes the messiah as "a man of sorrows and acquainted with grief," and in fulfilling those words, Jesus bore our griefs and carried our sorrows (Is 53:3–4). Jesus is the one who will give those who mourn in Zion "a garland instead of ashes . . . the mantle of praise instead of a faint spirit" (Is 61:3). And after the Last Supper, Jesus promised his disciples: "Truly, truly, I say to you, you will weep and lament, but the world will rejoice; you will be sorrowful, but your sorrow will turn into joy. When a woman is in labor, she has pain, because her hour has come; but when she is delivered of the child, she no longer remembers the anguish for joy that a child is born into the world.

So you have sorrow now, but I will see you again and your hearts will rejoice, and no one will take your joy from you" (Jn 16:20–22).

As Christians, therefore, we will mourn. But not all mourning is the same. There's a toxic kind of mourning that has lost all hope. It's bitter and vindictive, mistrustful of love and truth. And it slowly consumes the soul. Yet there's another kind of mourning; the mourning of those who love truth and justice and see how these beautiful things are despised in the world. These mourners are different.[28] They weep for the man in the homeless shelter, the woman kicked out of her home because she's pregnant, the gay teenager caught between promiscuity and condemnation. They weep when people mock Jesus Christ and his Church. This is mourning as witness.

Thomas Aquinas identifies three more kinds of weeping and the ways in which Jesus provides consolation for each.[29] First, there's the grief we feel for our own sins and for those of others. It recognizes that sin grieves God and kills our souls. There's a reason that the Desert Fathers talk about the gift of tears, when the Holy Spirit so moves our heart that we shed tears because of our sins.

Second, there's the grief caused simply by living in this world with its many sorrows. With good reason we tell the Virgin Mary that we send up our sighs, "mourning and weeping in this valley of tears." Even when we aren't immediately hurt by our sins, we're acquainted with suffering. Our parents die, leaving us orphaned. We lose a job or our investments for no reason. Some of us lose children. But God promises that we'll be consoled with the joy of eternal life. The book of Revelation describes heaven as a place where God will wipe away every tear from our eyes, "and death shall be no more, neither shall there be mourning nor crying nor pain any more, for the former things have passed away" (Rev 21:4). He promises us that our wounds will be healed and that we'll know joy forever.

There's a third kind of mourning that's unique to Christians: the sorrow of those who accept the cross of Jesus Christ in this life, die to the world, and prefer the joys of God to worldly offerings. This kind of mourning comes from those who hurt because of their commitment to Jesus. Being disciples makes their lives harder. Maybe it's enduring ridicule from doctors because they're not on the birth control pill and they've had their fourth kid. Maybe their tithing means they can't take a vacation they hoped for. Or maybe it's taking a pay cut because working more would take them away from their family. Christ calls us to die to ourselves, and that always hurts. But if our hearts are open, we receive great consolation from the Holy Spirit, the one Jesus sends to comfort us in fulfillment of this Beatitude.

All the Beatitudes are about suffering, but this one homes in on it like a laser. It allows us to meet suffering with confidence in Jesus because he's gone before us on the same path. Christ, too, endured ridicule, material loss, and the pains of his mission. He was tortured and put to death on a cross, but he rose from the dead. The same body that died on the cross was transformed. His scars became trophies of love. His wounds became glorious. Jesus' resurrected body conquered suffering.

By faith in him, our suffering becomes a source of purification. It strips the clutter from our minds and brings us to the raw truth of life, leaving us with the choice between faith and hope in Jesus or, alternatively, despair. Even more than that, suffering becomes an instrument by which our love becomes more Christlike. It becomes a means of our salvation.[30] Or at least it can be, if we have faith. The Beatitudes aren't self-help platitudes. Without Jesus, suffering is meaningless evil. But with him we find consolation, and more.

Blessed are those who hunger and thirst for righteousness, for they shall be satisfied.

By and large, modern America is a land of abundance. Grinding hunger and material scarcity are not visceral experiences for most U.S. citizens. Moreover, we've figured out many ways of keeping ourselves amused. Billions of dollars are spent every year not on life's essentials, but on cars, pets, handbags, cable TV, movies, Facebook, Twitter, and other amusements. Whole industries exist to cater to our appetites. And yet surrounded by our wealth, we remain dissatisfied. We may live in a land of plenty, but, as Augustine would say, we find our hearts to be a land of want.

Our hunger for happiness isn't new. Nor is our attempt to satisfy that hunger with material things. Many centuries ago Saint Gregory the Great noted that we experience a desire for material goods before we possess them, and they attract us strongly. Then we attain them, and we find that after a brief satisfaction, we typically end up disgusted.[31] By contrast, Gregory continues, we don't value spiritual goods until we've tasted them. But experiencing them arouses our desire. It makes us seek them further. This hunger doesn't lead to full satisfaction either, but there's no disgust.[32] That's the feeling we have when we leave a retreat wanting more, but feeling full, or when the Mass makes us desire heaven but also empowers us to love those around us here and now.

This Beatitude reminds us that only spiritual things finally satisfy us. It calls us to detach ourselves from material appetites by adopting the posture of the Beatitudes: poverty, humility, meekness. This will involve a good deal of self-denial and willingness to accept suffering. But the paradox of the Beatitudes is that there's no other way to happiness.[33]

Now that we've talked about hunger, what about righteousness? Righteousness comes from being in proper relationship with God. Under the Old Covenant, that meant binding ourselves to the precepts of the Jewish law in all of its intricacies. Under the New Covenant, it means walking by faith in Jesus Christ, which unites us to his righteousness.[34] The fact that righteousness comes by faith underscores that for the Bible, justice is not an abstract ideal of equality. It's not distant and blind, like our statue of the blindfolded Lady Justice with her scales. Rather, justice is about being in right relationship with others, first and foremost with God, who is the source of righteousness and justice.[35]

To the extent that sin persists in the world, unrighteous relationships will always afflict us. The poor will be persecuted. The powerful and "enlightened" will scoff at God. Those who hunger and thirst for righteousness will never be satisfied in this life. But their ache will drive them on to share the mercy and love of God with others. Their hunger for the spiritual won't drive them away from the earthly. Rather, it will make them love earthly things *rightly*. And knowing that their righteousness comes from God alone will give them the Gospel freedom to work for him and not for themselves.

Holiness is not about earning points. Rather, good works flow forth from faith, hope, and love.[36] True disciples acknowledge their hunger for happiness by striving forward along the path to heaven, confident that when they see God face-to-face, the Beatitude promise will be fulfilled, and they will be satisfied.

Blessed are the merciful, for they shall obtain mercy.

Right after the Beatitude focusing on God's righteousness and justice, we have another focusing on mercy. The Latin word for mercy, *misericordia*, captures it well. It means being moved in our hearts at the misery of others. It means a persistent attitude of kindness and forgiveness toward others. People often oppose justice and mercy, even in God. They'll talk about the mercy of God winning out over the justice of God, as though God wants to punish us on the one hand but feels sorry for us on the other.

But God doesn't have conflicted feelings the way we do. His justice and mercy go hand in hand. They complement each other. In fact, mercy is the musical key in which God's justice is played. God manifests his mercy by tempering his justice, but never by being unjust. If God's mercy were in some way to diminish his righteousness or ours, it would be a false pity. God loves us too much to let us remain anything less than perfect, which is why he sent his Son out of mercy to lead us into his righteousness.

The previous Beatitudes we've looked at describe particular needs or painful situations. But this Beatitude and the two that follow it describe qualities that merit a reward.[37] We often think of mercy as a feeling, like pity or empathy, and impulses like those are certainly part of mercy. But ultimately, mercy—like hope as we discussed in the previous chapter, and like peace and purity in the subsequent Beatitudes—is more than a feeling. It's about what we *do*, and what makes us act the way we act. It's rooted in our will.[38]

True mercy, as Pope Francis saw so vividly in creating the 2015–16 Jubilee Year of Mercy, disrupts our normal calculations about justice. We tend (understandably) to see things as rights and wrongs, and we want to fix or punish wrongs vigorously. We aren't interested in letting our opponents off the hook. We see that instinct clearly in Saul Alinsky's *Rules*. So many of his tactics are designed to break and humiliate the opponent, leaving him reduced to nothing, all in the name of bringing about a more just society.

Mercy takes a different tack. As Servais Pinckaers writes: "Mercy favors justice not only in action but also in the heart. In the eyes of the merciful the greatest misery is not to suffer injustice but to commit it and to end up by loving it. Beyond supposed unjust actions, mercy considers the person, always capable of returning to justice with the help of God's grace, and continues to love him in spite of the wrongs he does . . . This is mercy's work: to fight injustice with its own weapons and so to conquer it in our own heart and in the hearts of others."[39] Notice that mercy doesn't give up and accept injustice, just as God doesn't accept our sin and call it virtue. Rather, mercy opposes injustice with love. That's far more radical than any demonization Alinsky could devise.

Mercy begins with a deep awareness of one's own need for it. Whereas Alinsky first sees injustice in others, the man of mercy first sees sin within himself. But we also see how much mercy we've received from God in Christ's passion, the sacraments, and the love we know in our families and in the Church. Having received great mercy, we can give much away. As Pinckaers remarks, "Having thus driven out harshness and the spirit of revenge, the merciful man will know better than anyone how to discern the best way to promote true justice."[40] Acting in mercy means acting according to God's justice in the spirit by which God himself acts. It gives us a glimpse into the nature of God and allows us to live his divine life in our own ordinary lives.[41]

Blessed are the pure in heart, for they shall see God.

Remember how we talked about the Beatitudes building on the Old Covenant and Jewish law? Here is a good example. Think about Psalm 24, which describes going up to the Temple to worship the Lord: "Who shall ascend the hill of the Lord? And who shall stand in his holy place? He who has clean hands and a pure heart, who does not lift up his soul to what is false, and does not swear deceitfully . . . Such is the generation of those who seek him, who seek the face of the God of Jacob" (Ps 24:3–4, 6). This Psalm reminds us that purity is a vital trait for those who come to worship the Lord in the liturgy. In the Old Covenant, this frequently—but not exclusively—took the form of performing rituals. In the New Covenant, Jesus focuses on the purity of our hearts.[42]

GIVEN THE HYPERSEXUALIZED NATURE of today's culture, when we think of purity, we usually think of sexual purity. And thinking of sexual purity, we typically focus on abstinence. So purity somehow transforms into *not* experiencing a thing we want to experience. This is a distortion. Purity is about wholeness or integrity. It means that the body, mind, heart, and soul are rightly ordered toward God. Every element of who we are is doing its part to bring us to union with God, which is our ultimate happiness. Given the strength of the sexual desires we all feel, rightly acting on those desires is a key part of maintaining purity. For single people and celibates, as we noted earlier in these pages, it means offering those desires up to God and seeking to channel them in our love and service for others.

As a priest and bishop, that means that I should spend myself in being a good father to the members of our local Church. For married couples, purity means giving oneself to one's spouse in every way. For them, chastity naturally involves sexual intimacy. But purity of heart isn't limited to matters of sex. It's about not letting lesser loves or sins distract us from the Lord. We need to guard our hearts not just against lust and pornography, but also against gossip, anger, pride, greed, and selfishness. This keeps us on a path to God with his grace, and it leads us to the joy of one day seeing him.

Purity, then, comes from having our bodies, minds, hearts, and souls conformed to Jesus Christ, united in purpose by his love. This means that in our lives we need to walk the path of servanthood that Jesus walked. We need to love as he loved. And we need to cling to the promise that if we do that, then by his help we will come before the face of God and receive the full joy for which we were created.

Blessed are the peacemakers, for they shall be called sons of God.

Our understanding of purity as conformity to Jesus Christ helps us understand this Beatitude. As Augustine said, peace is the tranquility of order. It's not a warm, unfocused feeling, but the calm that results when everything is working as it should. And things work as they should when they're conformed to the designs of God. God shows us what a man of peace looks like in Jesus Christ, who models the truth of what it means to be a human being. So peacemakers are those who live their lives conformed to Jesus. They make Christ's order and peace present in their lives, which further conforms the world to them as well.

If we're wondering how best to work for peace, then, the answer is surprisingly simple: Go to confession. Read the Word of God. Worship the Lord in Mass. Love and respect your husband. Revere and protect your wife. Treasure your children. Pay your employees a just wage. Obviously, there are many other vital ways of bringing peace to the world. But for every Christian, a Christlike life is the first step to building peace in the heart, the family, and the world.

Note that Christ's peace isn't what we might expect. On the one hand, Jesus tells those he heals to "Go in peace." On the other, he warns that he hasn't come to bring peace, but rather division and a sword (Lk 12:51). Jesus' peace makes no compromise with the sin in our hearts and in our world. He gives us *his* peace—but not as the world gives it (Jn 14:27).

It's helpful to keep in mind a distinction Father Pinckaers makes between cowardly and noble peace.[43] Cowardly peace is filled with fear. It avoids conflict by evasion and compromise. Cowardly peace is a great temptation for all of us today. We feel "established" and settled in American life, and we like it. We'd rather not lose our privileges or change the way things are, so we're ready to follow Christ less zealously in order to hang on to our comforts. But this kind of peace never lasts. It's a lie. And as our culture grows more hostile to the forms of serious Catholic faith, it will be impossible to maintain.

In contrast, noble peace joyfully takes on commitments and boldly proclaims the truth. It's full of justice and love. It comes from knowing that we're beloved sons and daughters of God because we've been united to the Son of God by faith, hope, and love. And no power on earth can separate us from God's love (Rom 8:38–39).

Blessed are those who are persecuted for righteousness' sake, for theirs is the kingdom of heaven. Blessed are you when men revile you and persecute you and utter all kinds of evil against you falsely on my account. Rejoice and be glad, for your reward is great in heaven, for so men persecuted the prophets who were before you.

This Beatitude drives home a truth easily forgotten: If we try to live the Christian life, we'll be persecuted. At first, that may seem implausible. Today, many Catholics live in the suburbs like other Americans. Their children attend good schools. They've largely fit in. So when our culture turns against us or when people revile what we believe, we're shocked.

We've forgotten that Jesus promised that if we're faithful to him, even in a kind and loving way, other people will hate us. That means that if we're true to the Catholic faith, people will try to silence us. They'll work to force us out of the public square. They'll press us to compromise on our moral convictions. As we've seen, this is already happening in the United States in today's increasing attacks on religious liberty and efforts to coerce Catholic ministries and organizations to collaborate with destructive policies and disordered behaviors, and to violate their religious identities. And it will get worse before it gets better.

Yet as much as we encounter disdain for our faith in our own nation, the situation is far worse for Christians in other parts of the world.[44] Several years ago, Archbishop Amel Shamon Nona wrote a letter to Christians in the West. Nona is the head of the Church in Mosul, Iraq. In 2010 he was appointed archbishop when his predecessor was murdered gruesomely. The day after he came to the city, Christians began to be murdered, including the father of a young man who was praying with him in church. Many Christians in the city fled. The brutal violence of Muslim extremists made him wonder how he could strengthen the faithful members of his Church who remained in Mosul. How do you live the faith in a time of savage persecution? Archbishop Nona came to this conclusion:

I realized that, above all—in the face of suffering and persecution—a true knowledge of our own faith and the cause of our persecution is of fundamental importance. By deepening our sense of what it means to be Christians, we discover ways to give meaning to this life of persecution and find the necessary strength to endure it . . . From the moment when we are waiting for death, under threat from someone who may shoot us at any time, we need to know how to live well. The greatest challenge in facing death

because of our faith is to continue to know this faith in such
a way as to live it constantly and fully—even in that very
brief moment that separates us from death.

My goal in all this is to reinforce the fact that the Christian faith is not an abstract, rational theory, remote from
actual, everyday life, but a means of discovering its deepest
meaning, its highest expression as revealed by the Incarnation. When the individual discovers this possibility, he or
she will be willing to endure absolutely anything and will
do everything to safeguard this discovery—even if this
means having to die in its cause.

In China, India, North Korea, and many Muslim nations,
harassment and bloody persecution of Christians are now common. As free members of the body of Christ, we need to live
our faith all the more zealously for those who cannot. The witness of the early martyrs reminds us that as much as a passion-
ately Christian life is difficult, it's also a life of joy.[45]

The Beatitudes are not an easy road to follow. But they're the
path to extraordinary and infectious joy. They show us how to
live and share the faith in bitter times. They teach us that true
happiness is union with God, and that the path to happiness is
one of poverty of spirit, meekness, hunger, mercy, purity, peace,
and courageous witness. They offer us a grand adventure. It's
ours to accept or refuse.

CHAPTER 10

REPAIR MY HOUSE

You are come together today, fathers and right wise men, to hold a council . . . but I wish that, at length, mindful of your name and profession, you would consider of the reformation of ecclesiastical affairs; for never was there more necessity and never did the state of the Church more need endeavors.

—JOHN COLET, remarks to the leadership of the Catholic Church in England, 1512

E VERY PERSON IS PRECIOUS IN THE EYES OF GOD. BUT Christianity is not simply a religion for individuals. Jesus didn't come to be our private life coach or to have us follow him on our own. He came to build a family that would set the world on fire with God's love.

We need to turn now to what it means to be a member of that family we call the Church. We need to examine what it looks like to live our Christian vocation together, because that's the most fruitful way to fully witness our faith. But first, we should probably consider three of the problems that make it hard for us to do that: the cults of individualism, institutionalism, and clericalism.

Individualism is the idea that we can find God adequately on our own. We've all had friends tell us "I'm spiritual, but not

religious." By that they usually mean they find purpose and communion with some higher power without the baggage of a religious tradition or other people telling them what to believe. This
may sound appealing. But it isn't Christianity. As one scholar
put it, "spirituality is about man's search for God, while Catholicism is about God's search for man."[1]

As we've seen, American life has always had a deep individualist streak. The first colonists were shaped by Reformation
theology and hard frontier experience. So it's no surprise that
many Americans have a strongly individualistic approach to
their faith. And Catholics—who've been breathing American air
for generations—are no exception. Many come to Mass, but they
aren't active in their parish. Nor do they try to share the Church
with others.

All of us are prone to the second problem, *institutionalism.*
U.S. Catholics are used to the Church as a large institution. We
have big buildings. We run a huge network of schools, hospitals, parishes, charities, and ministries. It's easy to abdicate our
personal sense of mission to the official religious machinery. It's
easy to tie up our energies in bureaucracy. Catholics also tend
to think of their Church as part of the permanent furniture of
American daily life. Even if we drift away from the faith, even
if we never donate a dime, we want our childhood parish to stay
open on the corner—for nostalgia's sake.

And the Church is not just a physical institution, of course,
but a social one as well, with strong ideas about helping the poor
and building the common good. In that, we assume that the
Church will be reasonably accommodated by the government.
After all, plenty of self-described Catholics already serve in
national leadership roles.

A third problem we find in the Church is *clericalism.* Clericalism is a peculiar kind of codependency. It distorts the roles

of both priest and people. On the surface, clericalism is an excessive stress on the role of ordained leadership in the Church,
and a demeaning of the lay vocation. And history has plenty of
ugly examples to support that view.

But the American reality is more complex. If "Father" is
responsible for everything, and if "Father" has some unique and
reserved access to holiness, then "Father" is also blamable for
everything—and everyone else is off the hook in terms of his
or her obligations of discipleship. That can be a very convenient
alibi. Lay Christians are right to complain when they're treated
as second-class citizens in the Church. Especially today, there's
no excuse for it. But with rights come duties. And in Baptism,
the missionary duties apply to all of us. As Benedict XVI said
some years ago, "[The Church needs] a change in mindset, particularly concerning laypeople. They must no longer be viewed
as 'collaborators' of the clergy but truly recognized as 'co-
responsible' for the Church's being and action, thereby fostering the consolidation of a mature and committed laity."[2]

Individualism, institutionalism, and clericalism are all
detours from a genuinely Christian life. Yes, a personal walk
with God is vital. Yes, Catholic institutions are important. And
yes, our priests, deacons, and religious have an irreplaceable
role of leadership and witness in the work of the Church. But
each of these things can also become a weed that chokes our
discipleship (see Mt 13:22).

Deep change—some of it deeply problematic—is already
happening in our culture. And that means change has come to
the Church. This change is uniquely painful because it involves
the convergence of many compounding factors: the decline
of traditional religious faith among the young; rapid technological and social shifts; a culture of noise that drowns out
the Christian message; a falling off in Church practice; aging

and overbuilt infrastructure; an increasingly hostile legal and political environment; and ambitions and divisions within the Church herself.

Bluntly put, the habits of thought that have traditionally guided the Church are inadequate to the very different pastoral terrain American Catholics will face in the next ten to twenty years. The Church of tomorrow won't look like the Church of today, much less of memory. And most of us aren't ready to deal with the emerging new realities.

From the cross at San Damiano, Jesus spoke the words "Repair my house" to Saint Francis. As Francis came to see, Christ meant rebuilding not just a ruined chapel, but the wider Church. Francis's reform of the medieval Church—and through the Church, of the medieval world—began in obedience, not rebellion. And it grew one soul at a time. In our own day, like Saint Francis, we need to repair the Lord's house. We need to prepare for the likelihood of a smaller, poorer Church. But even more, we need to ensure that in the years ahead she is a more vigorous, more believing, more explicitly missionary Church.

That means cultivating in our clergy and laypeople a better sense of who and what the Church is, separate and distinct from the culture around us—a family of families; an intimate community of Christian friendship with a shared vocation to sanctify the world; a mother, teacher, and advocate; the path to eternal joy; and an antidote to the isolation and radical individualism of modern democratic life. It means recovering a sense of Catholic history and identity; a deepened habit of prayer and adoration; a memory of the bitter struggles the Church endured in this country; a distaste for privilege; and a love for personal and institutional asceticism.

The "power" of the Church resides not in her public statements or material resources, her structures or social services, but in her ability to form and lead her people—and to be their first loyalty. When Catholics trust their leaders and believe their teaching, the Church is strong. When they don't, or when they lose sight of who and what the Church is, she's weak. This is why bishops are so gravely accountable for their actions and inaction. It's also why Catholics who undermine trust in Church teaching sin so seriously against their own Baptism.

To recover the Church's identity, we first need to recall our own. Our lives are a gift of God's love. As Catholics, we believe that God himself is a Trinitarian communion of persons united in essence and in love. Before his election as pope, Joseph Ratzinger described that love beautifully:

> [God] loved me first, before I myself could love at all. It was only because he knew me and loved me that I was made. So I was not thrown into the world by some operation of chance . . . and now have to do my best to swim around in this ocean of life, but I am preceded by a perception of me, an idea and a love of me. They are present in the ground of my being . . . God is there first and loves me. And that is the trustworthy ground on which my life is standing and on which I myself can construct it.[3]

Unlike the rest of creation, God made us in his image and likeness so that we, too, can live in communion, both with God and other people. The world tells us that we exist to satisfy our will; that we become more human by getting or taking what we want. Jesus taught the opposite. He shows us that being an image of God means living in communion founded on self-gift.

Jesus warned that those who seek to cling to their lives will lose them, but those who lose their lives for his sake and for the sake of God's kingdom will find them (Mt 16:25; Lk 9:24). The

Second Vatican Council and Saint John Paul II echoed this in their constant calls for us to make a gift of ourselves to God and to others. Only in making our lives offerings of love do we grow more human and become the persons God created us to be.[4]

The Church, then, is a communion of persons filled with the Holy Spirit, who give themselves in love to each other and to God, together. Their communion—when it's lived zealously and joyfully—shows the world the loving communion that exists in God himself. In this communion, we're called to help each other achieve holiness. Different people have different roles to play. And these don't exist in competition with one another, but are complementary and placed at the service of others.[5]

We're also called—every one of us—to bring the Gospel to all those we encounter. We can't confine the love of God to our family, our parish, or our particular culture. Rather, we all have "the exalted duty of working to assure that each day the divine plan of salvation is further extended to every person, of every era, in every part of the earth."[6]

SOME KEY PASSAGES OF Scripture shed light on what this looks like. We can turn first to 1 Corinthians 12. This is where Paul describes the way the gifts of the Spirit allow us to work together for our mutual growth in Christ. This passage is so familiar that we can easily become dulled to its significance. So it's important to read it carefully, as though encountering it for the first time:

> To each is given the manifestation of the Spirit for the common good . . . All these are inspired by one and the same Spirit, who apportions to each one individually as he wills. For just as the body is one and has many members, and all

the members of the body, though many, are one body, so it is with Christ. For by one Spirit we were all baptized into one body—Jews or Greeks, slaves or free—and all were made to drink of one Spirit.

For the body does not consist of one member but of many. If the foot should say, "Because I am not a hand, I do not belong to the body," that would not make it any less a part of the body. And if the ear should say, "Because I am not an eye, I do not belong to the body," that would not make it any less a part of the body. If the whole body were an eye, where would be the hearing? If the whole body were an ear, where would be the sense of smell? But as it is, God arranged the organs in the body, each one of them, as he chose. If all were a single organ, where would the body be? As it is, there are many parts, yet one body.

The first thing to note is that the gifts we receive from God are for the common good. Paul lists a number of such gifts, including prophecy, healing, and service. But we can grow the list even more. Marriage, for example, is meant for more than just a husband and wife; it's also meant to build up the Church and to spread the Gospel. As Paul reminds us, no one can say that he or she has no role in the Church. We're all part of the same body, pursuing the same holiness, with gifts from the same Spirit that God has given according to the plan he has for the world. We're *all of us* called to serve and preach the Gospel to each other.

When we sincerely seek to do that, the Church is strong, even when her numbers are few. The early Church Fathers were fond of comparing the Church to a field with a variety of plants. As Saint Ambrose wrote: "In this field there are the priceless buds of virginity blossoming forth, widowhood stands out boldly as the forest in the plain; elsewhere the rich harvest of weddings blessed by the Church fills the great granary of the world with abundant produce, and the wine-presses of the Lord Jesus overflow with the grapes of a productive vine, enriching Christian marriages."[7]

To use another metaphor, Jesus says that the kingdom of heaven is like a householder who goes out to hire laborers to work in his vineyard (Mt 20:1). We're all laborers at work in the vineyard of the Lord. As Saint Gregory the Great urged the people of Rome, "Keep watch over your manner of life, dear people, and make sure that you are indeed the Lord's laborers. Each person should take into account what he does and consider if he is laboring in the vineyard of the Lord."[8]

We should also recall the parable of the talents, in which a hard master gives different servants different amounts of silver to watch over while he is gone (Mt 25:14–30). To one he gives five talents, to another, two, and to the last, one. When he returns and finds that the first two servants have invested their money and made more, he rewards them. But when he discovers that the man who received only one talent was afraid and didn't put it to use, he takes it from him and gives it to the man who doubled his five talents.

Our God isn't harsh, but he's given us many good gifts: money, health, time, our vocation, the sacraments—the list goes on. These gifts were not given lightly, but so that we could use them for God's glory and for the love of our brothers and sisters. No one's gifts and talents are so insignificant that they can't be put to good use for God's kingdom. Life is short. Our time in this world is brief. One day, we'll each be called to account for our stewardship. God will ask us what we did with our gifts and why. Did we use them to build up the Church, or to indulge ourselves? Did we share them, or did we hoard them? On that day, we want to be led out of the smallness of our hearts and into the joy of our master (see Mt 25:21).

Jesus uses three images to describe using our gifts for God's kingdom: salt, light, and leaven, or yeast. He says the kingdom of heaven is like "leaven which a woman took and hid in three measures of meal, till it was all leavened" (Mt 13:33). He also tells his followers: "You are the salt of the earth; but if salt has lost its taste, how shall its saltiness be restored? It is no longer good for anything except to be thrown out and trodden under foot by men. You are the light of the world. A city set on a hill cannot be hid. Nor do men light a lamp and put it under a bushel, but on a stand, and it gives light to all in the house. Let your light so shine before men, that they may see your good works and give glory to your Father who is in heaven" (Mt 5:13–16).

Note the logic at work here. Yeast mixes with flour and makes dough rise. We sprinkle salt on our food, and the meal tastes better. We turn on the lights of a dark room so we can see. The yeast, salt, and light aren't the focus of our attention. Rather, they impart their qualities to something else to make it better. And so it should be with the work of the Church in the world.

One of the most important—and beautiful—biblical passages describing the Church comes when Jesus lays out his vision of Christian life after the Last Supper account in the Gospel of John:

> I am the true vine, and my Father is the vinedresser. Every branch of mine that bears no fruit, he takes away, and every branch that does bear fruit he prunes, that it may bear more fruit. You are already made clean by the word which I have spoken to you. Abide in me, and I in you. As the branch

cannot bear fruit by itself, unless it abides in the vine, neither can you, unless you abide in me. I am the vine, you are the branches. He who abides in me, and I in him, he it is that bears much fruit, for apart from me you can do nothing. If a man does not abide in me, he is cast forth as a branch and withers; and the branches are gathered, thrown into the fire and burned. If you abide in me, and my words abide in you, ask whatever you will, and it shall be done for you. By this my Father is glorified, that you bear much fruit, and so prove to be my disciples. As the Father has loved me, so have I loved you; abide in my love. If you keep my commandments, you will abide in my love, just as I have kept my Father's commandments and abide in his love. These things I have spoken to you, that my joy may be in you, and that your joy may be full. (Jn 15:1–17)

A grapevine has two distinct parts. The leaves, fruit, and green branches come out of the old gnarled wood of the vine itself. These branches must be cut back, sometimes brutally, so that the vine will produce more and better fruit. We in the Church are the many branches that come from Christ, the vine, and we must remain in Christ if we want to experience his divine life.

The verb "abide" (in Greek, *meno*) is very important to John. It suggests us living together in a deep unity with Jesus. The branch has nothing that the vine has not given it. It receives all its life from the vine. Separated from it, the branch withers and dies. Connected to it, the branch lives and brings forth beautiful fruit. We must be connected to the Body of Christ, the Church, in order to receive the Holy Spirit through her. We do this by letting the Spirit work in and through us, keeping Christ's commandments and loving as he loved. It's our unity with Christ in the Spirit that allows us to work for the building up of his Church.[9] The point of this work and the Christian life as a whole is not burden and drudgery, but joy.

Jesus gives us commandments and invites us to be members of the Church so that our joy might be full. Living in communion with him and those united to him is what we were created to do. Hence, "the Church is not here to place burdens on the shoulders of mankind, and she does not offer some sort of moral system. The really crucial thing is that the Church offers him [Jesus Christ]. That she opens wide the doors to God and so gives people what they are most waiting for and what can most help them. The Church does this mainly through the great miracle of love, which never stops happening afresh."[10]

We become engrafted to Christ the Vine when we enter the Church in Baptism. Baptism is an underappreciated sacrament, probably because so many of us were baptized as children and have no memory of the event. We take it more as a given than as a gift. As a result, many parents come to a better understanding of Baptism only by witnessing the Baptism of their own children. It's in Baptism and in Confirmation that we receive the gift of the Holy Spirit.

John Henry Newman describes Baptism as the sacrament that makes us like the Ark of the Covenant, because it brings the glory of God in the form of the Holy Spirit down to dwell in us.[11] All other sacraments and vocations stem from Baptism and from its missionary mandate. In Baptism, Jesus designates each of us to proclaim the truth about him as a prophet. He calls on us to order the world to his glory as a king. And he anoints each of us a priest to offer him the spiritual sacrifice of our life and love—to take the pain and toil and beauty of the world and raise it back up to him in worship.[12] This is a great dignity, a high calling, and an immense gift.

✤

HAVING OUTLINED THE MEANING of our life in the Church
and our baptismal calling, we can turn to three ways in which
we can live out that calling. The first is through works of charity. We can too easily think of our charitable works as the same
sort of good efforts made by secular people or institutions. But
that's a mistake. Scripture gives us a different picture. Note
Jesus' famous words in Matthew 25:31–46:

> When the Son of man comes in his glory, and all the angels
> with him, then he will sit on his glorious throne. Before
> him will be gathered all the nations, and he will separate
> them one from another as a shepherd separates the sheep
> from the goats, and he will place the sheep at his right hand,
> but the goats at the left. Then the King will say to those at
> his right hand, "Come, O blessed of my Father, inherit the
> kingdom prepared for you from the foundation of the
> world; for I was hungry and you gave me food, I was thirsty
> and you gave me drink, I was a stranger and you welcomed
> me, I was naked and you clothed me, I was sick and you vis-
> ited me, I was in prison and you came to me." Then the righ-
> teous will answer him, "Lord, when did we see thee hungry
> and feed thee, or thirsty and give thee drink? And when
> did we see thee a stranger and welcome thee, or naked and
> clothe thee? And when did we see thee sick or in prison
> and visit thee?" And the King will answer them, "Truly, I
> say to you, as you did it to one of the least of these my breth-
> ren, you did it to me." Then he will say to those at his left
> hand, "Depart from me, you cursed, into the eternal fire
> prepared for the devil and his angels; for I was hungry and
> you gave me no food, I was thirsty and you gave me no drink,

I was a stranger and you did not welcome me, naked and
you did not clothe me, sick and in prison and you did not
visit me." Then they also will answer, "Lord, when did we
see thee hungry or thirsty or a stranger or naked or sick or
in prison, and did not minister to thee?" Then he will answer
them, "Truly, I say to you, as you did it not to one of the least
of these, you did it not to me." And they will go away into
eternal punishment, but the righteous into eternal life.

The biblical scholar Gary Anderson helps us draw two key
points from this text. First, charity to the poor has the power to
open the gates of heaven. This is because charity is a sacramental act. Jesus tells us that when we give to those in need, we give
to him. When we reach out to the poor in love, we encounter
him. Recall the story of Saint Martin of Tours, who when con-
fronted with a shivering beggar divided his cloak and gave away
half. That night he dreamed of Christ, who was wearing the
piece of cloak he'd given away.

Second, we tend to think of works of charity separately from
the Mass, but for the early Christians the two were tied intimately together.[13] Anderson explains: "In the Eucharist, one represents the love Christ showed the world by the self-offering of
his life. In alms-giving, the layperson has the opportunity to
participate in this divine act by imitating God's mercy in his or
her daily actions."[14]

Anderson offers us two more ways to think about our works
of charity. First, charity is an expression of faith. It declares what
we believe about the world and the God who created it. Consider Mother Teresa. People were drawn to her because she lived
with a deep trust in God and his love for the poor. Her acts of
love proclaimed that God is love: "They reveal to us the hidden
structure of the universe."[15] Second, and more radically, Jews

and Christians have often thought of charity as giving God a kind of loan. When a woman gave alms to a beggar, she wasn't just giving money to a person. She was making a loan to God. Her acts of charity were like enduring prayers for mercy that the Lord would not ignore.[16]

We mustn't think of this in a crude way, as though we can manipulate God by our good works. That would be pointless. God can't be used as an instrument of anyone's will. Rather, God inspires us to love the poor and then gives us the "reward" that we earn by his help.[17] We call them works of charity, after all, because they're performed with the love the Holy Spirit gives us, and the Holy Spirit is charity itself. The beauty of charity is that it forms both those who give and those who receive, and it grows in the exchange. In giving our love, we're "rewarded" with more love to give.

That's how God's love works: He gives love to us, we respond with acts empowered by that love, and then we and those we love grow in love. This dynamic exists in another vital part of Christian life: *friendship.* As C. S. Lewis saw many years ago, friendship is suspect in a hypersexualized culture, where any nonsexual love between two close friends can seem dubious. But Christian friendship is immensely important. We need the Church as a whole to be our family. But we also need particular friends, close friends, with whom we can share our interests, joys, and troubles while following Jesus Christ. Even in the strongest marriages, spouses need more than each other. We're on a journey to a heavenly home, and we need all the help we can get.

Societies in the past have seen friendship as a great good worthy of contemplation. Aristotle made friendship the culmination of his famous *Nicomachean Ethics.* Ancient thinkers like Cicero wrote lavishly on the theme. And in the so-called Middle

Ages—the term "Middle Ages" is an Enlightenment vanity—
an English monk named Aelred of Rievaulx read Cicero's work.
He knew good material when he saw it. So Aelred decided to
blend the Roman statesman's thought with the wisdom of the
Gospel. His insights can help us understand what Christian
friendship is and the benefits that it brings.

A medieval monk might sound irrelevant to our own time
and concerns. But Aelred was like us in surprising ways. In his
youth, he was torn by conflicting loves and friendships. Some
of them were sinful. These hurt him deeply, but he found the
love of Jesus Christ to be a source of healing. Aelred writes that
true Christian friendship begins with two people who are drawn
to some quality of holiness or virtue they see in each other. Since
both persons love Jesus Christ and want to build their friendship on their love of Christ, Jesus is, in a real sense, the third
person in their friendship.

The love that the two friends share helps them love Christ
more. And as their intimacy increases, so their intimacy with
Christ also grows.[18] As the friends go through life, they encourage each other in holiness. They also correct each other. They
enjoy each other's company. They share each other's fears and
confidences. Aelred's description of one friend praying for the
other, and the love of one's friend moving into one's love for
Jesus Christ, is striking:

> And thus a friend praying to Christ on behalf of his friend,
> and for his friend's sake desiring to be heard by Christ,
> directs his attention with love and longing to Christ; then it
> sometimes happens that quickly and imperceptibly the one
> love passes over into the other, and coming, as it were, into
> close contact with the sweetness of Christ himself, the friend
> begins to taste his sweetness and to experience his charm.

Thus ascending from that holy love with which he embraces a friend to that with which he embraces Christ, he will joyfully partake in the abundance of the spiritual fruit of friendship, awaiting the fullness of all things in the life to come. Then, with the dispelling of all anxiety by reason of which we now fear and are solicitous for one another, with the removal of all adversity which it now behooves us to bear for one another, and, above all, with the destruction of the sting of death together with death itself, whose pangs now often trouble us and force us to grieve for one another, with salvation secured, we shall rejoice in the eternal possession of Supreme Goodness; and this friendship, to which here we admit but few, will be outpoured upon all and by all outpoured upon God, and God shall be all in all.[19]

Despite the strife of the world and their own flaws and failures, friends enjoy a foretaste of the peace and rest we'll experience fully in heaven. Their communion together in Christian love mirrors that communion of the Trinity toward which their friendship leads them. Aelred is clear that this type of friendship is not possible to share with many people, maybe three or four at most over the course of a lifetime. But it's important for all Christians to have such deep, Christ-centered friendships that help them grow closer to God.

AELRED'S NOTION OF SPIRITUAL friendship also helps us understand the dynamics of Christian marriage, the third way we can live out our vocation in the Church. The idea that a man and woman united in the love of Jesus Christ can draw closer to God through their love is central to the Sacrament of Matrimony. That's why Vatican II said that "authentic married love is caught up into divine love."[20] The Apostle Paul describes the relationship between Christ and the Church as a marriage, and he teaches that Christian marriages are icons of that union and Jesus' complete self-emptying love (Eph 5:21–33). This means that when we're baptized, we become part of the body that is espoused to Christ. A spousal covenant between Christians, then, takes place within the spousal covenant of Christ and the Church. The love between spouses "is elevated and assumed into the spousal charity of Christ, sustained and enriched by his redeeming power."[21]

The catechism for the 2015 World Meeting of Families explained it this way: "In the case of marriage, when husbands and wives give themselves to one another with a love that imitates Jesus, their gift of self to each other is part of the work of Christ, joining in the same spirit of Jesus' own gift of himself for the Church. When the spouses exchange their vows in church at their wedding liturgy, Christ receives their nuptial love and makes it part of his own Eucharistic gift of self for the Church and the Father who, pleased by the offering of the Son, gives the Holy Spirit to the spouses to seal their union."[22]

These are more than just religious-sounding words. They have intensely practical consequences. Because married love is so closely united to Christ's love for the Church, it requires making Christlike sacrifices and is a "cruciform self-sacrificial communion."[23] Through this cruciform communion, spouses are more united to Jesus Christ.[24] By giving and receiving love, even in their ordinary obligations, Vatican II notes, spouses "are penetrated with the Spirit of Christ, who fills their whole lives with faith, hope and charity. Thus they increasingly advance toward their own perfection, as well as toward their mutual sanctification, and hence contribute jointly to the glory of God."[25]

Couples live out the call to holiness given to them in Baptism

through their marriage, and they live out their baptismal priesthood, too. In marriage, their daily lives become "spiritual sacrifices acceptable to God through Jesus Christ" (1 Pet 2:5).[26]
Because of the dynamics of love, this makes them more of a man
and woman; through dying to themselves, they live more richly.[27]

This vision of marriage, like the nature of the Church herself, is radically alien to the spirit of our times. Marriage, again
like life in the Church, is in many ways "a long walk of mercy."[28]
It requires that spouses bear with each other in forgiveness and
love (Col 3:13) and offer their bodies to each other in a chaste
and holy way.[29]

And just as the Church must bring new life in Jesus Christ
into the world, so a vital part of marital love is being open to
the gift of children. One of the ways in which a good Christian
marriage mirrors the divine is that, just as God's love overflowed
into creation, so the love of man and woman should overflow into
new life. The family is the "domestic Church" where parents
preach the word of God to their children by example and instruc-
tion.[30] It's a school of deeper and more fruitful humanity.[31]

Vatican II teaches that one of the key graces a couple will
receive through the Sacrament of Matrimony is God's aid in
fulfilling the "sublime office of being a father or mother."[32]
The Latin word the Council Fathers use for "office" is *munus*,
which also means "service," "duty," and "gift." A *munus* is an
honor to receive and a burden to bear. The *munus docendi* is the
teaching office that every bishop holds, the gift of grace and the
responsibility he has for upholding the truths of the Catholic
faith in his local Church. Parents have a *munus* for doing exactly
the same thing in their homes.[33]

Marriages aren't just for parents and children, though. Like
the Sacrament of Holy Orders, marriage is devoted to the salvation of others and confers a special grace for a particular mis-

sion to serve the people of God and evangelize the world. Spouses are called to make their homes places of charity and mercy so that they can be empowered to go out and spread the Gospel. They're also called to invite others into their homes, so others, too, can experience the love of Jesus Christ, especially those without a family of their own.

As American culture becomes more estranged from Christian faith, Catholic homes need to become countercultural sanctuaries where visitors can taste the joy and freedom of the Lord. True hospitality is not a small thing. In a lonely, cynical, distracted culture, it's a massively important thing. It's a vital form of Christian life and a means by which Christ's love can reach others.

In 1512, the English priest and educator John Colet—a friend of Erasmus and Thomas More—delivered a blistering sermon to a convocation of leading clergy in his country. Speaking just five years before the start of the Reformation, he pressed his brothers to turn away from ambition, comforts, and worldliness and to reform the Church *by reforming their own lives.* His audience was bishops and priests. But his message applies equally to every Catholic believer, and just as urgently now as then.

Which is why, at this point, readers may have noticed that, in a chapter on "repairing God's house," they'll find no new ideas for projects, programs, studies, procedures for nominating bishops, committees, structures, offices, synods, councils, pastoral plans, changed teaching, new teaching, budget realignments, sweeping reforms, or reshuffled personnel.

None of those things matter. Or rather, none of them is essential. The only thing essential, to borrow a thought from the great Leon Bloy, is to be a saint. And we do that, as a Church and as individuals, by actually living what we claim to believe, and believing the faith that generations of Christians have suffered and died to sustain.

If we want to repair God's house, if we want to renew the Church, we need to start with a reform of our own hearts, with an unflinchingly honest look at ourselves. And we certainly have a motive to do so: We can count on demanding times ahead. However we manage it, we need to be bolder and more loving in our Catholic witness, both personally and as a family of faith.

Because anything else, no matter how pious its veneer, is dead weight.

CHAPTER 11

A LETTER TO DIOGNETUS

E VERY MINUTE OF EVERY DAY, ETERNITY PRESSES IN ON US. Time passes, and our own time in the world is limited. So it is for every person we love. For Christians, then, certain questions become urgent. In the light of eternity, what does God ask from us? And what does it mean to be the "people of God" today, in a distracted and unbelieving age?

We've looked at many of the challenges now facing Catholics in America. We've also seen that the Church may be very different in size and influence over the next several decades. To bear a compelling witness to Jesus Christ, Catholics will need to be different as well—different, more resourceful, and far more deliberate in living our particular vocations with zeal and joy. So what does that look like? Where can we turn for guidance?

For answers, we might start with a letter written eighteen hundred years ago to a man named Diognetus.[1] It's a curious document for several reasons. First, it's not from one of the apostles.

Nor from any great, early Christian figure. Nor do the Church
Fathers refer to it much. In fact, we're not really sure who wrote
it. All we know is that sometime in the second century, a Christian in what is now Turkey wrote an explanation of the faith
to a man named Diognetus—and we're not even certain who
Diognetus was.

For all that we don't know about it, though, we do know
that it survives as a great apology for the faith, an account of
what Christians believe and why. Many have thought that the
Letter to Diognetus offers the single best description of what the
Church should look like living in the world. It gives helpful
guidance for dealing with the problem that every generation of
Christ's disciples ends up facing: i.e., how to be in the world but
not of it, faithful pilgrims living in a land that is not their home.

When the *Letter to Diognetus* was written, paganism was
strong. Christianity was new to the religious scene. Rome tended
to see the young Christian cult as dangerous and disloyal. In his
Annals, Tacitus, the great Roman historian and senator, described
the new sect as a "destructive superstition" filled with "hatred
for the human race." Jewish communities saw Christ-followers
as heretical and blasphemous, the fevered work of misguided
disciples of a minor rabbi. As a result, Christians were a distrusted minority in the empire, often locked in bitter theological disputes with the Jews, who were, in many places, more
numerous and better respected by the Romans.

It makes sense, then, that a Roman might want to learn more
about these strange Christians—what they actually believed and
did, what was true about their cult and what was malicious
rumor. Diognetus' questions seem to have hinged on the following points: Why do Christians not acknowledge the pagan dei-
ties as gods, but at the same time not practice Judaism? Why

had this new way of life appeared at this juncture in history, and not before? And what was the source of the loving affection that so many Christians had for one another?

These questions in turn implied two key facts about the early Christians. First, they didn't fit into the categories that pagan society had to offer. In a sophisticated empire comfortable with many gods (so long as they reinforced the state), their faith was somehow different. And second, this odd new religion made Christians care for one another in a tangible way that impressed those who encountered it.

If Diognetus wants to understand this new religion, our anonymous author says, he must "pack away all the old ways of looking at things that keep deceiving you. You must become like a new man from the beginning, since, as you yourself admit, you are going to listen to a really new message." Those of us today for whom the good news is old news would do well to recall just how radical Christianity was, and always is. For a start, it rejected the whole order of pagan religion practiced by the Greeks, Romans, and many other peoples. Christians looked at statues of the gods and saw them simply as sculptures; lumps of marble, bronze, and clay. They found it ridiculous that Romans would guard them day and night, like any other valuable possession.

The author of the *Letter* clearly had in mind the words of Psalm 115:4–8: "Their idols are silver and gold, the work of men's hands. They have mouths, but do not speak; eyes, but do not see. They have ears, but do not hear . . . feet, but do not walk; and they do not make a sound in their throat." Of the pagan gods, the *Letter*'s author writes: "Those who make [these lifeless idols] are like them; so are all who trust in them."

Pietas (piety) was a celebrated Roman virtue, and Romans

accused Christians of being atheists—not in the modern sense of believing in no gods, but rather in refusing to accept the gods that everyone else worshiped. For American Catholics, this might sound familiar. Earlier in our nation's history we were distrusted because of our fidelity to the Pope, which many saw as unpatriotic loyalty to a foreign prince. In a robustly Protestant society, we were disdained for our rosaries and sacraments. In a post-Christian age, the alienation is of a different sort.

Today's idols come in the shape of the human will and private appetites, wrapped in a pious refusal to judge anyone else's behavior, the better to escape being judged oneself. As long as nobody else gets hurt, the reasoning goes, personal behavior is a matter of individual moral sovereignty. But of course, this is delusional. As every parent soon discovers, all of our personal flaws and actions ripple out to affect others, starting with the young, who have the fewest defenses.

As "rights" to disordered desires and behaviors spread, they take on the protection of law and the robes of public respectability. The more problematic the behavior, the more sacred grows the liturgy of alibis. The killing of unborn children becomes a woman's right to choose. Marriage and family are sacrificed to the "equality" of same-sex relationships. Parents are applauded for helping their children change gender, something seen as an act of child abuse just decades ago. And as these strange things flower, the language of tolerance and diversity invariably hardens into repression against "haters"—those who hold to older biblical ideas of right and wrong.

The reason this happens is simple. No man, no society, and no nation can serve two masters. Evil cannot abide its critics. Evil does not want to be tolerated. It needs to be vindicated. It demands to be seen as right.

So it was in the second century. So it remains today. As a

friend once said, "Modern man doesn't want to be saved. He wants to be affirmed."

CATHOLICS WHO SEEK TO live their faith seriously don't fit in the categories secular society provides because the Gospel itself doesn't. The *Letter to Diognetus* reminds us that Christian faith isn't "an earthly discovery" or a "mortal thought" that we hand down. Rather, "it was really the Ruler of all, the Creator of all, the invisible God himself, who from heaven established the truth and the holy, incomprehensible word among men, and fixed it firmly in their hearts."

God did this, of course, by sending that holy Word to us in the person of Jesus of Nazareth. The divine message begins with the Incarnation. The One who made the heavens, who ordered the sun and moon, and who governs all of creation came to us not as an overwhelming ruler, but as a man. His coming shows God's kindness and gentleness. It teaches us that God seeks to persuade us to love him, not to compel us. But because of sin, we can't respond perfectly to that invitation. So Jesus took upon himself the burden of our sins, suffering death on the cross and rising again to new life.

The author of the *Letter* is eloquent in his joy: "O sweetest exchange! O unfathomable work of God! O blessings beyond all expectation! The sinfulness of many is hidden in the Righteous One, while the righteousness of the One justifies the many that are sinners. In the former time he had proved to us our nature's inability to gain life; now he showed the Savior's power to save even the powerless, with the intention that on both counts we should have faith in his goodness, and look on him as Nurse, Father, Teacher, Counselor, Healer, Mind, Light, Honor, Glory, Might, Life . . ."

These truths, the *Letter* argues, explain the puzzling ways that make Christians distinct. In accepting the Gospel, our author writes, "think with what joy you will be filled! Think how you will love him, who first loved you so! And when you love him, you will be an imitator of his goodness. And do not be surprised to hear that a man can become an imitator of God. He can, because God wills it."

This faith in the saving work of Jesus Christ, combined with their love for him, drove early Christians to lives of radical charity. They loved greatly because they knew themselves to be greatly loved. The example of Jesus showed them that God is not a demanding idol, not an artifact of human fear, but the Author of self-emptying and self-sacrificing love.

This new view of God showed the early Christians that being happy did not "consist in lording it over one's neighbors, or in longing to have some advantage over the weaker ones, or in being rich and ordering one's inferiors about. They had a joy that others did not." Rather, they recognized that what they had received came as a gift from God, and they saw their care for the poor as a way of imitating God who had given them so much.

This impulse to care for the poor may seem normal to us now. But as historians of the period such as Peter Brown have noted, it was utterly new to the Roman world. Even today, many people help others only because of guilt or social pressure; or they expect public authorities to do it for them; or they don't really engage with the poor as fellow human beings at all.

But we Christians have a very particular reason for any good works we do. We can love other persons as living, unique, unrepeatable images of God's own love, imbued with his dignity. And we can share with them the same love we've received ourselves. When we do this, we truly act as members of Christ's body in the world. In the *Letter*'s beautiful wording: "This

[Jesus] is he who was from the beginning, who appeared new and was found to be old, and is ever born young in the hearts of the saints." Our acts of Christian love make Jesus present again in the world.

In the *Letter*'s most famous section, the author describes in greater detail what living in imitation of God's love looks like. We'll examine the section in parts to better digest the contents. First, the author writes:

> For Christians cannot be distinguished from the rest of the human race by country or language or customs. They do not live in cities of their own; they do not use a peculiar form of speech; they do not follow an eccentric manner of life. This doctrine of theirs has not been discovered by the ingenuity or deep thought of inquisitive men, nor do they put forward a merely human teaching, as some people do. Yet, although they live in Greek and barbarian cities alike, as each man's lot has been cast, and follow the customs of the country in clothing and food and other matters of daily living, at the same time they give proof of the remarkable and admittedly extraordinary constitution of their own commonwealth. They live in their own countries, but only as aliens. They have a share in everything as citizens, and endure everything as foreigners. Every foreign land is their fatherland, and yet for them every fatherland is a foreign land. They marry, like everyone else, and they beget children, but they do not cast out their offspring. They share their board with each other, but not their marriage bed. It is true that they are "in the flesh," but they do not live "according to the flesh." They busy themselves on earth, but their citizenship is in heaven. They obey the established laws, but in their own lives they go far beyond what the laws require.

In a way that would be shocking to us, early Christians really *were* like people living in a foreign country. The spirit of their surrounding culture was alien to what they had now come to believe. But notice how they responded. They criticized their culture where it went astray, as we've seen in the *Letter*'s harsh words for idolatry. But they didn't abandon or retire from the world. They didn't build fortress enclaves. They didn't manufacture their own culture or invent their own language. They took elements from the surrounding society and "baptized" them with a new spirit and a new way of living.

If a Christian who lived at the time of the *Letter* wanted to have an object in her home that showed her Christian faith, she'd find something with a conventional symbol that could be given a Christian interpretation. The theologian and historian Robert Louis Wilken describes how this would work: "When placed in a Christian home, a symbol which had one meaning to the Romans was invested with a Christian meaning: the dove for gentleness; the fish for Jesus Christ, Son of God, Savior; the shepherd for *philanthropia* or Christ the good shepherd. In buying and displaying objects such as lamps or rings or seals, Christians created the first Christian art (of which we have knowledge), but what the symbols represented lay in the eyes of the beholder, not in the object." As far as Roman society was concerned, early Christianity could sometimes seem invisible.[2]

So again, the essential thing for the earliest Christians was not having a unique culture that communicated the faith. Rather, it was taking elements from the wider society and making them Christian. Notice, too, that they didn't condemn pagan culture root and branch, but sought out those aspects of society they might make obedient to Christ (see 2 Cor 10:5).

Yet for all their adaptability, for all their efforts to follow the customs of their countries, something very different persisted about Christians: They knew, and deeply believed, that their primary citizenship was in heaven. They would obey earthly rulers whenever possible. But their highest loyalty belonged to the King of Kings. They would render unto Caesar the things that were Caesar's. But they never forgot that they themselves belonged to God. They understood that imitating Christ meant going against the grain. So, for example, the *Letter* notes that Christians get married and have children, just as the other citizens around them do. But they refuse to abort their children or abandon weak infants to die. They share food with one another, but they respect chastity within marriage.

Eighteen centuries ago these were the astonishing markers that set Christians apart. If today the American soul has moved away from its biblical conscience, the *Letter to Diognetus* reminds us that the terrain of unbelief may be new, but it's not unfamiliar. Christianity was born in a world of abortion, infanticide, sexual confusion, and promiscuity, the abuse of power and exploitation of the poor. The early Christians' love for Jesus compelled them to choose a more excellent way, one that made them distinct, puzzling, and sometimes contemptible in the eyes of the wider culture. Like the apostle Paul, they let their everyday life in society attract others to the Gospel (as in 1 Cor 9:22–23). But they did not conform so much that they betrayed that Gospel.

These ancient brothers and sisters in Christ are more than an interesting anecdote from history. They live vividly now in our memories as an example. We need to heed Pope Francis's caution that the Church isn't an NGO or a social club. The Church must be herself in order to serve and save the societies in which she lives. The Swiss theologian Hans Urs von Balthasar wrote: "The Church must be open to the world, yes: but it must be the *Church* that is open to the world. The body of Christ

must be this absolutely unique and pure organism if it is to
become all things to all men. That is why the Church has an
interior realm . . . so that there *is* something that can open
and pour itself out."[3]

THE CHURCH WILL ALWAYS remain a sign of contradiction,
exactly like the Lord she loves and serves. Jesus warned his disciples to expect persecution. If we follow him, we shouldn't be
surprised when the world treats us as it treated him. The *Letter
to Diognetus* gives us a picture of how the love of Jesus enabled
early Christians to answer hatred with supernatural love:

> They love all men, and by all men are persecuted. They are
> unknown, and still they are condemned; they are put to
> death, and yet they are brought to life. They are poor, and
> yet they make many rich; they are completely destitute,
> and yet they enjoy complete abundance. They are dishon-
> ored, and in their very dishonor are glorified; they are
> defamed, and are vindicated. They are reviled, and yet they
> bless; when they are affronted, they still pay due respect.
> When they do good, they are punished as evildoers; under-
> going punishment, they rejoice because they are brought to
> life. They are treated by the Jews as foreigners and enemies,
> and are hunted down by the Greeks; and all the time those
> who hate them find it impossible to justify their enmity.

Reading passages like this, we can too easily imagine martyrdom as something from the distant past. But as we noted
briefly in chapter 9, that would be very far from the truth. The
twentieth century produced more martyrs than any other period
in the two-thousand-year history of our faith. And today Chris-

tians are the most persecuted and harassed religious community in the world.

We live at a time when Muslim extremists destroy Christian churches and holy sites, kidnap and enslave Christian women, and publicly slaughter Christian men in many parts of Africa and the Middle East—with only modest attention from American and European news media. One event did make the headlines, though: the twenty-one Coptic Christians beheaded in 2015 by ISIS in Libya. Masked murderers cut the men's throats on a video broadcast all over the world. The last words of some of them were "Lord Jesus Christ."

What happened next did not make headlines. On Christian television, Beshir Kamel, the brother of two of the murdered men, thanked ISIS for not editing out the men's last declaration of faith in Christ because it had strengthened his own faith. He then added that the families of those who were killed were "congratulating one another." He said: "We are proud to have this number of people from our village who have become martyrs . . . Since the Roman era, Christians have been martyred and have learned to handle everything that comes our way. This only makes us stronger in our faith because the Bible told us to love our enemies and bless those who curse us."

When the host asked whether he could forgive ISIS, Kamel relayed what his mother had said she would do if she saw one of the men who killed her son: "My mother, an uneducated woman in her sixties, said she would ask [him] to enter her house and ask God to open his eyes because he was the reason her son entered the kingdom of heaven." When the host invited him to pray for his brothers' killers, Kamel prayed, "Dear God, please open their eyes to be saved and to quit their ignorance and the wrong teachings they were taught."[4]

This is what the *Letter* means when it says that Christians are set apart by their love. This love makes no sense apart from Jesus Christ. It shows how Christian faith can turn ordinary men and women into heroes. Christians in the Middle East offer us a powerful lesson in how to live as Jesus lived. And their suffering also challenges us to come to their aid.

The Coptic martyrs and their families offer us two lessons. First, the religious liberty that Americans take for granted is actually quite rare in the world. Even in the United States, our freedom to preach, teach, and witness our Catholic faith is only as strong as our willingness to live the faith vigorously in our own lives, and to work and fight for it in the public square. The Church has no shortage of critics eager to smother her voice and constrain her mission.

But second, we can never forget that we fight for the God of Love. We need to engage with that spirit even those who hate us. The Coptic martyrs and their families—like the early Christians—call us to claim the more excellent way. They remind us that we should bless our persecutors and pray for their conversion, that we should even be thankful for the opportunity to suffer for the sake of Christ. Only that kind of radical love can, in the end, bring victory not on the world's terms, but the victory of genuine peace in Christ.

The next paragraph of the *Letter* may be the most remarkable of all:

> To put it simply: What the soul is in the body, that Christians are in the world. The soul is dispersed through all the members of the body, and Christians are scattered through all the cities of the world. The soul dwells in the body, but does not belong to the body, and Christians dwell in the world, but do not belong to the world. The soul, which is invisible, is kept under guard in the visible body; in the same

way, Christians are recognized when they are in the world, but their religion remains unseen. The flesh hates the soul and treats it as an enemy, even though it has suffered no wrong, because it is prevented from enjoying its pleasures; so too the world hates Christians, even though it suffers no wrong at their hands, because they range themselves against its pleasures. The soul loves the flesh that hates it, and its members; in the same way, Christians love those who hate them. The soul is shut up in the body, and yet itself holds the body together; while Christians are restrained in the world as in a prison, and yet themselves hold the world together. The soul, which is immortal, is housed in a mortal dwelling; while Christians are settled among corruptible things, to wait for the incorruptibility that will be theirs in heaven. The soul, when faring badly as to food and drink, grows better; so too Christians, when punished, day by day increase more and more. It is to no less a post than this that God has ordered them, and they must not try to evade it.

It's a bold, even preposterous, statement. How could a small, disreputable sect begin to claim such a thing? Christians had no historical provenance, nothing great they could point to that might support such a claim. The only thing that could validate such a statement was this: Jesus of Nazareth rose from the dead. If the Resurrection happened, then that fact changes everything.

If Jesus rose from the dead, then he is all he claimed to be. As the Easter Vigil liturgy proclaims, he is the Alpha and the Omega; all time and all the ages belong to him. He creates the world and gives it its meaning. He tells the world its story. As the great French theologian Henri de Lubac wrote, "Christianity is not one of the great things of history: it is history which is one of the great things of Christianity."[5]

This could be a source of inordinate pride for Christians, but it should never be so. As Benedict XVI pointed out many times, we don't possess the truth of Christ; we are first and foremost *possessed by* it. Being possessed by Christ's truth empowers us to live the Gospel with courage. Christians know that the underlying logic of the cosmos is one in which the very principle of existence is self-giving love. As one writer puts it, "Christians are a people both in and ahead of time. Christians are the people who know, and who ought to live as if they knew, that the Lord of history is in charge of history. Christians are the people who know how the story is going to turn out."[6] We know that it ends with the triumph and wedding feast of the Lamb.

Acknowledging Jesus as Lord of history means that history belongs to him. It's his project. We should love the good in the world and work for its salvation, but the outcome isn't finally in our hands. This means that "Christians can relax a bit about the world and its politics: not to the point of indifference or insouciance or irresponsibility, but in the firm conviction that, at the extremity of the world's agony and at the summit of its glories, Jesus remains Lord. The primary responsibility of Christian disciples is to remain faithful to the bold proclamation of that great truth, which is the truth that the world most urgently needs to hear."[7] Or, as John Henry Newman put it, "[The Church's task is] not to turn the whole earth into a heaven, but to bring down a heaven upon earth."[8]

Christians, then, have the task of leading the world to the truth about itself. But in our time—as in the time of Diognetus—the world doesn't want to hear it. The world hates the story Christians tell. It no longer believes in "sin." It doesn't understand the forgiveness of sinners. It finds the ideas of a personal God, immortality, grace, miracles, the Incarnation, the Resurrection, and the whole architecture of the sacraments and the "supernatural" more and more implausible. It sneers at the restraints the Gospel places on appetites and ego. And in place of the Christian narrative of history, it lowers the human horizon to a relentless *now* of distractions, desires, and suppressed questions about meaning.

This empty shell of a life leads in small, anesthetic steps to nihilism: In effect, the "truth" of our time in the world seems to be that there is no truth, that life has no point, and that asking the big questions is for suckers. The Lutheran theologian Robert Jenson has observed that we live in a world that has lost its story.[9] Thus the Church's task is to tell and retell the world its story, whether it claims to be interested or not.

Benedict XVI put it another way, focusing on the Eucharist. If Jesus is really present in the consecrated bread and wine, as Catholics believe, then the Eucharist is the event that is "at the center of absolutely everything. It is the event, not just of a single day, but of the history of the world as a whole, as the decisive force that then becomes the source from which changes can come. If we want the world to move forward a little, the only criterion in terms of which this can happen is God, who enters into our lives as a real presence. The Eucharist is the place where men can receive the kind of formation from which new things come into being."[10]

IN ORDER FOR THE Church to pursue her mission in preaching and the Eucharist, she asks two things of the world.

The Church asks the world to open its ears and consider the possibility of its redemption. She asks the world to hear her proposal of Jesus Christ and Christ's more excellent way. As Richard John Neuhaus wrote, "For the Catholic Christian, the world is not alien territory but a creation of love that has tragically alienated itself from its Creator. The mission of the Church is to call the world home . . . [We must] never tire of engaging [people], of persuading them, of pointing out in their lives the signals of the transcendent glory for which they were created. Never weary of proposing to them the true story of their lives."[11] Neuhaus also never tired of saying that the Church must make her proposal "winsomely, persuasively, and persistently, like a lover to the beloved."[12]

The Church also asks the world for the freedom to be herself, for the space to live out her particular mission in word, sacrament, and charity. This requires a state that limits itself through law and custom, a state that doesn't presume to invade all sectors of society.[13] This freedom is vital not only for the Church, but also for other bodies in society that exist between the individual and the state. In the last few years, as we've already seen, the state has encroached on the Church's autonomy again and again. We've come again to a place where the world is making it much harder for the Church to be herself.

So, what do we do? One option is to withdraw, to shake the dust from our feet and retreat to the margins. That won't work for two reasons. First, the world will come after us. It's not enough for an adulterer to divorce the wife he lied to, abused, and cheated on; he'd really prefer her to completely disappear. So, too, as people and cultures turn away from their former convictions, reminders of the past become both more haunting and more irritating. The Church and Christian beliefs will be resented simply because they exist, they have life, and they move faithful persons to act. And critics who attack the Church now will continue to do so more zealously.

Second, and more important, God calls us to be the soul of the world. As the *Letter to Diognetus* reminds us, the task to which God calls us is to hold the world together. When the world opposes Jesus Christ, we may end up being against the world. But in every such case, we're against the world for the sake of the world. After all, God so loved the world that he sent his only Son to save it, not to condemn it. If we want to follow Jesus, we must love the world too and remain in it, as he did, to work for its salvation.

But we can never afford to be comfortable. We need to renew our minds with the Gospel (Rom 12:2), and we need places and moments in our lives to help us achieve that renewal. Places do exist where the world's influence is diminished, where we can rest before returning to the mission. Practically speaking, this means working to renew our parishes, schools, and the small communities of which we're a part. It means making sure that, whatever schools they attend, our children learn to live and think as Catholics.

An Eastern Orthodox writer describes this as creating "countercultural places [that] we make for ourselves, together." This is vital for handing on the faith to our children. He continues: "If we do not form our consciences and the consciences of our children to be distinctly Christian and distinctly countercultural, *even if that means some degree of intentional separation from the mainstream*, we are not going to survive . . . The primary focus of orthodox [i.e., faithful] Christians in America should be cultural—or rather, countercultural—building the institutions and habits that will carry the faith and the faithful forward through the next Dark Age" (emphasis in original).[14]

This is wisdom, so long as we don't give up on the good still present in American society. We need to create places where Catholic culture can flourish and be handed down to the next generation.[15] After all, we've inherited a vast wealth of culture that Christians at the time of the *Letter to Diognetus* didn't have.

Today we Catholics do, in a sense, have our own language. Our lives are marked by a particular calendar. We feast and we fast. And of course we have the great works of Christian-inspired philosophy, theology, art, literature, music, and film. This profound Catholic culture is a blessing, and we need to recover and cultivate it. Catholic culture helps to keep our faith alive, and it marks us as different from the culture around us.

It also attracts thousands of others to the faith. Bland secular platitudes, consumer junk, and cheap nihilism feed nobody's soul. These things strangle the heart. The grandeur and beauty of Catholic culture, even when we need to excavate it from under a mountain of mediocre religious kitsch, is the outgrowth of our worship—our *cult*—of Jesus Christ.[16]

As Robert Louis Wilken writes, "If Christ is culture, let the sidewalks be lit with fire on Easter Eve, let traffic stop for a column of Christians waving palm branches on a spring morning, let streets be blocked off as the faithful gather for a Corpus Christi procession. Then will others know that there is another city in their midst, another commonwealth, one that has its face, like the faces of angels, turned toward the face of God."[17]

That's what it means for Christians to live as the soul of the world. We certainly do need to engage in political issues, vigorously, for the sake of our society and for the liberty of the Church. But more than that, we need to build the communities, the friendships, and the places in which we joyfully live out our faith. Above all, we need to be filled with a consuming passion for Jesus Christ—that blaze of love that has lit the human heart from the second century to our own and remains unlike anything else the world has ever seen.

If we truly love God, we'll evangelize the world he made, and whose soul he created us to be. After all, we're disciples and friends—not just servants, but friends—of the Lord of history, who died and rose again to save the world.

The Church will endure until the end of time. We have the Word of God on that. But how and where she survives is another matter. "The question," as one scholar suggested, "is whether her life *in our time* will be indifferent, fearful and corrupt, or a luminous proposal to the world of a more excellent way. The answer in our time, as so often in the past, may depend upon small communities that mirror to the world the light that came into the world, the light that has not and will never, never ever, be extinguished."[18]

CHAPTER 12

THE CITY OF MAN

Beauty is the battlefield where God and Satan contend for the hearts of men.

—DOSTOYEVSKY, *The Brothers Karamazov*

Late have I loved thee, Beauty so old and so new; late have I loved thee. Lo, you were within, but I was outside, seeking there for you, and upon the shapely things you have made I rushed headlong— I, misshapen. You were with me, but I was not with you. They held me back far from you, those things which would have no being, were they not in you.

—AUGUSTINE, *The Confessions*

A FRIEND ONCE TOLD ME THE STORY OF HOW SHE FIRST met God. She doesn't remember her age; she must have been about five or six. Her family lived in the countryside on the rim of one of our big eastern cities. And one July evening, cloudless, moonless, with just the hint of a humid breeze, her father took her out into the backyard in the dark and told her to look up at the sky.

From one horizon to the other, all across the black carpet of the night, were the stars—thousands of them, tens of thousands, in clusters and rivers of light. And in the quiet, her father said, "God made the world beautiful because he loves us."

That was more than sixty years ago. My friend grew up and learned all about entropy and supernovas and colliding galaxies and quantum mechanics and the general theory of relativity. But still, when she closes her eyes, she can see that carpet of stars and hear her father's voice: *God made the world beautiful because he loves us.* Creation is more than an accident of dead matter. It's a romance. It has purpose. It sings of the Living God. It bears his signature. And it's our home.

The story of my friend offers a few lessons we might want to consider as these reflections draw to a close.

First, the most powerful kind of witness doesn't come from a classroom or pulpit. It doesn't need an academic degree or special techniques. Instead, it grows naturally out of the lives of ordinary people—parents and spouses and friends; people confident in the love that God bears for them and eager to share it with others; people who know the world not as a collection of confused facts but as a symphony of beauty, truth, and meaning.

Second, nature is sacramental. It points to things outside itself. God speaks and creation sings in silence. We can't hear either if we're cocooned in a web of manufactured distraction, anxiety, and noise. We can't see the heavens if our faces are buried in technologies that turn us inward on ourselves. Yet that's exactly what modern American life seems to promote: a restless and relentless material appetite for "more" that gradually feeds selfishness and separates each of us from everyone else.

Third and finally, every experience of real beauty leads us more deeply into three key virtues: *humility*, because the grandeur of creation invites awe and lifts us outside ourselves; *love*, because the human heart was made for communion and for sharing joy, and only the Author of life can satisfy its longings;

and *hope*, because no sadness, no despair, can ultimately survive the evidence of divine meaning that beauty provides.

If the world taking shape around us today seems to make
us strangers in a strange land—strangers in our own land—
that's because it does. If, while preaching freedom, the world
seems filled with cynicism, ugliness, blasphemies big and small,
and sadness, that's because (too often) it is. What the modern
world really wants, wrote Josef Pieper, "is flattery, and it does
not matter how much of it is a lie." But since every lie is an act
of violence against reality and a deforming of the truth, the
world also wants the right to disguise the lying, so "the fact of
being lied to can be easily ignored." The result is predictable:
"The common element in all of this is the degeneration of
language into an instrument of rape."[1]

And that rape is carried out not just against the dignity of
the human spirit, but against the beauty of the earth itself. Just
as the face of a beloved shines with the inner light of the person's soul, so the world as a sacrament shines with the face of
God. The atheist culture of our age, says Roger Scruton, has a
number of motives—but one of them is the desire to escape
from the eye of judgment. And we escape from the eye of
God's judgment by mutilating the face of his world.

Thus the spoiling of the earth with waste and the brutaliz-
ing of our human habitats with ugly art and buildings are not
just clumsy mistakes of progress, but desecrations. As Scruton
notes, "Sacred places [like a sacramentally understood natural
world] are the first places to be destroyed by invaders and icon-
oclasts, for whom nothing is more offensive than the enemy's
gods." We should recognize "that much of the destruction of our
environment today is *deliberate*, the result of a willed assault on
old and despised forms of tranquility."[2]

We need to ask why.

LIFE AS A BISHOP—or at least the life of this bishop—doesn't leave much time to spend on poetry. But some years ago a friend lent me a volume of Rainer Maria Rilke poems, and, of course, Rilke's work can be quite beautiful. In it, I found these lines of his verse:

Slowly now the evening changes his garments
held for him by a rim of ancient trees;
you gaze: and the landscape divides and leaves you
one sinking and one rising toward the stars.

And you are left, to none belonging wholly,
not so dark as a silent house, nor quite
so surely pledged unto eternity
as that which grows to star and climbs the night.

To you is left (unspeakably confused)
your life, gigantic, ripening, full of fears,
so that it, now hemmed in, now grasping all,
is changed in you by turns to stone and stars.[3]

Philosophers and psychologists have offered many different theories about the nature of the human person. But few have captured the human condition better than Rilke does in those twelve lines. We are creatures made for heaven, but we are born of this earth. We love the beauty of this world, but we sense there's something more behind that beauty. Our longing for that "something" pulls us outside of ourselves.

Striving for "something more" is part of the greatness of the human spirit, even when it involves failure and suffering. In the words of Saint John Paul II, something in the artist, and by extension in all human beings, "mirrors the image of God as

Creator."[4] We have an instinct to create beauty and new life that comes from our own Maker. Yet we live in a time when, despite all of our achievements, the brutality and indifference of the world have never been greater. And that cruelty is *also* the work of human hands. So if we're troubled by the spirit of our age, if we want to change the current course of our culture and challenge its ruling ideas, then we need to start with the author of that culture. That means examining man himself.

Culture exists because man exists. Men and women think, imagine, believe, and act. The mark they leave on the world is what we call culture. In a sense, that includes everything from work habits and cuisine to social manners and politics. But most of us focus in a special way on those elements of culture that people consciously choose to create; things like art, literature, technology, music, and architecture. These are what most of us think about when we first hear the word "culture."

That makes sense, because all of these things deal with communicating knowledge that's both useful and beautiful. The task of an architect, for example, is to translate abstract engineering problems into visible, pleasing form; in other words, to turn disorder into order, and mathematical complexity into a public expression of elegance and strength. We are social animals. Culture is the framework within which we locate ourselves in relationship to other people. Through it, we find meaning in the world and then, in turn, transmit meaning to others.

In his *Letter to Artists*, John Paul II wrote that "beauty is the visible form of the good, just as the good is the metaphysical condition of beauty." There is "an ethic, even a 'spirituality' of artistic service which contributes [to] the life and renewal of a people," because "every genuine art form, in its own way, is a path to the inmost reality of man and of the world."

He went on to say that "true art has a close affinity with the world of faith, so that even in situations where culture and the Church are far apart, art remains a kind of bridge to religious experience . . . Art by its nature is a kind of appeal to the mystery. Even when they explore the darkest depths of the soul or the most unsettling aspects of evil, artists give voice [to] the universal desire for redemption."

Christianity is an *incarnational* religion. We believe that God became man. As we've seen, this has huge implications for how we live, and how we think about culture. God creates the world in Genesis. He judges it as "very good" (Gen 1:31). Later he enters the world to redeem it in the flesh and blood of his son (Jn 1:14). In effect, God licenses us to know, love, and ennoble the world through the work of human genius. Our creativity as creatures is an echo of God's own creative glory. When God tells our first parents, "be fruitful and multiply, and fill the earth and subdue it" (Gen 1:28), he invites us to take part, in a small but powerful way, in the life of God himself.

The results of that fertility surround us. We see it in the great Christian heritage that still underpins the modern world. Anyone with an honest heart will grant that the Christian faith has inspired much of the greatest painting, music, architecture, and scholarship in human experience. For Christians, art is a holy vocation with the power to elevate the human spirit and lead men and women toward God.

Having said all this, we still face a problem. And it's this: God has never been more cast out from the Western mind than he is today. Additionally, we live in an age when almost every scientific advance seems to be matched by some new cruelty in our entertainment, cynicism in our politics, ignorance of the past, consumer greed, subtle genocides posing as rights like the cult of abortion, and a basic confusion about what—if anything distinctive at all—it means to be human.

Science and technology give us power. Philosophers like Ludwig Feuerbach and Friedrich Nietzsche give us the language to deny God. The result, in the words of Henri de Lubac, is not atheism, but an *anti-theism* built on resentment.[5] In destroying God, man sees himself as "overthrowing an obstacle in order to gain his freedom." The Christian understanding of human dignity claims that we're made in the image and likeness of God. Thomas Aquinas said that "In this [likeness to God] is man's greatness, in this is man's worth, in this he excels every creature."[6] But this grounding in God is exactly what the modern spirit rejects as an insult to human sovereignty.

Of course, most people walking the planet have never read Nietzsche. Nor will they. Few have even heard of Feuerbach. But they do experience the benefits of science and technology every day. And they do live inside a cocoon of marketing that constantly teases their appetites, makes death seem remote, and pushes questions about meaning and morality down into matters of private opinion.

The result is this: While many people in the developed world still claim to be religious, their faith—in the words of the Pontifical Council for Culture—is "often more a question of religious feeling than a demanding commitment to God."[7] Religion becomes a kind of insurance policy for eternity. Too often, it's little more than a convenient moral language for daily life. And what's worse is that many people no longer have the skills, or even the desire, to understand their circumstances, or to think their way out of the marketing cocoon.

Part of what blocks a serious rethinking of our current culture is the "knowledge economy" we've created. In its statement *Towards a Pastoral Approach to Culture*, the Pontifical Council for Culture saw that the constant flow of "information provided by [today's] mass media . . . affects the way things are perceived: What people come to know is not reality as such, but what they are shown. [The] constant repetition of selected items of information involves a decline in critical awareness, and this is a crucial factor in forming what is considered public opinion." It also causes "a loss of intrinsic value [in the specific] items of information, an undifferentiated uniformity in messages which are reduced to pure information, a lack of responsible feedback, and a . . . discouragement of interpersonal relationships."

As we've already seen, all of this is true. For all of its great benefits, modern technology can isolate people as often as it brings them together. It weakens community as easily as it builds it up. It also forms the human mind in habits of thought and expression that are very different from traditional culture based on the printed word. And that has implications both for the Word of God and for the Church.

There's also another important point here that even strong religious believers can feel awkward talking about.

Referring to artists, John Paul II said, "In shaping a masterpiece, the artist not only summons his work into being, but also . . . reveals his own personality by means of it." In other words, "works of art speak of their authors; they enable us to know their inner life." This is normal. But it also poses a danger.

A key temptation of our age is the desire for power. It's most obvious in our politics and science, in the constant erosion of our respect for the weak, the infirm, the unborn, and the disabled. But the impulse to pride—that hunger to smash taboos and inflate the self—appeals in a special way to artists and other creators of both high and popular culture. Genius can breed vanity. Vanity breeds conflict. Conflict breeds suffering. And the vanity of creative genius has a pedigree that leads back a very long way.

✖

IT'S RATHER ODD THAT in the wake of the bloodiest century in history—a twentieth century in which scores of millions of human beings were shot, starved, gassed, blown apart, and incinerated with superhuman ingenuity—even many religious leaders are embarrassed to talk about the devil (Pope Francis is a notable exception). In fact, it's more than odd. It's revealing.

Mass murder and exquisitely organized cruelty are not just exceptionally sad "mental and social health" problems. They're crimes and sins that cry out to heaven for justice, and they carry the fingerprints of an Intelligence who is personal, gifted, calculating, and powerful. The devil is implausible only if we imagine him as the black monster of medieval paintings, or think Dante's *Inferno* is meant as a literal road map to hell. Satan was vividly real for Jesus. He was very real for Paul and every other great saint throughout history. And, in Christian belief, he's profoundly formidable. If we want a sense of the grandeur of the Fallen One before he fell, the violated genius of who Satan really is, we can take a hint from the Rilke poem *The Angels*:

> . . . *when they spread their wings*
> *they waken a great wind through the land:*
> *as though with his broad sculptor-hands*
> *God was turning*
> *the leaves of the dark book of the Beginning.*

This is the kind of Being—once glorious, then consumed by his own pride—who is now the Adversary of humanity. *This* is the Pure Spirit who betrayed his Creator and his own greatness. *This* is the Intellect who hates the Incarnation because through it, God invites creatures of clay like us humans to take part in God's own divinity. There is nothing sympathetic or noble about Satan; only tragedy and loss and enduring, incandescent fury.

In 1929, as the great totalitarian murder regimes rose to power in Europe, the philosopher Raissa Maritain wrote a now largely forgotten essay called *The Prince of This World*. It's worth reading. We need to remember her words today and into the future. With no trace of irony or metaphor, Maritain argued:

> Lucifer has cast the strong though invisible net of illusion upon us. He makes one love the passing moment above eternity, uncertainty above truth. He persuades us that we can only love creatures by making Gods of them. He lulls us to sleep (and he interprets our dreams); he makes us work. Then does the spirit of man brood over stagnant waters. Not the least of the devil's victories is to have convinced artists and poets that he is their necessary, inevitable collaborator and the guardian of their greatness. Grant him that, and soon you will grant him that Christianity is *unpracticable*. Thus does he reign in this world.[8]

If we don't believe in the devil, sooner or later we won't believe in God. Try as we might, and as awkward as it might be for our own peace of mind, we can't cut Lucifer out of the ecology of salvation. The supernatural is real, and his existence is near the heart of this world's confusion, fears, sufferings, and spiritual struggles. True, Satan is not God's equal. He's a created being subject to God and already, by the measure of eternity, defeated. Nonetheless, he's the first author of pride and rebellion, and the great seducer of man. Without him the

Incarnation and Redemption make little sense, and the cross is meaningless. The devil is real. There's no escape from this simple truth.

We can underline that truth even more strongly. Leszek Kolakowski, the former Marxist philosopher who died in 2009, was one of the great minds of the last century. A fierce critic of the Church in his youth, and later a fan of John Paul II, Kolakowski was never traditional in his religious convictions. But he had few doubts about the reality of the devil. In his essay "Short Transcript of a Metaphysical Press Conference Given by the Demon in Warsaw, on 20th December 1963," Kolakowski's devil indicts all of us who call ourselves "modern" Christians with the following words:

> Where is there a place [in your thinking] for the fallen angel? . . . Is Satan only a rhetorical figure? . . . Or else, gentlemen, is he a reality, undeniable, recognized by tradition, revealed in the Scriptures, commented upon by the Church for two millennia, tangible and acute? Why do you avoid me, gentlemen? Are you afraid that the skeptics will mock you, that you will be laughed at in satirical late night reviews? Since when is the faith affected by the jeers of heathens and heretics? What road are you taking? If you forsake the foundations of the faith for fear of mockery, where will you end? If the devil falls victim to your fear [of embarrassment] today, God's turn must inevitably come tomorrow. Gentlemen, you have been ensnared by the idol of modernity, which fears ultimate matters and hides from you their importance. I don't mention it for my own benefit—it is nothing to me— I am talking about you and for you, forgetting for a moment my own vocation, and even my duty to propagate error.[9]

We live in an age that imagines itself as postmodern and post-Christian. It's a time defined by noise, urgency, restless action, utility, and a hunger for ever greater efficiencies and practical results. But there's nothing really new about any of this. Saint Paul would find our age rather familiar. For all the slogans about "hope and change" and "a future we can believe in" in American politics, our urgencies hide a deep unease about the future, a kind of well-manicured and selfish despair. The world around us has a hole in its heart, and the emptiness causes pain. Only God can fill it. In our Baptism, God called each of us to be his partners in that holy work. Like Saint Paul, we need to be "doers of the word, and not hearers only" (Jas 1:22). We prove what we really believe by our willingness, or our refusal, to act on what we claim to believe.

We need to remember that what we do proceeds first from who we are. Nothing is deader than faith without works (Jas 2:17), except perhaps for one thing: works without faith. The questions that determine everything else in our life as Christians are these: Do I really know God? Do I really love him? Do I seek him out? Do I study his word? Do I listen for his voice? Do I give my heart to him? Do I really believe he's there?

We have a duty as Catholics to study and understand the world around us. We have a duty not just to penetrate and engage it, but to convert it to Jesus Christ. That work belongs to all of us equally: clergy, laity, and religious. We're missionaries. That's our primary vocation; it's hardwired into our identity as Christians. God calls each of us to different forms of service in his Church. But we're all equal in Baptism. And we all share the same mission of bringing the Gospel to the world, and bringing the world to the Gospel.

Kolakowski's urbane and cynically helpful demon was right

in one key respect. The fundamental crisis of our time, and the special crisis of today's Christians, has little to do with numbers, or organization, or resources. It's a crisis of faith. Do we believe in God or not? Are we on fire with a love for Jesus Christ or not? Because if we're not, none of our good intentions matter. And if we are, then everything we need in doing God's work will naturally follow, because he never abandons his people.

Dante Alighieri, perhaps the greatest poet in history, is rightly remembered for the genius of *The Divine Comedy*. But one line shines more brightly than any other verse in his stunning work. He ends *The Paradiso* and the entire *Comedy* with these words: "The Love which moves the sun and the other stars."

The Love which moves the sun and the other stars. That Love is the nature of the God we preach. A God so great in glory, light, and majesty that he can emblazon the heavens with a carpet of stars and call life out of dead space; yet so intimate that he became one of us; so humble that he entered our world on dirt and straw to redeem us. We can be forgiven for sometimes running away from that kind of love, like a child who runs away from a parent, because we simply can't understand or compete with that ocean of unselfishness. It's only when we give ourselves fully to God that we grasp, finally, that we were made to do exactly that. Our hearts are restless until they rest in him. And so we should never be afraid to believe in God's love and to make it the basis for our lives; it took even a great saint like Augustine half a lifetime to finally admit that "late have I loved thee, Beauty so old and so new; late have I loved thee."

God calls us to set the world on fire with his Word. But he calls us first to love him.

❧

WAIT A MINUTE, THOUGH. Somewhere we took a wrong turn. We started out, some seventy thousand words ago, talking about American politics, identity, and history. Good practical stuff. So how did we end up in the weeds, worrying about beauty, art, poetry, and the devil? It might be true that "Beauty will save the world" (Dostoyevsky). And that "Every experience of beauty points to infinity" (von Balthasar). And even that "Man can live without science, he can live without bread, but without beauty he could no longer live" (again, Dostoyevsky). But frankly, so what? Beauty doesn't help us vote. In fact, it doesn't actually help us *do* anything.

There's certainly very little "beauty" in the following facts.

The Notre Dame law scholar Gerard Bradley has written compellingly about the "institutional martyrdom" now facing many U.S. Catholic institutions and ministries. Many of them took federal funds in a friendlier time. Now they face federal pressure to conform to policies that violate their Christian identity. But as Bradley notes, no public religious ministry is really safe, federal funds or not. And why is this happening? Much of it links to Catholic convictions about the dignity of life and human sexuality—notably the issues of abortion, contraception, gender identity, marriage, and family. These convictions are rooted not just in biblical revelation, but in reason and natural law.

Critics of the Church reduce all these moral convictions to an expression of subjective religious beliefs. And if they're purely religious beliefs, then—so the critics argue—they can't be rationally defended. And because they're rationally indefensible, they should be treated as a form of prejudice. Thus two thousand years of moral truth and religious principle become, by sleight of hand, a species of bias. Opposing same-sex marriage (so the reasoning goes) amounts to religiously blessed homophobia.[10]

There's more, though. When religious belief is redefined downward to a kind of private bias, then the religious identity of institutional ministries has no public value—other than the utility of getting credulous people to do socially useful things. So exempting Catholic adoption agencies, for example, from placing children with same-sex couples becomes a concession to private prejudice. And concessions to private prejudice feed bigotry and hurt the public. Or so the reasoning goes. Insufficiently "progressive" moral teaching and religious belief end up reclassified as hate speech.

All of the above makes a forceful case for Catholic political activism. It's also a damning indictment of scholars, journalists, and publications—some of them "Catholic"—that have belittled for years the Church's strong concerns about sanctity of life and sexual integrity issues. The right to life is the foundation of every other right, which makes intentionally killing an unborn child, or encouraging, enabling, or deliberately tolerating such a killing, a uniquely vile act.

Saying this, of course, absolves no one from working to help the poor, the immigrant, and the homeless. Quite the opposite. If we call ourselves Christians, we have duties on a whole range of urgent social concerns. But sexuality-related issues are not a separate, idiosyncratic corner of Catholic thought. They're deeply connected to much broader issues of personal and social morality and the organization of society. Thus fighting—vigorously—in the voting booth, in legislatures and the courts, and in the public square to protect our religious freedom, and the integrity of Catholic institutions and ministries, is a vital expression of our faith. It's also our constitutional right.

Yet as Bradley himself says, government and media pressure will make it harder for genuinely Catholic social service ministries to survive in the years ahead. U.S. Catholic institutions of the future will likely be "organized but informal networks of properly formed professionals, working for free or whatever people can pay out of their pockets."[11]

Moreover, as the John Paul II Institute scholar Michael Hanby argues:

> The [Church's] public and legal defense of religious liberty, as . . . conducted thus far, leaves the impression that these are one and the same freedom, so that the freedom of the Church finally depends upon the decision of the state. This constitutes a debilitating limit on the Christian imagination and a dangerous self-limitation of Christian freedom. For the freedom of the Church, properly speaking, comes not from the state but from the Truth revealed ultimately in Jesus Christ, and she remains free—irrespective of what the state decides—so long as she can see this Truth, because she is always free to offer herself in suffering witness to it.[12]

He continues:

> The indifference of [America's system of] liberal freedom to [matters of] truth insures that religious freedom *cannot* be understood from within the liberal order to be "first" [among the freedoms] . . . Rather it can only be seen as one freedom among many, one which is not likely to fare well when it comes into conflict with more "fundamental" rights such as the "right" to "build a family," the right of equal access, or the right to non-discrimination in employment. Because this conflict does indeed concern fundamental things, it is not

at all clear that the "tolerance" which Christians are seeking would be logically and legally possible, even if good will were in abundance, and the opponents of the Church wanted to grant it.

For Hanby, there's "no question that the Church should continue to resist the assaults on her juridical freedom through the judicial and legislative process." This is obvious and necessary. And it needs to be done not just for the sake of the Church, but for the sake of the best of those qualities that were, and in some ways still are, the American experiment. But three concerns need to guide our longer-term thinking:

First, the defense of Church freedom should not preclude a much greater effort to defend the truth of the human being, and to speak the truth about what our present sexual and social revolution portends.

Second, Church leaders must take better care to distinguish between the freedom that the Church has by nature and by grace, and the purely juridical freedom granted by the state and civil society. Her basic rights and liberty come from God and are not gifts of the government.

Third, the defense of Church freedom therefore depends not mainly on a legal or political strategy, but on a renewal of Catholic thought about nature, the human person, marriage, and even freedom itself in its relation to truth.

It's good advice for a U.S. political terrain now better suited to Fantasyland than the real world. As this book was being completed in the mid-2016 election season, one of the nation's two main political parties seemed committed to *America contra mundum* ("America against the world"), while the other doubled down on an entitlement state that's morally compromised, bleeding money, and can't be sustained. In a culture with an unofficial state religion of "choice," real choices were remarkably few.

And while America has always had an amazing ability to renew itself, some changes in the body politic are unlikely to be reversed. In 2013 Gallup polling, 75 percent of Americans voiced support for a greater influence of religion in national life . . . but that included the many among those surveyed who had no *personal* interest in religious faith.[13]

In other words, "Americans want religion," as one headline read, for "everyone but themselves." It's little surprise that in 2014, 23 percent of adult Americans self-described as atheists, agnostics, or persons with no religious affiliation. This was up sharply from 16 percent in 2007. "Nones" are now the fastest growing religious group in the country, with nonreligious congregations (nicknamed godless churches) appearing nationally. And they're increasingly organized as a political voice focused on "elevating science over belief" and keeping government and religion strictly separate.[14]

So where does that leave us as American Catholics? And again, where does beauty fit into any of this?

We need to revisit one last time the question weaving its way throughout these pages: Who is man?

※

"WHAT DO WE REALLY mean when we use the word *man* today? Whom are we speaking of when we defend human rights or engage in the human sciences?" These are the first words of Pierre Manent's provocative work *The City of Man*—its title a nod to Augustine's great masterpiece *City of God*. One of our era's best political thinkers, Manent notes that "Our speech is obsessed with man and sings his praises without inquiring who he is . . . Man commands humanity's attention everywhere today, yet never perhaps since the time of Homer has the question embodied in the word *man*" been so little explored or understood.[15]

The reason for the confusion isn't a mystery. The identity of man cannot be separated from the God who made him. And who is that God? For the Christian, God is not a "Supreme Being" within reality, but the Author of reality itself, outside the envelope of time and space, transcendent and utterly omnipotent and unknowable—except insofar as he chooses to show himself. He does that through creation, reason, his revealed Word, the community of believers we know as the Church—and above all, through his Word made flesh in his son.

What he shows us in Jesus Christ is not simply his own divine nature, but the face of man fully alive, the face of true freedom and love.

Humanity in its fullness—the complementarity of man and woman—shows its glory in lives of free will, self-awareness, and intellect, subordinated to love. We humans can choose ourselves, but at our best, we choose others. We humans can choose ourselves, but at our best, we choose to love. Love, even more than intelligence, is the genius of man. It's the way we share in the furnace of love that is the Trinitarian God himself. And as long and as well as we love, faith grows stronger by our actions, and hope has the soil in which to thrive.

What does God ask us to do in a seemingly post-Christian world? The first thing he asks from us is to realize that the words "post-Christian" are a lie, so long as the fire of Christian faith, hope, and love lives in any of us.

We can tag along as compliant fellow travelers with a secular culture that's now, in so many ways, better described as *apostate*. Lots of people already do.

Or, to borrow from the words of Rabbi Jonathan Sacks, we

can live as a conscious minority in a nation whose beliefs, culture, and politics are no longer our own, yet still nourish our identity, witness our faith with zeal, and add to the common good as the prophet Jeremiah did. This demands humility. It also requires courage and a refusal to be digested and bleached out by the world around us. As Sacks said in 2013, the task "isn't easy. It demands a complex finessing of identities. It involves a willingness to live in a state of cognitive dissonance. It isn't for the faint-hearted. But it is creative."[16]

Václav Havel put it even more forcefully when he said that the only way to fight a culture of lies, whatever form the lies take, is to consciously live the truth instead of merely talking about it. The power of living the truth does not consist in physical strength or threats, "but in the light it casts" on the "pillars [of a mendacious] system and on its unstable foundations."[17]

This was clearly the approach of the first Christians, who refused to pay tribute to the idols of the Roman state and sought instead to build a new life rooted in the truth of the Gospel. We can measure the character we ourselves need by their example.

One of the great pastors of the last century, writing about the tepid Christianity of his era, said that most people's faith was "like a farmer who needs a horse for his fields; he leaves the fiery stallion on one side, and buys the tame, broken-in horse. This is just the way men have tamed for themselves a usable Christianity, and it is only a matter of time and honest thought before they lose interest in their creation and get rid of it."[18]

The man who wrote those words was Dietrich Bonhoeffer, the great German Lutheran theologian. For Bonhoeffer, faith was not an academic discipline, or a personal hobby, or a collection of useful wisdom. It was the engine that powered his life. And so it needs to be with us. Knowing "about" Jesus Christ is not enough. We need to engage him with our whole lives. That means cleaning out the garbage of noise and distraction from our homes. It means building real Christian friendships. It means cultivating oases of silence, worship, and prayer in our lives. It means having more children and raising them in the love of the Lord. It means fighting death and fear with joy and life, one family at a time, with families sustaining one another against the temptations of weariness and resentment.

And what about beauty? Beauty can be admired. It can be venerated. It can inspire gratitude or awe. But it cannot be consumed as a product or "used" for instrumental purposes without defacing it. Beauty doesn't *do* anything . . . except the one most precious thing in life: It invites and elevates the soul beyond itself, beyond calculation, beyond utility, and thus reminds us what it means to be human.

Beauty, to borrow from Augustine's thoughts on the First Letter of John, is like the ring a bridegroom gives to his bride, a sign and seal of God's enduring love. It's the antidote to the deeper, demonic pornographies of our age: anger, despair, vanity, violence, cynicism. Roger Scruton describes beauty as the "present symbol of transcendent values." That's a big way of saying that beauty refreshes our hearts in this world while lifting us toward the next, "for here we have no lasting city, but we seek the city which is to come" (Heb 13:14).

The idea of the city is so powerful in man's imagination because it conjures up images of commerce, energy, progress, and community. The cities of man are living examples—signs to the world—of the best and also the worst in human nature. In Scripture, Sodom and Gomorrah are the wicked "cities of the plain." But Jerusalem is longed for and revered as the "holy city," the heart of life for God's people.

In the mind of Augustine, we were made for the City of God, but we pass through the City of Man on the pilgrimage of our lives. We will never have perfect justice in the earthly city because of sin. But we can make the world around us better or worse, more beautiful or more defaced, by what we do and how we live as "resident aliens."

As Augustine once wrote:

> The body by its own weight gravitates toward its own place. Weight goes not downward only, but to its own place. Fire tends upward, a stone downward. They are propelled by their own weights, they seek their own places . . . My weight is my love; by it am I borne wherever I am borne. By Your gift we are inflamed, and are borne upward; we wax hot inwardly, and go forward. We ascend Your ways that be in our heart, and sing a song of degrees; we glow inwardly with . . . Your good fire, and we go, because we go upward to the peace of Jerusalem.

My weight is my love. For Augustine, the fire of our love carries us upward on its heat. The more we love, the higher we rise toward heaven.

The point is this: Nations, too, have weight. The "weight" of a nation is the love that animates—or fails to animate—its treatment of the poor, the elderly, the person with disabilities, the unborn child.

Each of our lives lifts up or drags down the soul of the world. Each of our lives matters. What we do has consequences for our own eternity and those around us. In a City of Man that banishes God to the margins, it's little wonder that men and women, the work of his hands, are foreigners to each other and themselves, and aliens to their own nature.

We were made by God to receive love ourselves, and to show love to others—love anchored in the truth about the human person and the nature of human relationships. That's our purpose. That's why we were created. We're here to bear one another's burdens, to sacrifice ourselves for the needs of others, and to live a witness of Christian love—in all our public actions, including every one of our social, economic, and political choices; but beginning with the conversion of our own hearts. Every such life is the seed of a dozen others and begins a renewal of the world.

Who is man? What is his destiny? What do our lives mean? The questions aren't new.

O Lord, our Lord, what is man that you are mindful of him, and the son of man that you care for him? Yet you have made him little less than the angels, and you have crowned him with glory and honor." (Ps 8:1, 4–5)

The Word of God testifies to the goodness of creation, the gift that is life, and the glory of the human person. With this glory comes a duty. We are born for the City of God. The road home leads through the City of Man. So we are strangers in a strange land, yes.

But what we do here makes all the difference.

NOTES

1. Resident Aliens

1. Tom Phillips, "China on Course to Become 'World's Most Christian Nation' Within 15 Years," *Telegraph*, April 19, 2014.
2. Benedict XVI, *Christmas Greetings to the Roman Curia*, December 21, 2012.
3. On the origin of personhood, see Mark Shiffman, "The Loss of a Culture of Personhood and the End of Limited Government," *Front Porch Republic*, October 6, 2014. On the roots of the idea of the individual, see Larry Siedentop, *Inventing the Individual: The Origins of Western Liberalism* (Cambridge, MA: Harvard University Press, 2014).
4. Alexis de Tocqueville, *Democracy in America*, translated and edited by Harvey C. Mansfield and Delba Winthrop (Chicago: University of Chicago Press, 2000), 486. The Mansfield/Winthrop edition of Tocqueville is used throughout this text.
5. See Pierre Manent, "Democracy and Religion," in *Tocqueville and the Nature of Democracy* (Lanham, MD: Rowman and Littlefield, 1996), 83–107.
6. Tocqueville, *Democracy in America*, 418.
7. Thomas W. Smith, "Catholic Social Thought and Modern Liberal Democracy," *Logos* 11, no. 1 (2008): 15–48. See also Rowan Williams's 2002 Dimbleby Lecture, *Guardian*, December 19, 2002.

8. Francis, *Evangelii Gaudium*, no. 10.
9. Ibid., no. 85.
10. Cindy Wooden, "Pope Says Christians Should Have Restless Hearts Like St. Augustine's," *Catholic News Service*, August 28, 2013.
11. Romano Guardini, a major influence on Francis's thought, had a vivid understanding of Satan as a personal and malignant spiritual being. See Guardini's *The Faith and Modern Man* (New York: Pantheon Books, 1952), 139–54. See also Guardini's *The Lord* (Washington: Regnery Gateway, 1982), 132–39, and especially 604.
12. Augustine, *City of God*, book II, chapter 20.
13. Ibid., book XIV, chapter 28.
14. Ibid., book XIX, chapter 26.
15. For a discussion of Augustine's approach to politics, see Robert Dodaro, O.S.A., *Christ and the Just Society in the Thought of Augustine* (New York: Cambridge University Press, 2004). See also Jean Bethke Elshtain, *Augustine and the Limits of Politics* (Notre Dame, IN: University of Notre Dame Press, 1995).
16. John Milton, *Paradise Lost*, book I.
17. Lindsay Putnam, "*Charlie Hebdo* Cartoonist Doesn't Want You to Pray for Paris," *New York Post*, November 14, 2015.
18. Augustine, *De Trinitate.*
19. Nicholson in the 1983 film *Terms of Endearment.*
20. Stanley Hauerwas and William Willimon, *Resident Aliens: Life in the Christian Colony; A Provocative Christian Assessment of Culture and Ministry for People Who Know That Something Is Wrong* (Nashville: Abingdon Press, 1989), 2014.

2. Of Blessed Memory

1. Daniel J. Boorstin, *America and the Image of Europe: Reflections on American Thought* (Gloucester, MA: Peter Smith, 1976), 70.
2. Nicholas von Hoffman, "God Was Present at the Founding," *Civilization*, April/May 1998.
3. Alexander Kazam, "By Design and Choice: French Political Theorist Pierre Manent Reflects on Europe and the American Founding," *National Review Online*, August 21, 2012.
4. George Grant, *Technology and Empire* (Toronto: House of Anansi Press, 1969), 17.
5. Napp Nazworth, "Robert George: Immigrant Gratitude Demonstrates American Exceptionalism," *Christian Post*, August 5, 2012. See also

Robert George, "Immigration and American Exceptionalism," in his *Conscience and Its Enemies: Confronting the Dogmas of Liberal Secularism* (Wilmington, DE: ISI Books, 2016), 67–68.

6. Matthew J. Franck, "Christianity and Freedom in the American Founding," in *Christianity and Freedom*, vol. 1: *Historical Perspectives*, edited by Timothy Samuel Shah and Allen D. Hertzke (New York: Cambridge University Press, 2016), 264, 271.

7. John Witherspoon, "Dominion of Providence over the Passions of Men," sermon in Princeton, NJ, May 17, 1776.

8. Hugh Heclo, *Christianity and American Democracy* (Cambridge, MA: Harvard University Press, 2007), 32–33.

9. Franck, *Christianity and Freedom*, 284.

10. Tocqueville, *Democracy in America*, 43.

11. W. Bradford Wilcox and Robert I. Lerman, "For Richer, for Poorer: How Family Structures Economic Success in America," www.aei.org /publication/for-richer-for-poorer/, October 28, 2014; and Ed Stetzer, "Marriage, Divorce, and the Church: What Do the Stats Say, and Can Marriage Be Happy?" *Christianity Today*, February 14, 2014.

12. Jessica Gavora, "Obama's 'Julia' Ad and the New Hubby State," *Washington Post*, May 11, 2012.

13. Robert Kraynak, "The American Founders and Their Relevance for Today," *Modern Age*, Winter 2015.

14. Alasdair MacIntyre, *After Virtue: A Study in Moral Theory* (Notre Dame, IN: University of Notre Dame Press, 1984), 213.

15. Catholics were obviously numerous in Spanish America—an important, but also a different, part of the nation's story.

16. Stanley Hauerwas, "The End of American Protestantism," *ABC Religion and Ethics*, July 2, 2013.

17. Pastoral Letter (1840), Fourth Provincial Council of Baltimore, in *Pastoral Letters of the American Hierarchy: 1792–1970*, edited by Hugh J. Nolan (Huntington, IN: Our Sunday Visitor, 1971), 87–107.

18. Charles J. Chaput, O.F.M. Cap., *Render Unto Caesar: Serving the Nation by Living Our Catholic Beliefs in Political Life* (New York: Doubleday, 2008), 92–93, 130–31.

19. Charles Morris, *American Catholic: The Saints and Sinners Who Built America's Most Powerful Church* (New York: Random House, 1997), 67–69, 135.

20. Pastoral Letter (1919), *Pastoral Letters of the American Hierarchy*, 238.

21. "The Present Crisis" (1933), ibid., 292, 294.
22. Letter of December 22, 1941, ibid., 378–79.
23. Morris, *American Catholic*, 277.
24. John H. Lang, "From Kristallnacht to the Kindertransport to, Finally, America," *Wall Street Journal*, November 8, 2015.
25. Morris, *American Catholic*, 281.
26. John Courtney Murray, S.J., "Catholics in America—a Creative Minority?" *Epistle* 21 (1955): 36–41.

3. Why It Can't Be Like It Was

1. Patrick Deneen, "The Power Elite," *First Things*, June/July 2015.
2. Madeline Buckley, "Threats Tied to RFRA Prompt Indiana Pizzeria to Close Its Doors," *Indianapolis Star*, April 3, 2015.
3. For a more extensive analysis of pornography and its effects, see James Stoner and Donna Hughes, editors, *The Social Costs of Pornography: A Collection of Papers* (Princeton, NJ: Witherspoon Institute, 2010).
4. "Porn Sites Get More Visitors Each Month Than Netflix, Amazon and Twitter Combined," *Huffington Post*, May 4, 2013.
5. Norman Doidge, "Acquiring Tastes and Loves: What Neuroplasticity Teaches Us About Sexual Attraction and Love," excerpted from his book *The Brain That Changes Itself* (New York: Penguin, 2007), and collected in Stoner and Hughes, *The Social Costs of Pornography*, 35.
6. Thomas Jefferson, "Letter to James Madison: The Earth Belongs to the Living," Paris, September 6, 1789.
7. Christian Smith, with Kari Christofferson, Hilary Davidson, and Patricia Snell Herzog, *Lost in Transition: The Dark Side of Emerging Adulthood* (New York: Oxford University Press, 2011), 9, 10, 11, 69, 147.
8. Nicolette Manglos-Weber and Christian Smith, "Understanding Former Young Catholics: Findings from a National Study of Emerging Young Adults" (Notre Dame, IN: Institute for Church Life and Center for the Study of Religion and Society, University of Notre Dame, 2015), 14.
9. Smith, *Lost in Transition*, 15.
10. Mary Eberstadt, *How the West Really Lost God: A New Theory of Secularization* (West Conshohocken, PA: Templeton Press, 2013), 133.
11. Ross Douthat, *Bad Religion: How We Became a Nation of Heretics* (New York: Free Press, 2012), 70, 71.
12. Ibid., 72.
13. Pierre Manent, *Seeing Things Politically: Interviews with Benedicte Delorme-Montini* (South Bend, IN: St. Augustine's Press, 2015), 171.
14. George Grant, *Technology and Empire*, 22–23.

15. Pew Research Center, "America's Changing Religious Landscape," www
.pewforum.org/2015/05/12/americas-changing-religious-landscape,
May 12, 2015.

16. Pew Research Center, "The Religious Affiliation of U.S. Immigrants:
Majority Christian, Rising Share of Other Faiths," www.pewforum.org
/2013/05/17/the-religious-affiliation-of-us-immigrants/#affiliation,
May 17, 2013.

17. Ibid.

18. Data taken from Pew Research Center 2013 (33 percent) and Boston
College / Center for Applied Research in the Apostolate (CARA) 2014
(40 percent) studies. Total U.S. Catholic population estimate by CARA,
2015.

19. "Boston College Study: Hispanics Vital to Future of Catholic Church,"
Boston College Chronicle, May 8, 2014. See also Hosffman Ospino, *Hispanic Ministry in Catholic Parishes: A Summary Report of Findings from
the National Study of Catholic Parishes with Hispanic Ministry* (Huntington, IN: Our Sunday Visitor, 2015), 8–9.

20. Joshua Bolding, "Diffusion of Faith: Immigrants Are Transforming
American Christianity," *Deseret News*, January 12, 2012.

21. Ibid.

22. Alan Dunn, "Average America vs. the One Percent," *Forbes*, March 21,
2012.

23. Agustino Fontevecchia, "Forbes' 2016 Presidential Candidate Wealth
List," *Forbes*, September 29, 2015.

24. Jacob Davidson, "Wealth Inequality Doubled Over Last 10 Years, Study
Finds," *Time*, June 25, 2014.

25. "Class in America: Mobility, Measured," *Economist*, U.S. edition, February 1, 2014.

26. Eli Lehrer and Lori Sanders, "Moving to Work," *National Affairs*,
Winter 2014.

27. Zygmunt Bauman, *Consuming Life* (Malden, MA: Polity Press, 2007),
18, 21, 29.

28. James Poulos, "Losing Liberty in an Age of Access," *New Atlantis*,
Summer/Fall 2014.

29. Ibid.

4. The Topography of Flatland

1. L. Frank Baum, *The Wonderful Wizard of Oz* (New York: Sterling
Children's Books, 2005), 3–4; original text published in 1900.

2. Benedict XVI, *Caritas in Veritate*, no. 48.

3. Benedict XVI, *Angelus*, December 12, 2012.
4. Francis, *Laudato Si*, no. 44.
5. J. R. R. Tolkien, *The Silmarillion*, 2nd ed., edited by Christopher Tolkien (New York: Ballantine Books, 1999), 3–4.
6. Matthew Dickerson and Jonathan Evans, *Ents, Elves and Eriador: The Environmental Vision of J. R. R. Tolkien* (Lexington: University of Kentucky Press, 2011), 24.
7. Bob Tita, "Motorized Walking Gear Gets Approval," *Wall Street Journal*, March 11, 2016.
8. Ben Popper, "Understanding Calico: Larry Page, Google Ventures, and the Quest for Immortality: Radical Life Extension Is a Dream Shared by Many Top Googlers," *Verge*, September 19, 2013.
9. *Caritas in Veritate*, no. 69.
10. *Laudato Si*, no. 131.
11. *Caritas in Veritate*, nos. 11, 29, 70.
12. Paul Newall, "Thomas Lessl: Science and Rhetoric," *Galilean*, June 7, 2005; reposted June 15, 2010. See also Lessl's *Rhetorical Darwinism: Religion, Evolution and the Scientific Identity* (Waco, TX: Baylor University Press, 2012).
13. Jean-Marie Lustiger, *The Promise* (Grand Rapids, MI: Eerdmans, 2007), 100.
14. George Grant, *Technology and Empire*, 17.
15. Ibid., 25.
16. Ibid., 27.
17. Leon R. Kass, M.D., "A More Perfect Human: The Promise and the Peril of Modern Science," presented for the "Insight" series at the U.S. Holocaust Memorial Museum, March 17, 2005.
18. Leszek Kolakowski, "The Idolatry of Politics," collected in his *Modernity on Endless Trial* (Chicago: University of Chicago Press, 1990), 146.
19. Kass, "A More Perfect Human."
20. Larry Siedentop, *Inventing the Individual*, 352–53.
21. David Gelernter, "The Closing of the Scientific Mind," *Commentary*, January 1, 2014.
22. Thomas Nagel, *Mind and Cosmos: Why the Materialist Neo-Darwinian Conception of Nature Is Almost Certainly False* (New York: Oxford University Press, 2012).
23. Andy Crouch, "Steve Jobs: The Secular Prophet," *Wall Street Journal*, October 8, 2011.
24. Edwin A. Abbot, *Flatland: A Romance of Many Dimensions* (New York: Penguin, 1998), originally published in 1884.

5. Love Among the Eloi

1. Pascal Bruckner, *Perpetual Euphoria: On the Duty to Be Happy* (Princeton, NJ: Princeton University Press, 2010), 11, 12, 14.

2. All samples are drawn from Pascal Bruckner, *The Temptation of Innocence: Living in the Age of Entitlement* (New York: Algora Publishing, 2000).

3. Bruckner, *Perpetual Euphoria*, 52.

4. Michel Houellebecq, *Platform* (New York: Vintage, 2004); original French version (Paris: Flammarion, 2001).

5. Andrew Cherlin, *The Marriage-Go-Round: The State of Marriage and the Family in America Today* (New York: Alfred A. Knopf, 2009), 16–22.

6. Ibid., 24–35, 114.

7. See the discussion of Reich's ideas and influence in Carlo Lancellotti's excellent translation of Augusto Del Noce, *The Crisis of Modernity* (Montreal: McGill–Queen's University Press, 2014), especially 216.

8. Michael Hanby, "The Brave New World of Same-Sex Marriage: A Decisive Moment in the Triumph of Technology over Humanity," *Federalist*, February 19, 2014.

9. See Nancy Jo Sales, "Tinder and the Dawn of the 'Dating Apocalypse,'" *Vanity Fair*, September 2015; Scott Calvert, "'Sexting' Case Rocks Colorado Town," *Wall Street Journal*, November 9, 2015; ashleymadison .com, one of many adultery dating sites; Veronica Dagher, "Why Postnups Are Rising," *Wall Street Journal*, March 12–13, 2016; Sue Schellenbarger, "A Sense of Loss That's Hard to Explain to the Boss," *Wall Street Journal*, November 11, 2015; Kate Taylor, "Sex on Campus: She Can Play That Game Too," *New York Times*, July 12, 2013.

10. Del Noce, *Crisis of Modernity*, 158; for the fullness of his argument, see the chapter "The Ascendance of Eroticism," 157–86.

11. Lead editorial, "The New Intolerance," *Wall Street Journal*, March 31, 2015.

12. Margaret Hagen, "Transgenderism Has No Basis in Science or Law," *Public Discourse*, January 13, 2016; Paul McHugh, "Transgenderism: A Pathogenic Meme," *Public Discourse*, June 10, 2015; Walt Heyer, "50 Years of Sex Changes, Mental Disorders and Too Many Suicides," *Public Discourse*, February 2, 2016. See also sexchangeregret.com and waltheyer.com for alternative testimony from transgender voices.

13. The first three of these stories are from the *Philadelphia Inquirer*, appearing from June 2014 through April 2015, but others followed through 2016. "Heather Has Two Genders," by Meghan Cox Gurdon, appeared in the *Wall Street Journal*, September 15, 2014.

14. Melanie Phillips, "It's Dangerous and Wrong to Tell All Children They're 'Gender Fluid,' " *Spectator*, January 30, 2016.

15. Scott Pruitt, "Why We're Suing Over Obama's Transgender Power Play," *Wall Street Journal*, June 1, 2016.

16. Mickey Mattox, "Marquette's Gender Regime," *First Things*, April 2016.

17. Charles Murray, *Coming Apart: The State of White America, 1960–2010* (New York: Crown Forum, 2012), 158.

18. Mitch Pearlstein, *Broken Bonds: What Family Fragmentation Means for America's Future* (New York: Rowman and Littlefield, 2014), 23.

19. Ibid., 24.

20. Tocqueville, *Democracy in America*, 486.

21. Ibid., 487.

22. Murray, *Coming Apart*, 69.

23. Ibid., 167.

24. Ibid., 240–47.

25. Robert Nisbet, *The Quest for Community* (Wilmington, DE: ISI Books, 2010), 248.

26. Roger Scruton, *The Face of God* (New York: Bloomsbury, 2012), 102.

27. Roger Scruton, *The Soul of the World* (Princeton, NJ: Princeton University Press, 2014), 90–91.

28. Daniel M. Bell Jr., *The Economy of Desire: Christianity and Capitalism in a Postmodern World* (Grand Rapids, MI: Baker, 2012), 105–6.

6. Nothing but the Truth

1. Justin McBrayer, "Why Our Children Don't Think There Are Moral Facts," *New York Times*, March 2, 2015.

2. Ibid.

3. Tocqueville, *Democracy in America*, 244.

4. Ibid., 244.

5. Ibid., 404.

6. Ibid., 244.

7. Ibid., 406.

8. M. Scott Peck, M.D., *People of the Lie: The Hope for Healing Human Evil*, 2nd ed. (New York: Touchstone, 1998), 66.

9. Ibid., 75.

10. Ibid., 69.

11. Ibid., 76.

12. Ibid.

13. Ibid., 162.

14. Harry Frankfurt, *On Bullshit* (Princeton, NJ: Princeton University Press, 2005), 64.

15. Leonard Wong and Stephen J. Gerras, "Lying to Ourselves: Dishonesty in the Army Profession," U.S. Army War College Strategic Studies Institute Monograph, February 17, 2015. From the website Synopsis.

16. Ibid., 2.

17. Ibid., ix.

18. Regan McMahon, "Everybody Does It," *San Francisco Chronicle Magazine*, September 9, 2007.

19. Ibid.

20. Ibid.

21. Ibid.

22. Marilyn Chandler McEntyre, *Caring for Words in a Culture of Lies* (Grand Rapids, MI: Eerdmans, 2009), 1–2.

23. Ibid.

24. John Ayto, *Dictionary of Word Origins* (New York: Arcade, 2011), 543.

25. George Orwell, "Politics and the English Language," in *The George Orwell Reader: Fiction, Essays and Reportage* (New York: Harcourt, 1984), originally published in 1948, 363.

26. James Campbell, "The Spanish Cockpit," *Wall Street Journal*, April 19–20, 2014.

27. George Steiner, *Language and Silence: Essays on Language, Literature and the Inhuman* (New York: Atheneum, 1982), essay originally published in 1958, 100–101.

28. Josef Pieper, *Abuse of Language, Abuse of Power* (San Francisco: Ignatius Press, 1992), 32–33.

29. McEntyre, *Caring for Words*, 56–57.

7. Darkness at Noon

1. Alasdair MacIntyre, *After Virtue: A Study in Moral Theory* (Notre Dame, IN: University of Notre Dame Press, 1984), 1–2.

2. Ibid, 5.

3. Ibid., 261.

4. Ibid., 58.

5. Ibid., 59.

6. Ibid., 24.

7. Ibid., 68.

8. Ibid., 85.

9. Ibid., 35.

10. Ibid., 86.

11. See the decade-long study by MIT scholar Natasha Dow Schull, *Addiction by Design: Machine Gambling in Las Vegas* (Princeton, NJ: Princeton University Press, 2012).

12. Christian Smith, *The Sacred Project of American Sociology* (New York: Oxford University Press, 2014), ix–x.

13. Ibid., 7–8.

14. Ibid., 9–11.

15. For a more thorough critique of the rise of social science and its influence on American life, see Christopher Shannon, *Conspicuous Criticism: Tradition, the Individual, and Culture in American Social Thought, from Veblen to Mills* (Baltimore: Johns Hopkins University Press, 1996).

16. Alasdair MacIntyre, "Social Science Methodology as the Ideology of Bureaucratic Authority," in Kelvin Knight, editor, *The MacIntyre Reader* (Notre Dame, IN: University of Notre Dame Press, 1998), 53.

17. Christopher Lasch, *Haven in a Heartless World: The Family Besieged* (New York: Basic Books, 1979), 189.

18. Leo Strauss, "Liberal Education and Mass Democracy," in Robert Goldwin, editor, *Higher Education and Modern Democracy: The Crisis of the Few and Many* (Chicago: Rand McNally, 1967), 73–96.

19. Ibid.

20. Matthew Crawford, *The World Beyond Your Head: On Becoming an Individual in an Age of Distraction* (New York: Farrar, Straus and Giroux, 2015), 257.

21. George Dyson, *Darwin Among the Machines: The Evolution of Global Intelligence* (Reading, MA: Addison-Wesley, 1997), 10.

22. Robert Kraynak, "Justice Without Foundations," *New Atlantis*, Summer 2011.

23. Ibid.

24. Ibid.

25. Philip Hamburger, "The History and Danger of Administrative Law," *Imprimis: A Publication of Hillsdale College*, September 2014.

26. David Brooks, "The Organization Kid," *Atlantic Monthly*, April 2001.

27. Ibid.

28. William Deresiewicz, *Excellent Sheep: The Miseducation of the American Elite and the Way to a Meaningful Life* (New York: Free Press, 2014), 3.

29. Mark Shiffman, "Majoring in Fear," *First Things*, November 2014.

30. Charles Péguy, *Notre Patrie: Oeuvres en Prose (1898–1909)* (Paris: Pleiade, 1957), 834; see also Marjorie Villiers, *Charles Péguy: A Study in Integrity* (New York: Harper and Row, 1966), 194.

31. Regarding Confederate monuments, see Cain Burdeau, "Monumental Fight," *Philadelphia Inquirer*, March 27, 2016. On Alexander Hamilton, see Terry Teachout, "Rapping the Legend," *Wall Street Journal*, April 21, 2016. On corporate political activism, see Monica Langley, "Tech CEO Turns Rabble Rouser," *Wall Street Journal*, May 3, 2016, quoting Georgia State Senator Josh McKoon. On American history, see Lynne V. Cheney, "The End of History, Part II," *Wall Street Journal*, April 2, 2015. On philanthropies and democracy, see James Piereson, "Philanthropies Target Democracy for 'Saving.' Watch Out," *Wall Street Journal*, July 24, 2014. On attacks on the insufficiently progressive, see Lloyd Cohen, "The Posthumous Attacks on Scalia Begin," *Wall Street Journal*, May 5, 2016; note that in the case of George Mason University's law school, the attacks failed. Note also the similar spirit directed at the (still living) Justice Clarence Thomas in the HBO film *Confirmation*; see Stuart Taylor Jr., "The Hollywood Hit-Job on Justice Clarence Thomas," *Wall Street Journal*, April 17, 2016.

32. Editorial, "Little Sisters of the Government," *Wall Street Journal*, November 10, 2015.

33. Sample headlines from the *Wall Street Journal*, September 2014 through May 2016.

34. Greg Lukianoff and Jonathan Haidt, "The Coddling of the American Mind," *Atlantic Monthly*, September 2015; Jefferson quoted therein.

35. Arthur Koestler, *Darkness at Noon* (New York: Bantam Books, 1968), 210–11.

36. Tocqueville, *Democracy in America*, 663.

8. Hope and Its Daughters

1. *Catechism of the Catholic Church* (CCC), no. 1817.

2. Richard John Neuhaus, *American Babylon: Notes of a Christian Exile* (New York: Basic Books, 2009), 216.

3. CCC, no. 1818.

4. Romanus Cessario, O.P., "The Theological Virtue of Hope (IIa IIae, qq. 17–22)," in Stephen J. Pope, editor, *The Ethics of Aquinas* (Washington, DC: Georgetown University Press, 2002), 232.

5. Robert Barron, *The Priority of Christ: Toward a Postliberal Catholicism* (Grand Rapids, MI: Brazos Press, 2007), 277.

6. Neuhaus, *American Babylon*, 224.

7. See Hugh of St. Victor's treatise on the betrothal gift of the soul, in Paul Rorem, *Hugh of St. Victor* (New York: Oxford University Press, 2009), 156.

8. Cessario, in *Ethics of Aquinas*, 236, 238. Cessario concludes: "In summary, the graced Christian believer possesses the cognitive certitude of faith that a mercifully omnipotent God offers the gift of salvation to all men and women and, as long as one personally appropriates this truth held by faith, the affective certitude of hope enables the believer to live a life of mature confidence in God's power" (239–40).

9. *Spe Salvi*, no. 7.

10. John Henry Newman, *Parochial and Plain Sermons* (San Francisco: Ignatius Press, 1997), 922.

11. Ibid., 923.

12. Ibid., 294.

13. Neuhaus, *American Babylon*, 217.

14. Ibid., 218–20. Thomas Aquinas articulates this by saying that despair is "neither a sentiment nor a mood, but an error in faith-judgment that supposes that God will not provide what is required for the wayfarer to reach salvation" (Cessario, in *Ethics of Aquinas*, 240).

15. Cessario, in *Ethics of Aquinas*, 240.

16. Ibid., 240.

17. See *Summa Theologica* II–II.21.4c.

18. CCC, no. 2091.

19. Quoted in Christopher Lasch, *The True and Only Heaven: Progress and Its Critics* (New York: W. W. Norton, 1991), 43.

20. Ibid., 47–48. In a similar way, the French political theorist Pierre Manent describes the way in which we want to be modern but lack a robust conception of what modernity actually entails. This leaves us striving toward a goal that we don't fully understand and never fully determine. See Manent, "City, Empire, Church, Nation: How the West Created Modernity," *City Journal*, Summer 2012.

21. Ibid., 42.

22. Ibid., 45.

23. "Since man always remains free and since his freedom is always fragile, the kingdom of good will never be definitively established in this world. Anyone who promises the better world that is guaranteed to last for ever is making a false promise; he is overlooking human freedom. Freedom must constantly be won over for the cause of good. Free assent to the good never exists simply by itself. If there were structures which could irrevocably guarantee a determined—good—state of the world, man's freedom would be denied, and hence they would not be good structures at all" (*Spe Salvi*, no. 24).

24. *Spe Salvi*, no. 22.

25. See Reinhold Niebuhr, *The Nature and Destiny of Man: A Christian Interpretation*, vol. 1: *Human Nature* (New York: Charles Scribner's Sons, 1941).

26. *Spe Salvi*, no. 44.

27. "For this reason, faith in the Last Judgement is first and foremost hope—the need for which was made abundantly clear in the upheavals of recent centuries. I am convinced that the question of justice constitutes the essential argument, or in any case the strongest argument, in favor of faith in eternal life. The purely individual need for a fulfilment that is denied to us in this life, for an everlasting love that we await, is certainly an important motive for believing that man was made for eternity; but only in connection with the impossibility that the injustice of history should be the final word does the necessity for Christ's return and for new life become fully convincing" (*Spe Salvi*, no. 43).

28. *Spe Salvi*, no. 10.

29. *Spe Salvi*, no. 2.

30. Neuhaus, *American Babylon*, 75.

31. *Spe Salvi*, no. 35.

32. Charles Péguy, *The Portal of the Mystery of Hope* (Grand Rapids, MI: Eerdmans, 1996), 9–11.

33. Ibid., 62.

34. Ibid., 66.

35. *Spe Salvi*, no. 12.

9. Rules for Radicals

1. Saul Alinsky, *Rules for Radicals: A Pragmatic Primer for Realistic Radicals* (New York: Vintage, 1989), originally published 1971, epigraph page.

2. Ibid., 61.

3. Ibid., 29.

4. Ibid., 36.

5. The Sermon on the Mount is, as the moral theologian Servais Pinckaers put it, "the summit upon which all revealed moral teachings converged." It contains and fulfills all those teachings' precepts. The Beatitudes are the heart of the Sermon on the Mount, and they are the key to understanding all of Jesus' teachings.

6. Servais Pinckaers, O.P., *The Pursuit of Happiness—God's Way: Living the Beatitudes*, translated by Mary Thomas Noble, O.P. (Eugene, OR: Wipf and Stock, 2011), 16.

7. Ibid., 13.

8. Ibid., 10–17.

9. Benedict XVI, *Jesus of Nazareth: From the Baptism in the Jordan to the Transfiguration* (New York: Doubleday, 2007), 67.

10. Pinckaers, *Pursuit of Happiness*, 18.

11. Servais Pinckaers, O.P., *The Sources of Christian Ethics*, translated by Mary Thomas Noble, O.P. (Washington, DC: Catholic University of America Press, 1995), 144.

12. *CCC*, no. 1718.

13. The *Confessions* are, in a sense, two stories woven into one. One is Augustine's confession of his own sin and inability to find happiness in the things of the world and in pagan wisdom. The other is a confession of praise to God because God has found Augustine and given him that happiness.

14. Augustine, *Confessions*, I.1.

15. Ibid., X.22–23.

16. *CCC*, no. 1721.

17. Ibid., no. 1724.

18. Ibid., no. 1820.

19. A common idea in Jesus' time and in the Old Testament was that in giving to the poor, the rich were lending to God. At the Day of Judgment, they would be repaid when the poor would proclaim their righteousness before God. For more on this idea, see Gary Anderson, *Charity: The Place of the Poor in the Biblical Tradition* (New Haven, CT: Yale University Press, 2013).

20. Pinckaers, *Pursuit of Happiness*, 40–41.

21. Benedict XVI, *Jesus of Nazareth*, 77.

22. Ibid., 44–52.

23. Ibid., 80–82.

24. Pinckaers, *Pursuit of Happiness*, 56–57.

25. Ibid., 61.

26. Ibid., 68.

27. Ibid., 71.

28. Benedict XVI, *Jesus of Nazareth*, 86–88.

29. Quoted in Pinckaers, *Pursuit of Happiness*, 76.

30. Ibid., 86–87.

31. Ibid., 94.

32. Ibid.

33. Ibid.

34. Benedict XVI, *Jesus of Nazareth*, 89.

35. Pinckaers, *Pursuit of Happiness*, 98–99.

36. Ibid., 110.
37. Ibid., 111.
38. Ibid., 117.
39. Ibid., 119.
40. Ibid., 120.
41. Ibid., 124.
42. Ibid., 127–31.
43. Ibid., 156.
44. John L. Allen Jr.'s book *The Global War on Christians* (New York: Image, 2013) offers a powerful, sobering account of this wave of persecution.
45. Thérèse of Lisieux once wrote: "I felt charity enter into my soul, and the need to forget myself and to please others; since then I've been happy!" Robert Barron comments: "I cannot think of a more succinct summary of the Christian way: the divine life, which can come only as a gift, changes us in such a way that we want to live for the other, and this conversion produces joy" (Barron, *Priority of Christ*, 308).

10. Repair My House

1. George Weigel, *Evangelical Catholicism: Deep Reform in the 21st-Century Church* (New York: Basic Books, 2013), 17.
2. Benedict XVI, Remarks to the Convention of the Diocese of Rome, May 26, 2009.
3. Joseph Ratzinger, *God and the World: A Conversation with Peter Seewald* (San Francisco: Ignatius Press, 2002), 26.
4. E.g., *Gaudium et Spes*, nos. 24, 41; *Mulieris Dignitatem*, no. 7.
5. See *Christifideles Laici*, no. 55.
6. *Lumen Gentium*, no. 33.
7. Quoted in *Christifideles Laici*, no. 55.
8. Quoted in *Christifideles Laici*, no. 2.
9. "Catholic action needs to be driven by contemplation in order to be Catholic. It needs to have the expansion of the kingdom of God as its end. We have to participate first in the Church's contemplation and then we can participate in her apostolate." Jacques Maritain, *Scholasticism and Politics*, translated and edited by Mortimer J. Adler (Indianapolis: Liberty Fund, 2011), 198–99.
10. Benedict XVI, *Light of the World: The Pope, the Church, and the Signs of the Times; A Conversation with Peter Seewald*, translated by Michael J. Miller and Adrian J. Walker (San Francisco: Ignatius Press, 2010), 176.

11. "By this new birth the Divine *Shechinah* is set up within him, pervading soul and body, separating him really, not only in name, from those who are not Christians, raising him in the scale of being, drawing and fostering into life whatever remains in him of a higher nature, and imparting to him, in due season and measure, its own surpassing and heavenly virtue. Thus, while he carefully cherishes the Gift, he is . . . 'changed from glory to glory, even as by the Spirit of the Lord.'" John Henry Newman, *Parochial and Plain Sermons*, 652. Newman also writes: "How the distinct and particular words of faith avail to our final acceptance, we know not; neither do we know how they are efficacious in changing our wills and characters, which, through God's grace, they certainly do. All we know is, that as we persevere in them, the inward light grows brighter and brighter, and God manifests Himself in us in a way the world knows not of. In this, then, consists our whole duty, first in contemplating Almighty God, as in Heaven, so in our hearts and souls; and next, while we contemplate Him, in acting towards and for Him in the works of every day; in viewing by faith His glory without and within us, and in acknowledging it by our obedience. Thus we shall unite conceptions the most lofty concerning His majesty and bounty towards us, with the most lowly, minute, and unostentatious service to Him" (653).
12. See *Apostolicam Actuositatem*, no. 3.
13. Anderson, *Charity: The Place of the Poor in the Biblical Tradition*, 6–7.
14. Ibid, 8.
15. Ibid., 3–4.
16. Ibid., 182–84.
17. Ibid., 189.
18. "Therefore, not too steep or unnatural does the ascent appear from Christ, as the inspiration of the love by which we love our friend, to Christ giving himself to us as our Friend for us to love, so that charm may follow upon charm, sweetness upon sweetness and affection upon affection. And this, friend cleaving to friend, in the spirit of Christ, is made with Christ but one heart and one soul, and so mounting along through degrees of love to friendship with Christ, he is made one spirit with him in one kiss." Aelred of Rievaulx, *Spiritual Friendship*, trans. Mary Eugenia Laker, S.S.N.D. (Kalamazoo, MI: Cistercian Publications, 1977), 3.20–21.
19. Aelred, *Spiritual Friendship*, 3.133–34.
20. *Gaudium et Spes*, no. 48.
21. John Paul II, *Familiaris Consortio*, no. 13.

22. *Love Is Our Mission: The Family Fully Alive* (Huntington, IN: Our Sunday Visitor, 2014), no. 105, catechism of the 2015 Eighth World Meeting of Families.
23. Ibid, no. 32.
24. "Christian marriage also represents for both consorts a way to attain an ever-increasing union with Jesus. As the bond has been concluded in Jesus and toward Jesus, the increase of conjugal love also means a growth of the love of Jesus." Dietrich von Hildebrand, *Marriage: The Mystery of Faithful Love* (Manchester, NH: Sophia Institute Press, 1984), 61.
25. *Gaudium et Spes*, no. 49.
26. *Familiaris Consortio*, no. 59. In this way, marriage is deeply connected to the Eucharist: "The Eucharist is the very source of Christian marriage. The Eucharistic Sacrifice, in fact, represents Christ's covenant of love with the Church, sealed with His blood on the Cross. In this sacrifice of the New and Eternal Covenant, Christian spouses encounter the source from which their own marriage covenant flows, is interiorly structured and continuously renewed. As a representation of Christ's sacrifice of love for the Church, the Eucharist is a fountain of charity. In the Eucharistic gift of charity the Christian family finds the foundation and soul of its 'communion' and its 'mission': by partaking in the Eucharistic bread, the different members of the Christian family become one body, which reveals and shares in the wider unity of the Church. Their sharing in the Body of Christ that is 'given up' and in His Blood that is 'shed' becomes a never-ending source of missionary and apostolic dynamism for the Christian family." *Familiaris Consortio*, no. 57.
27. In a dialogue with engaged couples, Pope Francis stressed this: "Matrimony is also a work of every day; I could say a craftwork, a goldsmith's work, because the husband has the task to make his wife more woman and the wife has the task to make her husband more man. To grow also in humanity, as man and as woman." "Francis' Dialogue with Engaged Couples," *Zenit*, February 14, 2014.
28. *Love Is Our Mission*, no. 62.
29. "At its roots, a happy marriage—the kind that endures over a lifetime—has more in common with the generous, patient, self-giving powers of celibacy than what Pius XII called 'a refined hedonism.'" *Love Is Our Mission*, no. 126.
30. *Lumen Gentium*, no. 11.
31. *Gaudium et Spes*, no. 52.
32. *Gaudium et Spes*, no. 48; see also *GS*, no. 50.

33. Nathaniel Peters, "The Domestic Church," www.firstthings.com/blogs /firstthoughts/2014/10/the-domestic-church, *First Things*, October 2014.

11. A Letter to Diognetus

1. All quotations from the *Letter to Diognetus* are taken from *Early Christian Fathers*, edited and translated by Cyril C. Richardson (New York: Touchstone, 1996), 205–24.

2. Robert Louis Wilken, "The Church as Culture," *First Things*, April 2004.

3. Hans Urs von Balthasar, *Truth Is Symphonic: Aspects of Christian Pluralism*, translated by Graham Harrison (San Francisco: Ignatius Press, 1987), 100.

4. Quotations and narrative taken from Mark Woods, "Brother of Slain Coptic Christians Thanks ISIS for Including Their Words of Faith in Murder Video," *Christianity Today*, February 18, 2015.

5. Henri de Lubac, S.J., *Paradoxes of Faith* (San Francisco: Ignatius Press, 1987), 145. Or, as Richard John Neuhaus put it: "[T]hink of it this way: If the culture of the Church—her teachings, practices, and habits of thought—is the culture that comprehends all reality, then it is not a matter of the Church's being countercultural but of the world's being countercultural in challenging the meta-culture of which it is a part. This is an audacious, some would say outrageously audacious, way of putting things. But it is an audacity that is inescapably implicit in saying that Jesus Christ is Lord, and he is Lord of all or he is Lord not at all. The *totus Christus* is Christ and his body the Church, and therefore our audacious claim for Christ necessarily entails an audacious claim for his Church." Richard John Neuhaus, *Catholic Matters: Confusion, Controversy, and the Splendor of Truth* (New York: Basic Books, 2006), 170.

6. George Weigel, "Diognetus Revisited, or, What the Church Asks of the World," in *Against the Grain: Christianity and Democracy, War and Peace* (New York: Crossroad, 2008), 68.

7. Ibid., 70.

8. Newman, *Parochial and Plain Sermons*, 832.

9. Robert Jenson, "How the World Lost Its Story," *First Things*, March 2010.

10. Benedict XVI, *Light of the World*, 157–58.

11. Neuhaus, *Catholic Matters*, 154–55.

12. As Benedict XVI put it, "Then I feel it is helpful to reaffirm that the Church does not impose but rather freely proposes the Catholic faith, well aware that conversion is the mysterious fruit of the Holy Spirit's

action." From "Church Does Not Impose but Freely Proposes the Faith," *ad limina* address to the Ordinaries of Central Asia, October 2, 2008.

13. Weigel, *Against the Grain*, 71.

14. Rod Dreher, "Christian and Countercultural," *First Things*, February 2015.

15. "In order to achieve their task directed to the Christian animation of the temporal order, in the sense of serving persons and society, the lay faithful are never to relinquish their participation in 'public life,' that is, in the many different economic, social, legislative, administrative and cultural areas, which are intended to promote organically and institutionally the common good. The Synod Fathers have repeatedly affirmed that every person has a right and duty to participate in public life, albeit in a diversity and complementarity of forms, levels, tasks and responsibilities. Charges of careerism, idolatry of power, egoism and corruption that are oftentimes directed at persons in government, parliaments, the ruling classes, or political parties, as well as the common opinion that participating in politics is an absolute moral danger, do not in the least justify either skepticism or an absence on the part of Christians in public life." *Christifideles Laici*, no. 42.

16. In his 2008 address to the cultural elite of France, Benedict XVI noted that this was how monks created European culture: "First and foremost, it must be frankly admitted straight away that it was not their intention to create a culture nor even to preserve a culture from the past. Their motivation was much more basic. Their goal was: *quaerere Deum*. Amid the confusion of the times, in which nothing seemed permanent, they wanted to do the essential—to make an effort to find what was perennially valid and lasting, life itself. They were searching for God. They wanted to go from the inessential to the essential, to the only truly important and reliable thing there is. It is sometimes said that they were 'eschatologically' oriented. But this is not to be understood in a temporal sense, as if they were looking ahead to the end of the world or to their own death, but in an existential sense: they were seeking the definitive behind the provisional ... What gave Europe's culture its foundation—the search for God and the readiness to listen to him—remains today the basis of any genuine culture." Benedict XVI, Meeting with Representatives from the World of Culture, Collège des Bernardins, September 12, 2008.

17. Wilken, "The Church as Culture."

18. Neuhaus, *Catholic Matters*, 169–70.

12. The City of Man

1. Josef Pieper, *Abuse of Language, Abuse of Power*, 26, 32.
2. Roger Scruton, *Face of God*, 123–24.
3. Rilke quotations are from *Rilke: Selected Poems*, with English translations and notes by C. F. MacIntyre (Los Angeles: University of California Press, 1968). Cited poems are "Evening" ("Abend") and "The Angels" ("Die Engel").
4. Quotations from John Paul II throughout this chapter are from his *Letter of His Holiness Pope John Paul II to Artists*, 1999.
5. See Henri de Lubac, S.J., *The Drama of Atheist Humanism* (San Francisco: Ignatius Press, 1995), 5, 24–25, and throughout.
6. Thomas Aquinas, *De Malo*, q. 5, a. I; cited in de Lubac, above.
7. *Towards a Pastoral Approach to Culture,* Pontifical Council for Culture, Vatican City, 1999.
8. Raissa Maritain, *The Prince of This World* (Toronto: Institute of Medieval Studies / Catholic Extension Press, 1933).
9. Leszek Kolakowski, *The Key to Heaven and Conversations with the Devil* (New York: Grove Press, 1972), 117–29, translated by Celina Wieniewska and Salvator Attanasio.
10. Gerard V. Bradley, "What's Behind the HHS Mandate?" *Public Discourse*, June 5, 2012.
11. Gerard V. Bradley, "The Future of Catholic Institutional Ministries in the United States," in *Unquiet Americans: U.S. Catholics and the Genuine Common Good* (South Bend, IN: St. Augustine's Press, 2016), 79–96.
12. Michael Hanby, "Reflections on the Cultural and Political Situation Confronting the Catholic Church in America," white paper commissioned by the author, May 2015; all Hanby references in this chapter are taken from this white paper.
13. "Americans Want Religion—For Everyone but Themselves," *American Interest*, June 6, 2013.
14. Laura Meckler, "Secular Voters Raise Their Voices," *Wall Street Journal*, June 4–5, 2016.
15. Pierre Manent, *The City of Man* (Princeton, NJ: Princeton University Press, 1998), 1.
16. Jonathan Sacks, "On Being a Creative Minority," 2013 Erasmus Lecture, *First Things* / Institute on Religion and Public Life, New York, October 21, 2013.
17. Václav Havel, "The Power of the Powerless," in *Open Letters: Selected Writings, 1965–1990*, translated and edited by Paul Wilson (New York:

Vintage Books, 1992), 125–214; drafted in Prague, October 1978, shortly before his arrest.

18. Dietrich Bonhoeffer, *No Rusty Swords: Letters, Lectures and Notes, 1928–36*, vol. 1, edited and introduced by Edwin H. Robertson, translated by Edwin H. Robertson and John Bowden (New York: Harper and Row, 1965), 309.

ACKNOWLEDGMENTS

Special thanks go to my literary agent, Bill Barry, for his patience, intelligence, and editing skill. Bill encouraged and shepherded the writing of *Render Unto Caesar* nine years ago, and it was a great pleasure to work with him again. He once mentioned that if he had a nickel for every writer with a great idea who later questioned his own sanity for starting on a book, he'd be a rich man. I had forgotten. Over the past eighteen months, I've had occasion to remember.

Bill opened the path to the excellent publishing team that president and publisher Steve Rubin leads at Henry Holt, and I'm deeply grateful for their competence and professionalism. This includes, especially, deputy publisher and marketing vice president Maggie Richards and senior editor Serena Jones, both of whom provided wonderful guidance for this project through the publishing process.

My thanks go as well to Gary Jansen, my former editor at

Random House and an early supporter of the ideas behind this book, a talent and a gentleman in every sense.

Thanks also to my friends at *First Things* magazine and the Institute on Religion and Public Life for permission to adapt portions of my 2014 Erasmus Lecture for the book's first chapter. Portions of chapter 12 are gratefully adapted from my 2010 remarks to the "Fifth Symposium Rome: Priests and Laity on Mission," sponsored by the Emmanuel Community and the Pierre Goursat University Institute, in collaboration with the Pontifical Institute *Redemptor Hominis.*

Many good minds reviewed parts of this text and offered their counsel and helpful criticism, or made valuable suggestions on the theme, or told me what else to read, or simply inspired me by their own impressive work and by their witness as Christians in the world. Among them in a particular way are Michael Hanby, David Scott, Meghan Cokeley, Rusty Reno, Matthew Franck, Gerard V. Bradley, Jonathan Reyes, Thomas W. Smith, Suann Malone Maier, Jayd Henricks, Daniel J. M. Cheely, Matthew O'Brien, Mark Shiffman, David L. Schindler, Kevin Hughes, Anna Bonta Moreland, Michael Moreland, Ken Myers, Edward Mannino, Jesus Fernandez-Villaverde, and Christopher C. Roberts. Whatever readers find worthwhile in this book, these friends have had a direct or indirect share in creating. Any mistakes or errors, obviously, are mine alone.

Thanks to Bill Rivers, who provided excellent research assistance while finishing his master's program at the University of Pennsylvania. Thanks also to my good friend Daniel Mark for connecting us.

I owe special gratitude to Nathaniel Peters and Brandon McGinley for their tireless and gifted help in developing the text. They brought the best of their own Catholic faith and considerable intellectual energies to a demanding task. Thanks also to David Mills for his early help with the project.

Finally, throughout my ministry as a bishop, I've been blessed with an exceptional and long-serving personal staff. This book would not exist without the largely invisible support and perseverance of Donna Huddell, Kerry Kober, and Francis X. Maier. They already know it, but I'll say it again: I will always be grateful.

Philadelphia
June 2016
Feast of Saints John Fisher and Thomas More

About the Author

CHARLES J. CHAPUT entered the Capuchin Franciscan religious community in 1965 and was ordained a priest in 1970. Pope John Paul II appointed him bishop of Rapid City, South Dakota, in 1988 and archbishop of Denver in 1997. In 2011, Pope Benedict XVI named him archbishop of Philadelphia. A member of the Prairie Band Potawatomi Tribe, he is the first U.S. archbishop of Native American heritage.

Archbishop Chaput served three years as a commissioner with the U.S. Commission on International Religious Freedom. He was an official U.S. State Department delegate to the 2005 Conference on Anti-Semitism and Other Forms of Intolerance in Cordoba, Spain, sponsored by the Organization for Security and Cooperation in Europe. The recipient of various religious liberty awards, he is a frequent public speaker and prolific writer.

In 2015, working with the Pontifical Council for the Family, he hosted the Eighth World Meeting of Families in Philadelphia. He subsequently served as a delegate to the 2015 Synod on the Family in Rome, where he was elected to a term on the Synod of Bishops' permanent council. In November 2016, he began a term as chairman of the U.S. bishops' Committee on Laity, Marriage, Family Life and Youth.